Florida A&M University, Tallahassee
Florida Atlantic University, Boca Raton
Florida Gulf Coast University, Ft. Myers
Florida International University, Miami
Florida State University, Tallahassee
University of Central Florida, Orlando
University of Florida, Gainesville
University of North Florida, Jacksonville
University of South Florida, Tampa
University of West Florida, Pensacola

The Values and Craft
of American Journalism

Essays from The Poynter Institute

Edited by Roy Peter Clark and Cole C. Campbell

University Press of Florida

Gainesville · Tallahassee · Tampa · Boca Raton

Pensacola · Orlando · Miami · Jacksonville · Ft. Myers

10 09 08 07 06 05   6 5 4 3 2 1

Library of Congress Cataloging-in-Publication Data
The values and craft of American journalism: essays from The Poynter Institute /
edited by Roy Peter Clark and Cole C. Campbell.
p. cm.
Essays, ten of which were originally published separately as booklets,
1992–1997, comprising the series Poynter Papers, now reedited,
with new essays added.
ISBN 0-8130-2467-6 (cloth)
ISBN 0-8130-2847-7 (pbk.)
1. Journalism—United States. I. Clark, Roy Peter. II. Campbell, Cole C.
III. Poynter Institute for Media Studies. IV. Poynter papers.
PN4853.V35   2002
070'.3—dc21   2001043725

The University Press of Florida is the scholarly publishing agency for
the State University System of Florida, comprising Florida A&M University,
Florida Atlantic University, Florida Gulf Coast University, Florida International
University, Florida State University, University of Central Florida, University of
Florida, University of North Florida, University of South Florida,
and University of West Florida.

University Press of Florida
15 Northwest 15th Street
Gainesville, FL 32611–2079
http://www.upf.com

In memory of Foster Davis
Reporter, Editor, Mentor, Friend

Ownership of a publication or broadcasting property is a sacred trust and a great privilege. . . . I'd rather be a newspaper editor than the richest man in the world.
Nelson Poynter

Contents

Foreword

"Keep the faith. Strive for excellence. Fight for the right."

Those words are the essence of this book. On the very day that I first sat at the keyboard to write this foreword, journalists everywhere were reminded starkly of their first principles by the impassioned resignation of a publisher. Jay T. Harris quit rather than impose upon his newspaper corporate profit goals that he believed to be diminishing its journalism. The words quoted above are from his farewell letter to the staff of the *San Jose Mercury News*.

They are noted not so much to laud Jay Harris—though his resignation over principle is laudable—as to celebrate the fact that Harris is a member of The Poynter Institute board of national advisers.

His principles are familiar to Poynter.

They are not, alas, nearly common enough in the early twenty-first century, an era in which individuals, institutions, and certainly corporations prize wealth with such single-mindedness as to blind many of them to more enduring values.

Journalism's enduring value is as a medium not of commerce but of self-government. It must, yes, be profitable to succeed as an instrument of community. Over the course of several decades, journalism leaders earnestly sought to amass media companies large enough, they theorized, to be insulated against takeover by businesses that had no tradition of caring about news. The irony is that some of these corporations have now made themselves appear to care little enough about news except as a commodity for profit growth. Public ownership is supplanting public interest. The commitment to shareholder value is corroding the concept of a sacred trust between journalists and their audiences.

The Poynter Institute was founded in 1975 by a journalist, Nelson Poynter, who so believed in the sacred trust that he gave his company, publisher of the *St. Petersburg Times* and of *Congressional Quarterly*, to a school that would preserve the publications' independence and promote his values. The school continues to honor Nelson Poynter by passing on his values to the several thousand professional journalists, journalism students and professors, and high school students who annually take part in Poynter seminars and conferences on craft skills and ethics.

Over its first quarter-century, Poynter has taught best practices of journalism and reinforced best instincts of journalists. In doing so, the institute has coincidentally created a large body of work reflecting on its principles. The scope of that instructive material was suddenly and urgently enlarged on September 11, 2001. The terror attacks magnified the public's understanding that news matters and heightened journalists' reliance on techniques of news coverage rooted in ethical values. Much of the best of our insight, but by no means all of it, is in this volume. More appears, constantly refreshed, on http://www.poynter.org, the school's website. We commend these works to anyone who cares to keep the faith, strive for excellence, and fight for the right.

James M. Naughton
President, The Poynter Institute

Acknowledgments

We extend our warmest gratitude to Susan Fernandez, the senior acquisitions editor of the University Press of Florida. She quickly saw the potential in this collection and became our shepherd, partner, and friend. Her professionalism and efficiency, and that of her colleagues at UPF, improved the book and made the best use of our talents and energy—all in the interest of our readers.

Special thanks go to our coworkers at The Poynter Institute: trustees, advisers, faculty, administrators, program assistants, librarians, those who maintain the facilities—all who contribute to making Poynter the influential school for journalists it has become. We will mention only one of them by name, Billie Keirstead, the production editor on the original Poynter Papers. Her dedicated service to Poynter, over a quarter century, stands for the work of one of the most helpful staffs ever assembled.

Vicki Krueger helped us prepare a clean manuscript and then turned her copyediting skills to making it better. She did these with the handicap of a right arm broken in a game of floor hockey. She turns out to be an ambidextrous copyeditor who can play with pain.

The Poynter Institute has been blessed with the resources of Nelson Poynter's company, the *St. Petersburg Times*. We can never thank enough the hard workers at our newspaper. Because of their efforts, Poynter can carry out its mission to help journalists everywhere in the interests of community and democracy.

If this collection has inspired a greater interest in The Poynter Institute, please consult our website at www.poynter.org. There you will find additional essays and reports on the craft and values of journalism, lists of resources, and directions on how to apply for Poynter's conferences and seminars.

Finally, we would be grateful to learn from any readers of the collection who have comments or criticisms to share. They can be addressed to rclark@poynter.org.

Introduction

Roy Peter Clark

This collection takes journalism seriously. The object of that last sentence is the key word: journalism. Not media, not mass communications, but journalism. Without a serious study of journalism, there can be no understanding of citizenship, democracy, or community.

The master narrative of this anthology is that journalism and democracy are coterminous, that they share common boundaries. Without journalism, democratic life dies from lack of oxygen. Without democracy, journalism loses its heartbeat. What is called journalism in a totalitarian system turns out to be propaganda.

The subplots of this collection include the ideas that the craft of journalism is a democratic practice; that community is sustained by journalism and helps sustain it; and that journalism is performed at the intersection of professional, commercial, and civic values.

Available for the first time in a single volume, these essays preserve some of the best conversations conducted about journalism at The Poynter Institute during the last decade. These conversations deserve to continue because they concern questions central to the common good. The hope is that journalists, educators, students, and citizens at large will travel down the paths cleared by these essays and engage the others and each other.

The history of these essays may be instructive. From 1992 to 1997, I edited a collection of ten booklets, known as the Poynter Papers. The shortest, the first one, was only thirteen pages. We thought that would become the model, but subsequent volumes grew, the longest to ninety-one pages. The original concept remained: The Poynter Institute would publish, and distribute at cost, short takes on topics important to journalists and those they serve.

An inventory of the original ten Poynter Papers reveals the range of interests cultivated during the 1990s by Poynter, a school for journalists that owns the *St. Petersburg Times*. They include leadership, ownership, community, visual journalism, ethics, reporting, writing, editing, scholastic journalism, and journalism as a liberal art. (If you add cultural diversity and new media to the list—as we've done in this volume—you have all of Poynter's concerns at your fingertips.) Five of the original papers were written by members of the Poynter faculty, five by professors who might be described as "friends of the Institute."

As editor, it was my intent to publish essays that could bridge the gap between the newsroom and the academy, that would be pitched to both practical scholars and reflective practitioners. The language would be both clear and thought provoking. The bridge was not an easy one to build, especially at a time when scholarly theory seemed so alienated from daily practice.

The Poynter Papers were designed to support the weight of important topics and were bound to last—more like tiny books than monographs. Some of them can be said to have a history of influence. An early essay by Jay Rosen helped spark the continuing debate about civic journalism and the proper role of journalists. Pegie Stark Adam's treatise on visual journalism came along at a perfect time: when editors and designers were trying to transform the newspaper into something both useful and beautiful. Essays on writing, such as the one by Donald M. Murray, helped build momentum in a reform movement in journalism that is now more than two decades old. The first and last reports confronted the issues at the nexus of business and journalism, at a time when traditional news values are in jeopardy. G. Stuart Adam's essay articulating a philosophy of journalism has fueled a conversation about journalism competencies and a reconsideration of how schools should be accredited. That's not bad for ten little papers.

Many of the fruits of this labor have occurred without much cultivation on my part. Publication was occasional rather than regular; topics were selected without strategic concern; in the absence of a marketing plan, papers were scattered far and wide and sometimes went out of print prematurely. As the editor of the series, I accept full responsibility for these deficiencies, and I am delighted that the Poynter Papers have made their mark in spite of them.

It was Cole C. Campbell, one of the nation's most thoughtful editors, who recognized the value in finding a new purpose and format for these essays. Reedited, organized by theme, and enhanced by several new pieces, the Poynter Papers are reborn into an anthology that supports Poynter's mission: to promote "excellence and integrity in the practice of craft and the practical leadership of successful businesses. It stands for a journalism that informs citizens, builds community, and enlightens public discourse."

Part I

Purpose and Culture

For most of the twentieth century, those concerned about journalism and democracy created a variety of frames for understanding who journalists were and what it was they were supposed to do. One debate, now thoroughly exhausted, concerned whether journalism was a profession or a craft or a trade. Other debaters struggled to understand how journalism reconciles its social purpose with its business interest. These explorations and conversations assumed new importance within the academy, where schools and colleges tried to figure out who should teach journalists and what the curriculum should look like. Journalism studies became mixed with advertising and public relations, complicated by scholarly interest in social science research and the emerging stature of communication and media studies.

G. Stuart Adam, one of Canada's most influential journalism scholars, turned his mind to these issues in a powerful way. During a sabbatical at The Poynter Institute, he drafted the essays that became "Notes Toward a Definition of Journalism" (1993). Adam's intellectual soulmate, James Carey, writes of his colleague's effort: "Stuart Adam here attempts to restore and expand our understanding of journalism, to examine its elements and purposes, to set it in relation to other modes of human understanding." In so doing, Adam elevates journalism to an important position in the liberal arts.

Poynter spent years building upon Adam's foundation. Roy Peter Clark began with a study of the language of journalism, not in its usual frame ("corruption by cliché") but in the context of its social and political purpose. That work became "The American Conversation and the Language of Journalism" (1994), an essay that garnered this praise from John

Sawatsky, one of Canada's most honored journalists: "This book deserves space on every library shelf alongside *The Elements of Style*. Every newsroom should stock this basic text, and give every reporter a copy, not to be read once, but again and again. Newspaper readers would be the real winners."

In February 1998, Poynter and the Committee of Concerned Journalists convened a conference on "Competence in the Newsroom." Drawing from Adam's seminal essay, Clark led the Poynter faculty in an articulation of ten areas of media competence: news judgment, reporting, language and narrative, analysis and criticism, visual literacy, technological competence, numeracy, cultural and civic competence, ethics, and law. By the year 2000, these categories had become the basis for reform of the standards by which schools of journalism were to be accredited.

If Adam and Clark can be said to "take journalism seriously," Cole C. Campbell takes their argument and magnifies it. In "Journalism Enlarged: Stuff That Matters" (2001), Campbell reveals why he is one of the most original thinkers among newspaper editors. Drawing upon the traditions of Joseph Pulitzer and Henry Luce, he argues that acts of journalism must be grounded in their highest purposes, to promote the public good. Moreover, he rejects what Brazilian scholar Paolo Freire might ridicule as the "banking model of journalism," that journalists merely deposit news, information, and entertainment into the minds of readers and listeners. That may be necessary, but it is insufficient to the task of democracy. In Campbell's new frame, citizens must be partners with journalists in building the public conversation on the stuff that matters.

Notes Toward a Definition of Journalism

Understanding an Old Craft as an Art Form

G. Stuart Adam

The Education of Journalists

I have taken my title from T. S. Eliot's *Notes Towards the Definition of Culture*, knowing, of course, that Eliot would shudder at the thought that his title and subject had in any way inspired mine. His shock would be well earned. Eliot was concerned in that work with the definition and preservation of a particular cluster of impulses and inventions out of which British culture was composed. As usual, he was on high ground, defending art, religious belief, and a caste society.[1]

My task is much more humble. Although I may be tempted into some of the conceits of art, I do not intend to involve God; and to the extent persons are on my mind as I write, they are a cast of characters, not a social caste. They are the reporters, writers, and critics who labor in the nation's newsrooms, magazine offices, and film documentary units, or who operate as free-lancers out of their own dens, and who are more commonly blamed, as Eliot might blame me, for being philistines rather than agents of culture. But I am pleased nevertheless to borrow part of his title. Like him, I am starting something, knowing full well that I cannot finish it. I am eager to make sense of my subject but am yet unsure where it will take me. Accordingly, these are my "notes toward a definition of journalism."

What follows is a discussion in which I identify, locate, and analyze the properties of journalism. I begin by providing a simple definition of journalism and then elucidate the concept of the Imagination in order to associate journalism with forms of expression, particularly fiction, that are intellectual or aesthetic or both. I conclude by identifying and analyzing the primary elements—news, reporting, language, narrative, and interpretative method—that mark it and distinguish it from other forms of expression.

I have several goals in mind, but first and foremost I want to lift the study of journalism in the university out of what I regard as a state of limbo. I want to define journalism in a way that will enable schools to participate more actively in its reform. I want to inspire a belief that journalism can be and often is an art form.

More specifically, my motives are those of a reformer, a teacher, and a scholar. To begin with, I believe that journalism is a fundamentally democratic art and through it, as others have observed, a free society engages in conversation with itself. So as a democrat, I want to protect and defend journalism as a free activity. But as a reformer, I want to strengthen the practice of journalism and, because I believe that we can change only what we understand, I am obliged to create a deeper understanding of what it is. As a teacher, I am required to do something that is alien to practitioners, and that is to bring to consciousness elements of craft that, once learned and incorporated, are barely recognized. A teacher must recognize such elements so that he or she can organize and communicate efficiently his or her knowledge. I must make explicit what is implicit, and that requires the creation of a language that comprehensively describes journalism's elements and dimensions.

As a scholar, I am interested in placing the field of journalism studies on what I regard as its proper ground. I have written about this elsewhere and argued, in summary, that the practical study of journalism in universities has been based on a notion of journalism that is too narrow and that research wings of journalism schools have been dominated for too long by the social sciences.[2]

These goals, motives, and roles are not truly divided or separate. They reflect a point of view I have developed in faculty meetings and conferences where the discussion has turned to the purposes and quality of journalism education. The focus of these discussions has usually been curriculum and research, and the context has been, for the most part, a consideration of the beliefs my colleagues express that professors should teach something called reporting, that students should receive an education in something called the liberal arts, and that it is in the interests of students to study a field, taught in the schools by scholars rather than practitioners, called mass communication or media studies.

No sensible person would deny the utility of reporting, liberal arts, and mass communication studies as categories to guide the development of a curriculum. But they are one thing as categories and another as operations. My disagreement with my colleagues turns on a consideration of how these beliefs have been operationalized. I have argued that reporting is defined far too narrowly to guide the development of an ambitious writer, that the liberal arts are not necessarily liberal anymore, and that the research and teaching conducted under the rubric of mass media studies or mass communication tend to deflect interest in journalism and direct attention to systemic, technological, or social concepts that are not immediately relevant.

In a nutshell, I believe that much of journalism teaching—whether it is concerned with professional practices or with social and political effects—is too functional and too divorced from the higher reaches of authorship and thought. Professional practitioners are inclined to define journalism in terms of limited newsroom conceptions and thus jettison any consideration of journalism's poetics or its ambitious forms; sociologists, communicologists, and political scientists are inclined to read journalism functionally rather than intrinsically and thus contribute to the leveling impulse that originates with the practitioners. Neither the practitioners nor the social scientists are sufficiently inclined to lift journalism out of the bureaucratic settings in which journalists are likely to operate. They fail to imagine journalism as the best journalists do as they make news judgments, engage in reporting, and compose accounts of the world. In the meantime, the liberal arts are organized for the most part within disciplines rather than across disciplines, and they contribute only randomly to the student's real education.

The dividend of all this is that students in journalism schools are too likely to end up stunted in their moral, intellectual, and aesthetic capacities, and too formed by bureaucratic needs rather than journalistic possibilities and obligations. Put a little differently, I believe that the language and concepts of traditional journalism instruction are either too lean or too bureaucratic to inspire passion or to encourage the creative spirit. A great opportunity is lost.

This is not a radical position. It is consistent with the findings of Everette Dennis and his highly influential *Oregon Report*, which was published in 1984, and it is more or less consistent with the point of view that led to the formation of a task force on journalism education by the Association for Education in Journalism and Mass Communication later in the decade. It published its report in 1989.[3]

The stronger of the two reports was the earlier one. Dennis and his colleagues simply declared that journalism education had failed to live up to the expectations that accompanied the foundation of the first university school of journalism in 1908 at Missouri. Among other things, the report said that although "journalism schools had begun with lofty ideals . . . many were little more than trade schools . . . following industry, not leading it," that "there is little connection between the [schools] . . . and the rest of the university," and that the "paradigm of journalism education has not changed much in forty years despite massive changes in mass communication."[4]

These reports mapped out a series of recommendations aimed at reforming the curriculum within the schools and strengthening the relationship between the schools and the wider university. But the prescriptions for change left the narrow definitions of journalism in place. Until there was a clear philosophical foundation for the study of journalism and some measure of consensus about the coordinates of this philosophy, the field would continue to be marked by a sense of failure and/or the uncertainty expressed in the reports.

So this paper has been conceived to provide a remedy for what seems to afflict journalism education. It is intended to put journalism studies on firm methodological foundations by putting the concept of journalism squarely into the foreground and placing institutional and systemic concepts such as media, press, and social structure into the background. I am promoting a more orderly approach to the practical and theoretical study of journalism in the academy by recommending that the study should begin with a searching interrogation of the concept of journalism itself.

So what are we referring to when we speak of journalism? The answer to this question is the principal subject of this paper and a recommended starting point for the organization of the field of journalism studies.

Journalism, Art, and the Imagination

A preliminary definition might go like this: Journalism is an invention or a form of expression used to report and comment in the public media on the events and ideas of the here and now. There are at least five elements in such a definition: (1) a form of expression that is an invention; (2) reports of ideas and events; (3) comments on them; (4) the public circulation of them; and (5) the here and now.

Let me comment on each of these elements, but save the first of them until the end so that I can dwell at greater length on the ideas of invention and what I think is invention's sponsor—the Imagination. The idea of the Imagination is central to the argument of this paper.

In the most fundamental sense, journalism involves reporting on ideas and events as they occur—the gathering and presentation of information on subjects that may vary each day from dogs that bite children to developments in ideas about the universe. The variety and range of journalistic subjects and treatments is suggested by a partial inventory of what was published in single editions of a daily, a weekly, a bimonthly, and a monthly in June 1991: the *New York Times* on June 11, the *Economist* in the week of June 15–21, *Rolling Stone* magazine on June 13, and the June edition of *Harper's*.

Page one of the *New York Times* included stories on the ticker-tape parade honoring the troops who fought in the Persian Gulf War, on the problems in the U. S. banking industry, on the decision to award professional baseball franchises to Miami and Denver, and on the decision by the Supreme Court to hear an appeal of a case originating in Minnesota involving a statute outlawing the display of symbols of racial hatred.

The *Economist* published "leaders" on the problems of economic growth, Iraq in the aftermath of the war, Japanese finance, confusing food labels, and civil liberties in Hong Kong; and, in the department its editors call American Survey, it published stories on health-care reform and on Japanese bashing at the Central Intelligence Agency. Other stories in other departments included an account of Poland's "anomalous" parliament, the debate in Germany about the venue of its capital, a feature with the diverting headline "Squid Are People Too," and another with the poetic headline "Arsenic and Cold Places."

Rolling Stone ran a story on the savings and loan problems, a step in the direction of the mainstream. But characteristically, its focus was on the entertainment scene, with notes on the musical group REM, a feature on a writer Mike Sager described as the "Pope of Pot," and a long and raunchy interview by Carrie Fisher with Madonna—a follow-up on the release of her film documentary on herself, *Truth or Dare*. The Madonna interview included views on oral and heterosexual sex.

Harper's published, as it regularly does, a set of readings, not all of which, speaking precisely, were journalistic. But two essays, one on banks and bankers and another titled "Reading May Be Harmful to Your Kids," and its regular index of absurdities and puzzles represented its editor's method of keeping Americans abreast of current issues.

Whatever else this journalism may be, some of it originating in the United States and some in Britain, it is the product of reporting—the gathering and presentation of slices and bits of human experience and thought selected from what N. K. Llewellyn once called the "aperceptive mass of behavior."[5]

So journalism involves, and is defined to some extent by, reporting. But it also involves criticism, or editorializing, or the conferral of judgments on the shape of things. Each of the items in the foregoing inventory—some more consciously than others—involved a judgment or an assessment of the significance, value, or worth of the actions of its subjects. The situation of the savings and loans banks was not only a debacle but a "scandal"; Madonna, not to mention her opinions, was "important"; REM makes good music; baseball and civil liberties matter. So journalism involves the application of the values we use to judge things, and those values are reflected in the selection of subjects and in the judgments conferred by journalists on how well the world they reveal is working. The concept of journalism embraces and gives a place to notions of commentary, judgment, and criticism.

Journalism is also public. We distinguish in our minds between voices that are specialized or private, as in correspondence, and voices conceived for public consumption. Journalism, along with novels, short stories, speeches, and proclamations, is created for public consumption. Thus its voice and vocabulary are colored by didactic responsibilities—by explicitness, by an absence of allusions that have meaning only in the private sphere, and by the absence of a vocabulary that has meaning solely within a specialized discourse, such as science.

If journalism is marked by its public voice, it is marked equally by its relation to the here and now. Michael Oakeshott, a British philosopher, once defined "the world of history [as] the real world as a whole comprehended under the category of the past."[6] The world of journalism, by contrast, may be the real world as a whole comprehended under the category of the present. I'll come to that later. In the meantime, may it be noted that journalism is avowedly about the present, not the past.

So the preliminary definition of journalism contains at least these four elements: reporting, judging, a public voice, and the here and now. These elements are straightforward—at least they arise out of a commonplace view of how journalism should be defined. But let me now turn to the first element of the original definition. I said journalism is a form of expression that is an invention. I will put it differently. It is a creation—a product of the Imagination—in both an individual and a cultural sense. It is a form of expression in which the imaginative capacities both of individuals and of a culture are revealed. The idea here is that although individual journalists speak individually in journalism, they speak through a cultural form that, although it is an invention, they did not invent.

I have used the words *invention, creation*, and particularly *imagination* in a way that may seem jarring. Journalism, after all, is about reality, not fantasy; there are no fairies or dreams in journalism, only the contours of nature and the dreary but familiar faces and words of our fellow beings. But I have chosen my words carefully and note that others connected to similarly earthly and empirical concerns have done so as well. C. Wright Mills, one of America's most accomplished sociologists, titled one of his best books *The Sociological Imagination*;[7] R. G. Collingwood, a British historian and philosopher, devoted a section to "The Historical Imagination" in his book *The Idea of History*.[8] Their points of view have inspired me, as have the points of view of such writers as Northrop Frye, the Canadian literary critic who wrote *The Educated Imagination*.[9] They each refer broadly to parts of human consciousness that are formed initially by what Oakeshott, in his essay, "The Voice of Poetry in the Conversation of Mankind," calls the "primordial activity" of imagining and are completed by elaborate and culturally sanctioned methods for framing such images.[10]

Oakeshott says that the self is activity and this activity is "imagining: the self making and recognizing images." So the not-self is composed of images, many of them: trees, chewing gum, cigarette butts, department stores, gas stations, dogs, cats, students, and colleagues. In order to see ourselves, he argues, we must see that before anything else we form images, and then through language or other forms of representation we create what he calls "arrest[s] in experience."[11] We give those images and thus, consciousness, specificity. This activity, he says, is primordial, and by this he means there is nothing antecedent to it. And so even sophisticated forms of representation—art and science, for example—are expressions of a primordial activity. Each of these are complex systems that bestow method and, thus, past experience on what in origin is a primordial activity.

So the forms of expression, whether sociological, historical, poetic, literary, or journalistic, are methods we use to form such consciousness. Mills was interested in how and in the name of what sociologists form images of society; Collingwood and Oakeshott, among other things, were interested in how historians form images of the past; Frye was interested in how literature builds images of the spirit and provides a home for the soul. I am interested in how journalists frame experience and form consciousness—in short, how a method is attached to the experience of the here and now.

A clue to how journalists form consciousness has been recorded by the distinguished American journalist and novelist Joan Didion. Her account of her own work corresponds nicely with Oakeshott's conceptions of the self's imagining:

I write entirely to find out what I'm thinking, what I'm looking at, what I see and what it means. . . .

When I talk about pictures in my mind I am talking, quite specifically, about images that shimmer around the edges. There used to be an illustration in every elementary psychology book showing a cat drawn by a patient in varying stages of schizophrenia. This cat had a shimmer around it. You could see the molecular structure breaking down at the very edges of the cat: the cat became the background and the background the cat, everything interacting, exchanging ions. . . . I am not a schizophrenic . . . but certain images shimmer for me. Look hard enough, and you can't miss the shimmer. It's there. You can't think too much about these pictures that shimmer. You just lie low and let them develop. . . . you try to locate the cat in the shimmer, the grammar in the picture.[12]

It is the "grammar in the picture" that suggests most vividly the journalist's impulse to construct an edifice of words on a primordial image.

Didion's novels and journalism provide examples of what she described in her essay on writing. Her reports on Miami, for example, published first in the *New York Review of Books* and then in a single volume, included the observations that

the entire tone of the city, the way people looked and talked and met one another, was Cuban. The very image the city had begun presenting of itself, what was then its newfound glamour, its "hotness" (hot colors, hot vice, shady dealings under the palm trees), was that of prerevolutionary Havana, as perceived by Americans. There was even in the way women dressed in Miami a definable Havana look, a more distinct emphasis on the hips and décolletage, more black, more veiling, a generalized flirtatiousness of style not then current in American cities.[13]

It is the images of the women's styles, more than the picture of the city, that suggest the shimmer. But all of it works. It calls to mind the words of Joseph Conrad in his famous manifesto on the art of writing. "My task," he wrote, "which I am trying to achieve is, by the power of the written word to make you hear, to make you feel—it is, before all, to make you see."[14] Didion's vision is clear and her use of language correspondingly vivid. She enables her readers to see.

One might say that it is tendentious to argue for a particular view of journalism by pointing to the achievements of Joan Didion. Her gifts are extraordinary; she is a poet of the craft—an artist. What about the routine and the commonplace—the five-paragraph story on the city page that records a vote in the local council on the municipal tax rate, or the brief that notes the submission of the annual report of the Humane Society? What about Associated Press style, the inverted-pyramid story, or the filler on page two that says that the production of sisal hemp on the Yucatán peninsula has risen by 10 percent in the last six months? What about the breathless accounts of shootings, stabbings, fires, accidents, traffic jams, and earthquakes?

There are at least three answers to such questions. But before answering them, it is necessary to do some owning up. Journalists work under varying conditions and deadlines. Some have much more time than others. But more to the point, just as the imaginative gifts of poets and novelists are unequal, so are the imaginative gifts of journalists. Some are much more creative than others. Some are artists, which means they can invent with the invention, and some are bureaucrats, which means they can reproduce the invention without inventing. But all are imaginative in the sense in which Oakeshott uses the word. They imagine and they fabricate images. With this admission and its qualification out of the way, the questions can be addressed.

First, the same principles of clarity, although perhaps not of complexity, apply in every story. A carefully constructed news story that follows the rules of narration we call the inverted pyramid can be a work of sculpture akin in its principles of rhythm and composition to Didion's account of Miami. The problems are not always so complex and do not necessarily call for such penetration; but clarity is always a requirement.

Second, from the point of view of the storyteller the most interesting stories come after proclamations announcing an accident, a disaster, or an earthquake. The day-after "follos" on the earthquake in California in October 1989 included this story by Jennifer Warren and George Ramos of the *Los Angeles Times*:

> For James Betts, the horror of Tuesday's earthquake peaked right around 8 P.M. It was then that the surgeon reached a frightened boy named Julio Berumen after slithering 20 meters on his belly through

a one-meter crawl space in the wreckage of a crumpled Nimitz Freeway.

Julio, 6, was pinned in a car, the weight of his mother's dead body upon him. After a quick look around, Betts and paramedics knew what had to be done.[15]

Most readers would know by now what is coming—the removal by surgical means of a boy from under the corpse of his mother. It is difficult; it fills us with shame and sorrow. But as Conrad once noted, "there is not a place of splendour or a dark corner of the earth that does not deserve . . . if only a passing glance of wonder or pity."[16] Journalism has many styles: the bulletin, the proclamation, and the announcement are only three of them. Lying in wait are more engaging narrative techniques and avenues of exploration that lead to the territories of splendor and of terror.

The third answer pulls us back clearly into the view that the analysis of Oakeshott's philosophy promotes and Didion's work illustrates. The world is born in our imaginations. This is not to say that acts of nature do not have an objective existence. It is to say that the experience of them—consciousness, in other words—is the work of the Imagination in both its rudimentary and its artistic incarnations. The transfer of consciousness from one human being to another through a story, any story—from a journalist to an audience—produces the forms of public consciousness that make collective existence possible. What is initially private becomes public, and so in journalism society is born and reborn every day. But this brings us to the functions of journalism—what journalism does rather than what it is. I want to concentrate on what it is.

We have touched now on styles and techniques, the devices and instruments of imagining, showing, and telling, and this suggests, as noted above, that there is more to journalism than simply a display of the imaginative qualities of single journalists. There are also styles to choose from or narrative procedures to adopt, and all of these belong to this broadly conceived form of expression we call journalism. Its elements and principles of design are a legacy of past experience, and although they must be reproduced and reconceived every time a journalist writes, the working journalist is never working in a vacuum. He or she is shaping new experience to established forms. Journalism is an imaginative form, like the poem or the novel, within which individual imaginations function.

I will discuss the properties of this expressive form in detail shortly, but note here that the history of journalism as we know it begins in the early seventeenth century in Europe's cities, particularly in London, where so-called *corantos* were first published in 1621.[17] It is possible, although it is a complex task, to map the evolution of the form from that time by following the contents of newspapers and tracing reportorial, narrative, and analytical methods through broadcasting to the present day. Seventeenth-century journalism was marked by the news brief and, during the discontents at midcentury, the violent essay.

Journalism in Britain in the eighteenth century evolved into something extraordinarily rich. It included the literary essays of Addison and Steele; the polemical writing of Lord Bolingbroke, Cato, and Junius; the legislative reports of Dr. Johnson in *The Gentleman's Magazine*; and, later, of Woodfall, one of the first Gallery reporters, in *The Public Advertiser*. By 1790, there were fourteen dailies and nine triweeklies in London alone.[18] So there was lots of journalism published, and much of it in form and content that an American or Canadian in the early twenty-first century can read with pleasure and insight. The modern world was being made and journalism was being made with it. Not only that. The modern world was being made and, through journalism, imagined in a modern way.

The world that was being made and imagined had two fundamental—one might even say mythic—properties that provided firm coordinates for journalism's content. One was the democratic state and, thereby, the democratically constituted legislature; the other was the community of citizens. The journalism of the eighteenth century in Britain and in North America reflected a fundamental interest in the civic domain and the activities of the people's representatives. The legislature and its affairs were very much in the foreground through the device of the political report. The journalism of the nineteenth century, while continuing to cast up images of the state and the legislatures, added more textured images of the community through the device of the human interest story. An invention mainly of American journalists and editors, the human interest story began the important phase of its career in the United States when the penny papers were launched in the 1830s. Together, the civic and the human interest stories continue to provide the foundations for modern journalism. The world that they reflect is like the world imagined by journalists from the beginning; and the way that they have imagined it has been consistently modern. From the beginning, the world was imagined by journalists through empirical techniques, just as the natural world was being imagined by those who were deserting religious myths and adopting scientific practices in the same period. These techniques, however crude and haphazard, grew into consolidated methods of reporting and generating facts.

Let me summarize what I have said about the Imagination and journalism. W. H. Auden says that a poem is a contraption with a guy inside of it.[19] Journalism is something like that. Each report, essay, editorial, or narrative documentary, however displayed in a publication by an editor or played in a broadcast by a producer, is the creation normally of an individual. Each item, however long or short, however simple or complex, is a composition in which experience is apprehended and rendered in narrative form by an individual. So journalism may be thought of in its particulars and in its various manifestations as single products of the imaginations of single individuals. There's a guy or a gal inside of it.

But it is also a contraption. This means that journalism is a creation in the broader—cultural—sense. The contraption is a form of expression, the templates of which reside in the culture and the principles of which have been invented and developed in the English-speaking world since the second decade of the seventeenth century. It is a form of expression that, along with the novel, narrative film, and modern social science, resides in the cultural storehouse where we put the procedures and techniques for creating public consciousness. It is the aspect of culture that inspires and directs the work of every journalist. To put it differently, it is the aspect of culture that is more or less immanent in the personal culture of every journalist and, correspondingly, more or less immanent in the institutional culture of every publication or broadcast unit. Considered culturally, journalism is a contraption with a method or a set of procedures and principles inside it. So what are the elements or essential principles of this contraption? This is the question to which I will now turn.

The Elements of Journalism

I have used the words *form* and *element* and am about to use the word *principle* to assist in this account of what I think journalism is.

I am not married to such words, although for the moment they seem helpful. Form refers simply to a type or class of thing—a genus, in this case, of expression—that has an internal structure and functions distinct from the internal structures and functions of other types of expression. Poetry is a form of expression; so is journalism. In poetry, there are sonnets, epics, limericks, and free verse; in journalism, there are news stories, sidebars, editorials, news features, backgrounders, think pieces, columns, narrative documentaries, and reviews. I am not identifying the subforms of journalism by reference to various media. I have referred to items that could be published in a newspaper or magazine, or broadcast on radio or television. In other words, I am trying to define journalism in terms of what it is rather than by the medium through which it is circulated. Now I am prepared to commit myself.

There are minimally five elements or principles of design in any piece of journalism that, although journalism may share some of these with other forms of expression and although the elements may be unequally represented in individual pieces, together mark and define it. In my view, journalism comprises distinctive elements or principles (1) of news, (2) of reporting or evidence gathering, (3) of language, (4) of narration, and (5) of meaning.

I have used the words *element* and *principle* synonymously. Speaking precisely, it is best to see them in this context as two sides of the same coin. A principle of design becomes an element when it is acted upon, operationalized, and embodied in a work of journalism. Put differently, the elements in the text reveal the principles that have guided its creation. It would be possible to write a full essay and then some on each of these elements or principles. Here, I will discuss each briefly in order to illustrate what I have in mind.

News: A Shift in the State of Things

At the core of what we call news are journalistic conceptions of events, time, and subject matter. Journalism is concerned with events in time or, to use the language I have already introduced, events in the here and now. Often these events are defined narrowly and in terms of conflict or, as the textbooks remind us, of the prominence of the major actors or the consequences for individuals in society.[20] The greater the consequences, the lesson goes, the higher the news value. But the starting point for journalism is an event, regardless of the scale of values on which it may be weighed and regardless of the breadth of meaning that we may give to the notion of an event.

By *event*, I am not referring to anything that happens. There are boundaries to the subjects and thereby to the events that journalism embodies. For example, the subjects of news and fiction are different, not only because one is documentary and the other pure invention, but because they operate in different territories. William Faulkner once said that the proper subject of fiction is the "human heart in conflict with itself."[21] He meant that fiction is primarily concerned with the interior lives of the characters an author imagines. In order to write a novel, an author has to do what a journalist can never do, and that is, as one commentator has observed, to "suspend the blur of events, to make passion an object for contemplation."[22] So the novelist follows a subject beyond the boundary of acts and events into the inner regions of mind and soul.

A journalist normally stops at that boundary. Journalism does not suspend the blur. In a sense it is the blur. Journalism is primarily about the events that the mysteries of passion or competition or love or hating produce—a fight, a foreclosure, a marriage, a war. It is about the manifest rather than the hidden, the objective rather than the subjective. News represents a shift or change in the state of the objective world, and a news story is an inquiry into this new state.

Furthermore, in the world of the manifest and the objective, at least two kinds of stories can be distinguished: the civic, having to do with politics, the conduct of public business, and the administration of society's major institutions and systems; and the human interest, having to do with events in the lives of individuals and the community of souls. Civic stories dominate the front page of the *New York Times*. For example, the edition of Tuesday, July 16, 1991, included the following headlines: "Big Bank Merger to Join Chemical, Manufacturer"; "Commerce Dept. Declines to Revise 90 Census Counts"; and "AIDS Tests Urged for Many Doctors." Each headline and story resonates with the idea of public business rather than private emotion. Not so with the human interest story.

The most obvious and natural setting for human interest stories is the tabloid, although I hasten to add that all major news organizations, including the *New York Times,* carry them. Human interest stories are constructed, for the most part, out of what humans do to each other beyond the boundaries of organized society and the state. Their motive, above all, is to divert by stirring emotions. Thus the *Chicago Sun-Times* of January 7, 1986, told "A Tale of True Love: He Expects Death, Gives Girlfriend His Heart." The dateline was Patterson, California, and the story, from AP, started with the words, "A 15-year-old boy who learned that his girlfriend needed a heart transplant told his mother three weeks ago that he was going to die and that the young woman should have his heart." The boy died; the transplant surgery followed. The girl survived.[23]

So the events that journalism records have boundaries of sorts. Journalism's view of the "pageant of creation" is, to start with, the view of a spectator to the manifest.[24] But as already noted, "the governing gaze," to borrow from Janet Emig, is not only directed at manifest events, either civic or human interest, but situated in the here and now.[25]

The clue to this is to be found in what functions as the news lead in hard news stories or the news points, which may or may not be the basis for the lead, in stories that are sometimes referred to as *soft*.

In a hard news story, narration begins normally in the lead and the lead embodies the notion of the latest. Thus, "Iraq on *Sunday* [my italics] delivered a new list of its nuclear facilities to UN inspectors" is the lead to a hard news story. The rest, which appeared on the front page of the *St. Petersburg Times* on Monday, July 15, 1991, is commentary and detail, not so much by the journalist who wrote it, but by President Bush of the United States and President Mitterand of France, who said "they might use military force if Iraq fails to disclose and then destroy its nuclear weapons."

If this had been my story, I probably would have led on the threat by the two presidents rather than on the delivery of the note to UN inspectors by Iraq. My reasons would have been partly because of the relative weight I would give to the two events recorded here—the delivery of the note and the utterance of the threat—and partly because of timeliness. As far as I can see, the threats followed the delivery of the note. The news is often nothing more than the last thing that happened in a chain of events.

So time counts. The lead in the story on Iraq incorporated the word *Sunday*. A second story at the bottom of the page on a computerized directory of the 3.5 million soldiers who fought in the Civil War turned on the time-word *soon*. It said, "Visitors to Civil War battlefields *soon* [my italics] will be able to ask a computer if their ancestors were Yankees or Rebels."

The elements of time and event are always present even when the boundaries of the event are blurred and the notion of time functions on a different calendar. Consider, for example, Pete Hamill's article on the Everglades that appeared in *Esquire* magazine in October 1990. A contribution to the magazine's "American Journal," the article was titled "The Neverglades." As with all of Hamill's writings, this piece was evocative and powerful.

At one stage in the narrative, Hamill recorded his memory of the wildlife when, as a youth, he first countenanced the Everglades:

I heard them, far off, almost imperceptible at first: thin, high, and then like the sound of a million whips cutting the air. They came over the edge of the horizon and then the sky was black with them. Birds.

> Thousands of them. Tens of thousands. Maybe a million. I shivered in fear and awe. . . . And then the vast dense flock was gone. The great molten ball of the sun oozed over the horizon.

Much later, he noted:

> I wasn't the first human to see the sky blacken with birds, I only felt that way. Once they came in the millions; dozens of species, including flamingos, great white herons, ibis, snowy egrets, pelicans, roseate spoonbills, and bald eagles with seven-foot wingspans, living in nests that were nine feet deep.

These passages appeared before and after the article's news point. It came in the 119th line and said, "The Everglades are in trouble." The detail of the news point's meaning was that a clash between developers and nature—an event of sorts—was being resolved or is being resolved *now* in favor of the developers. That's the news; the story, with all that powerful imagery, provides the detail.

I don't want to belabor this point unnecessarily, but it takes work to tune into the news and write it. The news is different from a story's subject. Subjects are one thing; the news is another. The Everglades can be thought of as a subject; that it is in trouble is news. Similarly, Michael Landon is a subject; his sickness and then his death were news.[26]

The news is a hook into journalism's subjects, regardless of what they are. Its weight is judged in relation to the weight of the facts and news involved in other events and in relation to the other facts of the story for which it provides the hook. It occurs when there is a change in the state of things—in the economy or politics or business or human relationships. To put it in words borrowed from Joan Didion, news is part of journalism's basic grammar. Without it, journalism itself is impossible to imagine.

Reporting: Facts and Information

If it is impossible to imagine journalism without imagining a principle of news, it is equally impossible to imagine it without reporting or, to put it in the language of my earlier list, without the principle and the operations of fact-gathering and assessment. Journalists are concerned with facts and information, and they follow, however crudely and randomly, an epistemological procedure. They construct a picture of fact and information.

The American writer Robert Stone has observed that a writer assumes, "above all, the responsibility to understand."[27] There are many ways to achieve understanding and belief. A psychoanalyst does it one way; a moral philosopher does it another way; a scientist does it in yet another way. The Czech novelist Milan Kundera has written that the "novel is a meditation on existence as seen through the medium of imaginary characters."[28] If we take Kundera as the authority, the writer of fiction "meditates" whereas a journalist reports. A journalist might meditate as well, but only after, and on what, he or she reports.

What journalists hear or see or smell is the authority for what they write. In this sense they are lock step in the empirical tradition we associate with science and with one strand of philosophy. John Hersey put it this way in a review that challenged some of the conceits of the so-called New Journalism and the "numbed acceptance of the premise that there is no difference between fiction and nonfiction."[29] He had been dismayed by the liberties Tom Wolfe, Norman Mailer, and Truman Capote had taken in *The Right Stuff*, *The Executioner's Song*, and "Handcarved Coffins," a story in Capote's larger collection titled *Music for Chameleons*. Among other things, Hersey said:

> I will assert that there is one sacred rule of journalism. The writer must not invent. . . . The ethics of journalism . . . must be based on the simple truth that every journalist knows the difference between the distortion that comes from subtracting observed data and the distortion that comes from adding invented data.[30]

Hersey used the verb *observe* for good reason. Observation is a central device of the reporter, one that the British critic John Carey makes the principle of inclusion in his book *The Faber Book of Reportage*. He notes in the introduction that "for my purposes reportage must be written by an eye witness." He goes on to say that "eye-witness evidence . . . makes for authenticity."[31] There is something to such a claim. Much of what is rich and authoritative in journalistic writing—think of Pete Hamill's description of the Everglades or Joan Didion's account of the dress of Cuban women in Miami—is the product of such observation.

However, every practitioner knows that much of what is published or broadcast originates in the analysis and summary of documents, whether published previously in newspapers and available on request from databases, or published in books and magazines, or broadcast on television and radio, or found in public records offices.

From the point of view of the investigative reporter, public records are gold mines. They include simple things such as phone books and city directories; they also include files in county courthouses where a journalist can often get access to the records of lawsuits, divorce files, wills and guardianship agreements, marriage licenses, real estate records (including deeds, mortgages, foreclosure notices, and tax records), and criminal records. City and county governments are likely to have records of auto and boat licenses, voter registration, hunting and fishing records, and so on.

An investigative reporter such as Jeff Good, formerly with the *St. Petersburg Times*, from whom this list was taken, has mastered forensic techniques that would humble a professional detective. As he notes, when all else fails, there is always the device of the state or federal Freedom of Information Act—a slow but nevertheless useful method for getting at well-buried material.

The opportunities created by the federal act are evident in a story published in June 1991 in the *St. Petersburg Times* on the investigation by J. Edgar Hoover and the FBI on the politics and connections of Claude Pepper, a congressional representative from Florida who throughout his career was an outspoken advocate of the rights of the elderly and the poor. Hoover and his colleagues evidently thought Pepper was a Communist and worked hard, but failed, to find a way to put him out of business. Written by Lucy Morgan, the story noted that the request for information dated from October 1989, shortly after his death. The documents were supplied in April 1991 and published, as noted, in June 1991.

If observation and the study of documents are primary devices of the reporter, so is the interview. In fact, the interview is the primary, although probably the least reliable, instrument. It would take some time to document this, but I would guess that most of what is published as news and most of what is factually wrong in newspapers is based on interviews. Regardless, many major stories, including the story of the Watergate cover-up, are based on interviews—in this case, with Deep Throat. Bob Woodward, one of the authors of the *Washington Post* articles that exposed the scandal in the executive branch of the U. S. government, is a prodigious interviewer. In an appendix to his book *Wired*, an account of the life of John Belushi, Woodward provides a list of more than 200 individuals he interviewed in order to construct his portrait of Belushi.[32]

Similarly, Gail Sheehy noted in the preface to her book *Character: America's Search for Leadership*, a collection of stories on candidates in the 1988 presidential campaign, that "I build my portrait of an individual on evidence culled from interviewing thirty, forty, or fifty people who have known him at different stages of his life—a parent, an uncle, a rivalrous brother, schoolmates; I seek the significant teacher, the high-school coach who forged him into a competitor, the first wife."

To construct her portrait of Gary Hart—it appeared first in *Vanity Fair* in September 1987—she interviewed, among others, Ann Warren, a high school date; Ralph Hartpence, Hart's uncle; and Aunt Emma Louise, Hart's mother's sister.[33]

The interview is at the heart of the practice of journalism. Sometimes interviews are conducted carelessly; sometimes they are conducted with a dedication to truth that would surprise the best historians or lawyers. And sometimes they are incorporated into systems of fact-gathering and discovery that would please the best empirical social scientists. I am thinking here of survey research published in newspapers, especially at election time. The random selection of interviewees and the preparation of questionnaires represent, in a sense, add-ons in reporting methods to the interview.

Acts of observation, the analysis of documents, and interviewing in journalism are intended to provide authoritative facts. They represent the operations of the principle of reporting. It is often necessary to check and crosscheck, to corroborate and double-corroborate in order to assert a fact with confidence. But in journalism, regardless of what some journalists might say or do, the principle requires that facts are authoritative. As John Hersey has said, "In fiction, the writer's voice matters; in reporting, the writer's authority matters."[34]

Language: The Plain Style

The clue that journalism has its own voice and style—that there are distinctive linguistic principles at work in journalism—is revealed by the fact that there are dictionary definitions of something called "journalese." *Webster's New World Dictionary* says that journalese is "a style of writing and diction characteristic of many newspapers, magazines, etc." Journalists can live with that. But the entry goes on to say that it is "a facile or sensational style, with many clichés." That's a little harder to accept.

Journalists who are proud of their craft are proud of their command of the language and endorse the point of view, inspired as much by George Orwell as by anyone, that they have an obligation to protect the language and guard it against its enemies. This means that they must resist using clichés, or what Orwell called "dying metaphors," or any inclination to numb the intellect's sharpness.[35] John Carey has said, in an extended commentary, that the "power of language to confront us with the vivid, the frightening or the unaccustomed is equaled only by its opposite—the power of language to muffle any such alarms."[36] Carey is right. I think all journalists must face up to the fact that there is a tension between the cognitive obligations the language is supposed to perform and the conditions under which it is used. The former inclines journalism to clarity, the latter to clichés.

There is also a tension between the need of journalism to sell itself and the need to provide a judicious reading of the day's events. The need to sell inclines the language to hyperbole; the need for judiciousness inclines the language to a kind of monotone—spare and efficient word choice to a fault. Good journalists know that these tensions must be resolved and the use of language turned into an art. Many succeed, but always within certain limits.

The limits are imposed by the public. Whatever else might be said about the language of journalism, it is fair to say that it is disciplined by its public and empirical character. Its vocabulary is the vocabulary of public discourse. It may strive to represent scientific ideas or the abstract notions of philosophy, but it does not adopt the vocabularies of those disciplines. It always uses a vocabulary that can be understood in the street or in the marketplace. Furthermore, it is always explicit in its references; it is laced with nouns, adjectives, and proper names; it is concrete, powerfully descriptive, and light on, although not devoid of, metaphors and similes. That does not mean it is devoid of beauty. It may well be beautiful. It has its own aesthetics—an aesthetics of originality, form, and efficiency, the last of these a product of the practical work it must do for us.

Hugh Kenner sums up these attributes by calling them together "the plain style."[37] It marks not journalism alone but much of prose fiction as well. But to say that it is plain is not to say that it is natural. Like the other forms of rhetoric, journalism is a contrivance, an artifice with its own palette pointing to the concrete and the experiential. Its great merit is that it is trustworthy. "The plain style," Kenner notes, "seems to be announcing at every phrase its subjection to the check of experience and namable things."[38] And so, "[h]andbooks and copy editors now teach journalists how to write plainly, that is, in such a manner that they will be trusted. You get yourself trusted by artifice."[39]

Narrative: The Story and the Storyteller

What applies to language applies with equal force to the operations of the narrative principle in journalism. But as with linguistic principles, there is more to the matter than meets the eye. To speak of narrative is to speak, as Robert Scholes and Robert Kellogg have reminded us, of a story and a storyteller.[40] The journalist creates both.

The storyteller in newspapers and news magazines is often disguised behind the device of an anonymous third person. That third person may be the publisher, the persona in the mind of the writer who states authoritatively that the war has ended or has been declared, or that the election campaign has begun or the vote tallied. *Time* magazine, when it was published by Henry Luce, was written in a uniform style so that it would appear, despite the many hands at work, that there was a single writer and a single voice—Mr. Luce's. That voice was clever, male, and a bit chummy, conferring judgments with the wisdom and insight of a true insider and expressing them confidently in an accessible prose style.

The *New York Times* in its way and the Associated Press in its also strive for uniformity and consistency in their news voices. The narrator in such organizations is likely to be less of an inside-dopester than a public authority with quasi-official status. True to its origins in seventeenth-century English gazettes, much of twenty-first-century news journalism in the English-speaking world retains elements of officialdom. The announcements from the White House and the results of a criminal trial each turn the narrator in journalism into an official of sorts who functions as a town crier or herald once did, but now with a stylized, polished, and routinized voice.

Of course, sometimes in journalism—when the journalist rather than the institution is speaking—the narrator is the journalist himself or herself. Occasionally, he or she appears as "this writer" or "this reporter" or simply as "I" or "me." Pete Hamill was an "I" in his story on the Everglades, as was Joan Didion in *Miami*. So the narrator is sometimes official-like and a part of the establishment; sometimes he or she is in an adversarial relationship to the same establishment; sometimes he or she is simply the journalist—his or her subjectivity revealed. But in every case the narrator is a presence who guides the reader through a story. He or she shows, tells, and explains.

The devices the narrator in journalism uses are those used by all storytellers: plot, characterization, action, dialogue, sequencing, dramatization, causation, myth, metaphor, and explanation. This may be understood simply by considering what all newspaper editors conventionally require in stories filed by apprentice reporters. They require, they say, five Ws—a who, a what, a where, a when, and a why. The *who* guides the writer to construct characters, the *what* to action, the *where* to sites, the *when* to a time line, and the *why* to motive or meaning.[41] The characters may exist simply as names attached to institutions—what James Ettema and Theodore Glasser call "authorized knowers"—or as carefully described individuals with clear voices, personalities, and physical shapes.[42]

The action may be rendered in an abbreviated or sustained form, the sites only alluded to, and the motive barely canvassed. The treatments may be shallow or profound, cursory or thorough. But in every case, the narrative the journalist constructs will contain these elements.

There are some twists. Stories in prose fiction normally begin at a beginning, and the middles and the ends fall into place according to the sequencing required by conventional time lines. In hard news, by contrast, the endings of events mark the beginnings of the stories. The lead is a conclusion of sorts and the rest is background.

It is not always so. Features very often start with setting shots—either physical or psychological. Narrative documentaries such as "South of Heaven," a seven-part series by Tom French published in the *St. Petersburg Times* in May 1991, is a good example. It was inspired as much by portraiture as by narrative, and the result was a story replete from the beginning with site and character descriptions.

"South of Heaven" is one of the most ambitious pieces of journalism ever published in a newspaper. French, a staff reporter with the *Times*, spent a year with the students and staff of a high school in Largo, a community north of St. Petersburg, Florida. A major theme of his documentary, implicit from the beginning, was that much more than academic learning goes on in high schools. Romance, ambition for status, confusion, and personal despair are as common as poems, foreign languages, and calculus. French's account revealed that high schools are in trouble because the society is in trouble and teachers are often required to be parents to a generation that includes too many orphans. He built his portrait by drawing detailed pictures of teachers, students, and parents and by weaving their individual stories into a single narrative. It is an impressive achievement.

The operations of the principle of narrative are normally less complex in newspaper journalism than they are in French's piece. That journalism is a public discourse inclines it, in narrative terms, to simplicity and explicitness. For example, efficiency and clarity are the principles that shape the construction of the hard news story, which stands at the opposite end of the spectrum. In narrative terms, the hard news story comprises actors, actions, and time sequences without the benefit of carefully drawn setting shots, scenes, character development, and suspenseful plot lines. But it is wrong to imagine journalism's narrative approaches as limited by the inverted pyramid. Between the inverted pyramid and the narrative documentary, a journalist may choose from many approaches.

Much of it will be underdeveloped from the point of view of the serious student of narrative. But it is useful then to shift ground and consider that the short, short stories in newspapers and broadcasts are stories within unfolding stories. Stories in newspapers and daily broadcasts especially are guided and constructed by reference to a metanarrative that at the most general level reveals society's story. At a less general level, they are guided by society's yet incomplete stories. They call for, as André Codrescu has noted, a follow-up that answers the childlike question, "What happened afterward? . . . What happened to the man who wrote the Hitler diaries or the man who faked the autobiography of the pope?"[43] To these we might add: What happened to the economy? What happened to women after the Supreme Court reconsidered *Roe v. Wade*? What happened to President Bush after he met concerned citizens on the lawn of the White House to discuss the state of the nation?

These events are marked by stories, follow-ups, and commentaries. The last of these may be discourses by editorialists on how we should evaluate such things. But they all fit together in metanarratives about society's progress, however many hands are engaged in rendering the descriptions and interpretations, however incomplete they may seem at the time. James Carey has noted that it is useful to think of the newspaper as a curriculum—to be judged, in other words, by how it follows a story day by day or month by month rather than by the character and substance of each story.[44] The curriculum fleshes out the detail and substance of a story—a narrative.

Meaning: Myth, Metaphor, Explanation

"South of Heaven" is compelling reading for a variety of reasons. It is carefully constructed and narrated; its imagery and characters are vivid and memorable; but more centrally, it contains an intellectual structure or principle of meaning that is, well, meaningful or persuasive. The principle of meaning is the last of my five elements.

The stories and the characters of "South of Heaven" are exquisitely aligned to a compelling idea that is the news of the series—the social system is disintegrating. The lives of the individuals described in the series reflect the forces of disintegration outside of the school—in the family, in race relations, and in the economy. The disintegration of failing individuals or the conflicts of successful ones, and the therapeutic and compensatory efforts of the teachers, are each an expression of such a theorized picture of society.

A similar idea organized Joan Didion's "Slouching Towards Bethlehem," an eloquent description written in 1967 of the comings and goings of the youthful inhabitants of Haight-Ashbury in San Francisco.[45] Didion's inspiration for that report and its principle of meaning was derived from "The Second Coming," a poem by W. B. Yeats in which the words "slouching towards Bethlehem" are part of its powerful cadence. In this poem, Yeats wrote gloomily that as the mythic gyre turns and widens, "things fall apart" and "the center cannot hold."

Didion secularized the notion of the gyre but held on to the observation that anarchy and atomization were everywhere. She said that the youths of Haight-Ashbury were hardly the bearers of a new communal vision, as they had sometimes been described in the press. Rather, they were the victims of America's disintegrating social system. The evidence for her belief was the halting and abstract language the flower children used. For Didion it was still an axiom that "the ability to think for one's self depends upon one's mastery of the language."[46] What she saw and reported, then, was the "desperate attempt of a handful of pathetically unequipped children to create a community in a social vacuum."[47]

Like all storytellers, journalists inscribe meaning on the facts and events they describe. The devices they use may vary. Some depend on myth—the myth of evil, for example—and/or metaphor. (Valentine stories are based on the metaphor of the heart.) Others depend on the secular explanatory devices of modern social scientists. Such devices are prominent in modern journalism.

For the most part, journalists are not highly conscious of the explanatory techniques they use. In this vein, James Carey has argued that while the answers to the how and the why of daily journalism are almost always hidden, daily journalists have a fairly fixed view of the causes of human behavior. "Because news is mainly about the doings and sayings of individuals," he says, "why is usually answered by identifying the motives of those individuals."[48] Rational motive is assumed to be the primary cause of behavior. Missing from the picture is a consideration of causes that transcend individuals and their motives and reflect deeper impulses in society and culture.

Such wider theories are not always missing. A reading of contemporary journalism that embraces more than the news pages reveals that there is as much variation in the intellectual cosmologies of journalists as there is in the cosmologies of social scientists and literary critics. I will identify four theories of human behavior in order to illustrate how the principle of meaning functions in contemporary journalism.

A first type, the interpretative method James Carey has identified, is an example of rational individualism. It is a theory that reads the world in terms of individuals and their mainly rational calculations. There is a kinship between this theory and traditional utilitarianism. That such a theory is dominant in a liberal-utilitarian culture is hardly surprising.

I would call a second type simply sociological. In the sociological method, events and behavior are explained primarily in the light of the composition of the social world as distinct from the unique psychological composition of individuals. The sociological method requires that the investigator read the impulses on which individuals act as the result of forces external to such individuals. These forces are to be found primarily in the domain of social organization and the structure of power. Individual actors are likely to be unaware—or to be falsely conscious—of the primary causes of their actions.

The third is a bit like the first. It works out of the category of the individual; however, it emphasized the nonrational. Dr. Sigmund Freud's presence may be noticed here. The unconscious, which is the product of experience and discovered in the detail of biography, is regarded as the source of the impulses that govern much of behavior. Individuals act out of unremembered psychic wounds that their current lives trigger.

The fourth is cultural—the method of Didion's "Slouching . . ." is a vivid example—and it is idealist in the technical sense. In Didion's cosmology, individuals are the embodiment of ideas and impulses that dwell in the culture. As in the sociological and the psychological, individuals are more the expressions of things than they are the source of things. But the things they are the expression of are to be found not so much in the society's organization or in an individual's psychic wounds, but in society's texts and language.

I have said all that needs to be said about rational individualism. In any case, James Carey covers it nicely. In the world of journalism that Carey analyzes, human actors are possessed of conscious motives and purposes, and human acts can be understood in light of them. Individual accounts of behavior are taken at face value. Human beings do what they intend for the reasons that they give. The unconscious or falsely conscious mark the other examples.

An example of the sociological method was published in the St. Peters-

burg Times on February 12, 1992, in an analysis of the reason Mike Tyson, the former world boxing champion, was convicted of rape while William Kennedy Smith, the nephew both of a senator and of a former president, was acquitted of a similar charge two months earlier. The story begins with these statements:

> William Kennedy Smith is a free man, about to walk through the halls of a university as a first-year medical student.
>
> Mike Tyson is living on borrowed time, out on bail awaiting a sentence that could put him in a prison cell for the rest of his life.

There were actually several approaches to the *why* of the acquittal and the conviction in this analysis. One approach took account of the evidence presented at the respective trials; another focused on the differences in the victims. (In the Kennedy case, the victim was picked up in a bar and was a 28-year-old single mother; the other was a Sunday school teacher and barely 18.) Yet another approach spoke of the skill of the respective prosecutors and lawyers for the defendants. However, the various approaches were themselves subject to an understanding provided in a single proposition attributed to Martha Burt, "a researcher for the Urban Institute, a non-profit policy and research organization in Washington." Ms. Burt said: "Smith is white, rich and a Kennedy. . . . Tyson is not white, not a Kennedy. He's rich, but he wasn't born into it."

So the primary way to understand these findings, according to the *St. Petersburg Times* writers, is to move from the categories of class and race to the fate of these single individuals. Marx, Weber, Michels, Pareto, and Mosca in their various ways have inscribed this explanatory method on the minds of social scientists and their disciples in the field of journalism. The jurors may have thought they were dispensing justice; to the writers of the *Times*, or at least to Ms. Burt, their actions embodied the predictable impulses of a society marked by racial divisions.

If Marx and Weber et al. in their various ways inhabited the minds of these St. Petersburg journalists and one of the principal sources, Sigmund Freud, then developmental psychologists and anthropological notions of a subculture provided the intellectual coordinates for Gail Sheehy's analyses of presidential candidates published in *Vanity Fair* starting in September 1987. In the introduction to the book in which the articles were republished, Sheehy wrote candidly that as a journalist she had been covering campaigns since 1968, but that as an author she had concentrated "on character and psychological development. In 1984, these two parallel tracks . . . came together. *Vanity Fair* magazine asked me to find out who Gary Hart really was."[49]

Sheehy was lucky, because by the time she was ready to publish Gary Hart's story, Hart's philandering and tastes in recreation had been discovered. She made *character* the true subject of her inquiry into Hart's life and sought, therefore, to ascertain what was most fundamental to his personality and behavior. She worked with complex intellectual materials.

> Character . . . refers to the enduring marks left by life that set one apart as an individual. Commonly, [they] are carved in by parental and religious imprinting, by a child's early interactions with siblings, peers at school, and authority figures. The manners of one's social class and the soil in which one grows up often remain indelible, and certain teachers and coaches or books and ideas may leave a lasting impression. . . . [W]hat matters . . . in a would-be leader, is how many of the passages of adult life have been met and mastered, and what he or she has done with the life accidents dealt by fate.[50]

It would be possible to argue with the results of Sheehy's analyses or to compare them with Didion's theories. But it is not possible to deny that in these articles she operated both as a journalist and a theorist with a carefully developed intellectual system. She operated as a journalist by interviewing former teachers, friends, parents, coaches, lovers, and associates in order to put together factual accounts of the lives of her subjects. But she also used the diagnostic techniques of a thoughtful psychologist. The pictures she formed of the characters of such individuals were pictures that the subjects themselves could not compose.

For example, Hart was undoubtedly unconscious of the impulses that drove him and gave him, as Sheehy was to conclude, "a pathological deficit of character [that] riddled the public man as thoroughly as it ruled the private one."[51] Sheehy argued that the impulses were established in his personality when, as a youngster in Ottawa, Kansas, he was cut off from normal friendships and the pleasures he might have derived from them by a cold and demanding mother who insisted that he conform to the strict codes of the Nazarene Church. Sheehy constructed a portrait of Hart in which the adult Hart could not escape the child who longed for forbidden pleasures. So regardless of his accounts of himself, the *why* of his behavior was to be found in the character of the child locked up in his soul.

By contrast, Didion's method of explanation focuses on the cultural as distinct from psychological. For Didion, what is unconscious resides not in the soul, as it did in Sheehy's Hart, but in society's primary texts or media. What is unconscious in human beings is ambient in the culture. Didion's meditation on Haight-Ashbury illustrates this method. But there is a better example of it in "Some Dreamers of the Golden Dream," a report published in the same collection. The site is the San Bernardino Valley in California. She writes:

> The future always looks good in the golden land, because no one remembers the past. Here is where the hot wind blows and the old ways do not seem relevant, where the divorce rate is double the national average and where one person in every thirty-eight lives in a trailer. Here is the last stop for all those who come from somewhere else, for all those who drifted away from the cold and the past and the old ways. Here is where they are trying to find a new life style, trying to find it in the only places they know to look: the movies and the newspapers. The case of Lucille Marie Maxwell Miller is a tabloid monument to the new life style.[52]

Lucille Miller was a murderer who discarded a husband in order to get a new one. She was unhappy. She did what the culture's axiology says you should do when you are finished with one thing and want another.

The study of all the major journalists and critics—from Walter Lippmann to Lewis Lapham—reveals something similar. Each works out of intellectual systems that shape both what they see and how they see it. They are not, of course, limited to theories of human action akin to the ones I have described. Their theories embrace, as it were, all that requires explanation. Typically, the systems contain conceptual templates that have been inscribed by such intellectual figures as John Stuart Mill, Max Weber, or Sigmund Freud. Sometimes they are grounded in the mythic and the metaphoric and can therefore be read more as literature than as social science. Thus, the operations of the principle of meaning in journalism vary according to who is writing and according to the explanatory or mythic systems that guide description and analysis. If there is a dominant method in daily journalism for conferring meaning, it is through the devices James Carey points to, in which causes and effects are read in terms of individuals possessed of motives acting more or less rationally. Such theorizing eschews references to social categories or even mythic notions of evil and virtue. But many journalists—some have been cited here—work in deeper intellectual cosmologies and thus confer meaning on their subjects in richer and more persuasive ways.

Conclusion

Let me end by summarizing the case I have tried to make and by suggesting some of the benefits that arise from reading journalism in my way. I have argued, first, that journalism is a form of expression that is the product of something called the Imagination. I have used the term *Imagination* in two carefully blended senses.

In the first sense, the Imagination is a property of individual human beings; it is, in short, their spontaneous consciousness-forming faculty. In the second sense, the Imagination is a property of culture. In this sense, it is made up of the methods and practices established in the culture for framing experience and forming consciousness. Language itself—but more relevant to the understanding I am attempting to promote—art, social science, fiction, and journalism are each examples of methods in culture for forming consciousness. In these various incarnations, the Imagination conceived as a property of culture connects the imaginations of individuals to society's consciousness-forming projects. Individual works of journalism comprise inquiries by individuals into the state of things. So journalism is a cultural practice, a section or part of the modern Imagination that in its broadest and most comprehensive sense includes all the devices we use to form consciousness. Journalism—or more precisely, the Journalistic Imagination—is the primary method of framing experience and forming the public consciousness of the here and now. Its principles are immanent, more or less, in every journalist and in every journalistic institution.

Second, I have named and analyzed the five principles of design that mark every piece of journalism. They are (1) news or news judgment, (2) reporting or evidentiary method, (3) linguistic technique, (4) narrative technique, and (5) method of interpretation or meaning. Clearly each of these principles of design is operationalized differently by different individuals and different institutions. But in my view, all journalists work off a palette composed of these principles. They exist in relation to the journalist as the principles of form and color exist in relation to painters, and they are embodied as elements, however inchoately, in every piece of journalism.

What is the use of all this? There are several uses, and I will conclude with a brief review of some of them. The first is that it enriches our vision of journalism. Whatever else the conception adumbrated in these remarks may be, it is richer than most, perhaps all, of the analyses of journalism. Most of what passes for the analysis of journalism—whether it is written by journalists or by social scientists—takes the journalism of the newsroom as a starting point and argues for its worth or meaning or significance in terms of what it does rather than what it is. The analysis of all the detail and especially the analysis of the work of journalism's poets or artists enable us to see truly what is going on. The payoff that comes from including journalism's more ambitious forms in the analysis is that it is possible to see more clearly what is inchoate in its less ambitious forms.

This broadening of the subject gives rise to a second benefit. By expanding the world of reference, it is easier to locate journalism in the territory of art and the humanities. Journalism is made; it doesn't just happen. So the language we use to see it and to teach it must be akin to the language of art. The language of art encourages students to enter the imagination of the artist and meditate on how the artist does what he or she does. In this sense, what I have written is simply a meditation on what I do. I am a journalist. I have tried in this piece to create a language that expresses what I and other journalists are doing as we work off our palettes. With the words and concepts I have used in this piece, I can say why I have written a news lead in a particular way, or why I have chosen to put this story on page one and another on page eight. I can say why one human interest story is a delight and another is not. I can tell you why a fact is authoritative, why a particular set of words are apposite, why a narrative line works, and why I see an event's meaning in a certain way.

A third benefit is that it enables us to be better critics of journalism. This system of analysis provides a straightforward guide to an analysis of journalistic achievements. It guides the critic to an assessment of the quality of news judgment in a journalistic piece, the authority of its facts, the clarity and originality of the language, the utility and success of its narrative technique, and the degree to which the journalist has penetrated and thereby interpreted the materials he or she has brought to light. Put differently, it engages the critic in the work of the editor rather than the work of the politician or bureaucrat. An editor measures achievements according to what is truly possible. A politician or bureaucrat measures impacts or effects, extrinsic rather than intrinsic goods.

What is good for the critic is good for the educator. As I noted at the outset, two major reports were written in the 1980s by American journalism educators on curriculum and teaching, and both contained critiques and suggestions for reform. It strikes me that neither hit the mark because the authors started and ended with both a limited view of journalism and an uncritical understanding of the broader university and its culture. For reasons I have already suggested, journalism education will look profoundly different when teachers of journalism add the perspectives of the artist and critic to the perspectives of the news journalist and the social scientist. In the schools themselves, such a cast of mind should encourage more systematic teaching of the elements of journalism in the class and lecture rooms and less reliance on hit-and-miss apprenticeship teaching in newsrooms. As important as the newsroom is—there is no implication here that it is not important—the class or lecture room is also important, and the systematic exploration of the language of journalism is best dealt with in the latter.

It should also encourage a more thoughtfully constructed set of connections with the other departments of the university. For example, historians put the past into perspective and encourage the development of a capacity to judge what matters; information scientists are in the business of finding facts, and historians, lawyers, and social scientists are in the business of assessing them; literary and composition theorists examine words, sentences, paragraphs, metaphors, rhythm, diction, dialogue, narrative, characterization, and dramatization; philosophers analyze systems of meaning. So the five principal elements of journalism may be imagined as starting points for laying out a curriculum that connects study in the schools and departments of journalism to classical disciplines and courses in the university at large. The task of journalism education in the university is to transmit journalism's principles—to see to it that these principles are immanent or, to put it differently, represented strongly in the mental equipment of novice journalists. In my view, the connection to the classical disciplines is direct and clear, and ought to be strengthened.

Finally, the approach I am recommending puts first things first. It is not journalists on their own who have written skimpy accounts of the journalistic palette and thereby diminished both the craft and what is necessary through curriculum to the formation of good journalists. My reading of journalism education has led me to conclude that social scientists have been likewise helpful. What I would construe as social science—the analysis of systems of interaction rather than the analysis of acts or methods through which artifice is produced—seems to have dominated the research wings of journalism schools. I am talking not just of the division between those who say they engage in quantitative as opposed to qualitative scholarship. I am talking, as I have already indicated, of the division between the analysis of the systems through qualitative or quantitative means, on the one hand, and the analysis of the creative acts of single individuals, on the other. Such acts may in turn give birth to systems, and they, too, may be studied. In the meantime, it is time to start at the beginning, to incorporate an understanding of the creative process more fully into the study of journalism, and to equip students with more appropriate capacities of execution and judgment.

To conclude, the study of journalism practices should be invigorated by the spirit of art and the humanities. The humanities, properly understood, celebrate creation more than power. They celebrate the highest achievements of the human imagination and meditate on them as starting points for civilized life and discourse. Journalism education and practice can benefit from a recasting within such a world. Put differently, as journalism is taught, it should be bathed in the light of the Imagination and the idea that journalism can be and often is one of our highest arts.

Notes

1. T. S. Eliot, *Notes Towards the Definition of Culture* (London: Faber and Faber, 1954). I am using the indefinite article in my title to suggest that the definition I am proposing may not be the only one.

2. G. Stuart Adam, "Thinking Journalism," in *Content for Canadian Journalists* (July/August, 1988); a version of this article appeared in the *Canadian Journal of Communication* 14, no. 2 (May 1989) under the title "Journalism Knowledge and Journalism Practice: The Problems of Curriculum and Research in University Schools of Journalism." See also "Journalism and the University: Reporters, Writers and Critics," in Kathleen Jaeger, ed., *The Idea of the University, 1789–1989,* (Halifax: Institute for Advanced Study, University of King's College, 1990), and "The World Next Door: A Commonwealth Perspective," *Gannett Center Journal* 2, no. 2 (Spring 1988).

3. Planning for Curricular Change: A Report on the Future of Journalism and Mass Communication Education, School of Journalism, University of Oregon, 1984 (Oregon Report); "Challenges and Opportunities in Journalism and Mass Communication Education: A Report of the Task Force on Journalism and Mass Communication Education," (AEJMC Task Force) in *Journalism Educator* 44, no. 12 (Spring 1989).

4. Oregon Report, 5, 10, 11.

5. N. K. Llewellyn, *The Bramble Bush* (New York: Oceana Publications, 1930), 56. Llewellyn, who was a lawyer, was quoting a psychologist.

6. Michael Oakeshott, *Experience and Its Modes* (London: Cambridge University Press, 1978), 124.

7. C. Wright Mills, *The Sociological Imagination* (New York: Oxford University Press, 1957).

8. R. G. Collingwood, *The Idea of History* (New York: Oxford University Press, 1959).

9. Northrop Frye, *The Educated Imagination* (Toronto: Canadian Broadcasting Corporation, 1980).

10. Michael Oakeshott, *The Voice of Poetry in the Conversation of Mankind: An Essay* (London: Bowes and Bowes, 1959), 17.

11. Oakeshott, *Experience and Its Modes*, 32.

12. Joan Didion, "Why I Write," in *The Writer and Her Work*, ed. Janet Sternberg (New York: W. W. Norton, 1980), 20.

13. Joan Didion, *Miami* (New York: Simon and Schuster, 1987), 52.

14. Joseph Conrad, "Preface" to *The Nigger of the Narcissus, Typhoon and Other Stories* (Hammondsworth, Middlesex: Penguin, 1986), 13.

15. Jennifer Warren and George Ramos (of the *Los Angeles Times*), "Devastation and Heroism," in the *Ottawa Citizen*, October 19, 1989, D1.

16. Conrad, 12.

17. Joseph Frank, *The Beginning of English Newspapers, 1620–1660* (Cambridge, Mass.: Harvard University Press, 1961).

18. A. Aspinall, "Statistical Accounts of the London Newspapers in the Eighteenth Century," *English Historical Review* 63 (1948): 201–32; see also Stanley Morison, *The English Newspaper: Some Account of the Physical Development of Journals* (London: Cambridge University Press, 1963), 197.

19. W. H. Auden, "Making, Knowing, Judging," in *The Dyer's Hand and Other Essays* (New York: Random House, 1962), 51.

20. I first encountered this formulation in Curtis MacDougall, *Interpretative Reporting* (New York: Macmillan, 1972); another source is Melvin Mencher, *News Reporting and Writing* (Dubuque, Iowa: Wm. C. Brown, 1977).

21. This quote comes from an essay by Thomas Gavin, "The Truth Beyond Facts: Journalism and Literature," in *The Georgia Review* 45, no. 1 (Spring 1991): 45.

22. Ibid.

23. The story is recorded in James Carey, "The Dark Continent of American Journalism" in *Reading the News*, ed. Robert Karl Manhoff and Michael Schudson (New York: Pantheon, 1987), 170.

24. The phrase "pageant of creation" is George Kelly's; it is quoted in Janet Emig, *The Web of Meaning, Essays on Writing, Teaching, Learning and Thinking* (Upper Montclair, N.J.: Boynton/Cook, 1983), 165.

25. Ibid., 160.

26. Landon's struggle with cancer of the pancreas was the cover story of *People* magazine, May 6, 1991.

27. Robert Stone, "The Reason for Stories: Toward a Moral Fiction," *Harper's Magazine*, June 1988, 71.

28. Milan Kundera, *The Art of the Novel* (New York: Harper and Row, 1986), 83.

29. John Hersey, "The Legend on the License," *The Yale Review* 75, no. 2 (February 1986): 296.

30. Ibid., 290.

31. John Carey, *The Faber Book of Reportage* (London: Faber and Faber, 1987), xxix.

32. Bob Woodward, *Wired* (New York: Pocket Books, 1984).

33. Gail Sheehy, *Character, America's Search for Leadership* (New York: William Morrow and Co., 1988), 18.

34. Hersey, 308.

35. George Orwell, "Politics and the English Language," in *The Collected Essays, Journalism and Letters of George Orwell*, vol. 1, ed. Sonia Orwell and Ian Angus (London: Secker and Warburg, 1968).

36. John Carey, xxxi.

37. Hugh Kenner, "The Politics of the Plain Style," in *Literary Journalism in the Twentieth Century*, ed. Norman Sims (New York: Oxford University Press, 1990).

38. Ibid., 189.

39. Ibid., 187.

40. Robert Scholes and Robert Kellogg, *The Nature of Narrative* (New York: Oxford University Press, 1966).

41. I heard this first from Roy Peter Clark, senior scholar at The Poynter Institute for Media Studies, who said that he first heard the idea of journalistic narrative formulated this way from Richard Zahler, a journalist who works in Seattle.

42. James Ettema and Theodore Glasser, "On the Epistemology of Investigative Journalism," *Communication* 8, no. 2 (1985): 188.

43. André Codrescu, "Of Unknown Endings and New Beginnings," *The Globe and Mail*, October 19, 1987, A7.

44. James Carey, "The Dark Continent," 151.

45. Joan Didion, "Slouching Towards Bethlehem," in a book with the same title (New York: Dell, 1967).

46. Ibid., 123.

47. Ibid., 122.

48. James Carey, "The Dark Continent," 180.

49. Sheehy, 11.

50. Ibid., 15.

51. Ibid., 39.

52. Joan Didion, "Some Dreamers of a Golden Dream," in *Slouching Towards Bethlehem*, 4.

2

The American Conversation
and the Language of Journalism

Roy Peter Clark

When most critics write about the language of journalism, they do so in a satirical vein. Using the pejorative term "journalese," they ridicule the journalist's addiction to bureaucratic clichés or hyperboles of action. To read a newspaper, they say, is to learn that all budget proposals face the "chopping block" and that all fires "rage."[1]

It is possible to define the language of journalism in a more ideal sense, to describe its most common characteristics, to understand its effects, to learn about its users and audiences, and to imagine how to teach it more effectively, in both classrooms and newsrooms. These are the goals of this essay.

The notes I am about to offer on the language of journalism apply, in my opinion, to all the narrative forms of journalism and to all journalistic media, and with some understandable exceptions, for all time. They apply as well to the reportage of eighteenth-century England as to *USA Today*. They apply to the *New York Times*, the *St. Petersburg Times*, and the *Times of London*. In spite of differences in readership, they apply to all of Toronto's heavenly bodies: the *Globe and Mail*, the *Star*, and the *Sun*. They apply as well to the captions under Rupert Murdoch's nudes as to the economic summaries in the *Wall Street Journal*. The language I am describing is the language of NBC, the BBC, CBN, NPR. It comes out of the mouths of Cokie Roberts, and Paul Harvey, and even Larry King and Geraldo Rivera. It communicates the meaning of long investigations and brief editorials, of film documentaries and sports briefs, of passionate commentaries and cold, neutral analyses. I cannot test this, except through translations into English, but I imagine the essential characteristics of the language of journalism can be found in all languages in which real news is conveyed, especially when readers are imagined as citizens.

The examples of journalism are so vast and varied that in any newspaper, on any day, you can find exceptions to the characteristics I am about to describe. We can view these exceptions two ways: as refreshing variations that validate the norms; or as mistakes of judgment and illustrations of bad writing.

Drawing upon the commentary of George Orwell, Hugh Kenner, William Strunk and E. B. White, William Zinsser, John Carey, and others, and upon my own literary analysis of modern and historical examples of journalism, I offer this list:

- The language of journalism is concrete and specific, especially when it comes to dogs and the names of dogs.
- The language of journalism is active.
- The language of journalism, if I may create a hybrid, is front-heavy.
- The language of journalism is democratic and, if I may say so, American.
- The language of journalism is different from speech, but more like speech than most other forms of prose.
- The language of journalism is plain.
- The most valued quality of the language of journalism is clarity, and its most desired effect is to be understood.

These qualities are made manifest in journalistic forms that can be called *stories* rather than *articles*.

The Name of the Dog

The language of journalism is concrete and specific. A saying at the *St. Petersburg Times* requires reporters to "get the name of the dog, the brand of the beer, the color and make of the sports car."

A man ties a bowling ball to the neck of a fluffy, white, three-legged dog and throws the dog into Tampa Bay. The mutt is rescued and, eventually, adopted. I can't explain why, but the story is incomplete, and barely satisfying, without the name of the dog. In fact, I'm more interested in the dog's name than the villain's name. Was its name Sid or Nancy, Butch or Fluffy, Aries or Ariel? The name of the dog makes the story real. (Local reporters nicknamed him Tripod!)

I remember a police story that came out of my end of town. It was a hot, oppressively humid Florida day, and things started to go badly inside a house on Sixty-third Avenue South. First the air conditioner broke down, making it unbearably sticky for husband, wife, and mother-in-law. Mother-in-law's irritation increased when the television set also went on the blink. (The reporter didn't tell me, but I wanted to know what she was watching at the time. Was it *Jeopardy* or *Wheel of Fortune* or *The Dating Game* or *One Life to Live?*)

The old woman complained to her son-in-law that the television was not working. So the son-in-law did what any Florida man would do under such circumstances: He shot out the screen of the television set with a handgun. What followed was a stand-off with police and his eventual surrender.

The reporter, Doreen Carvajal, does tell us, bless her, that the man's foul mood and subsequent violence were influenced by his imbibing twenty-four cans of beer that day. Black Label beer. Not Heineken or Budweiser or Coors. But Black Label.

No wonder he shot out the television.

In preparation for the execution of serial murderer Ted Bundy, reporter Christopher Scanlan flew to Utah to visit the family of one presumed Bundy victim. Years ago a young woman left the house and never returned. Scanlan found the detail that told the story of the family's unending grief. He noticed a piece of tape over the light switch next to the front door, so no one could turn it off. The mother always left the light on until her daughter returned home, and though years had passed, that light was kept burning, like an eternal flame.

In the introduction to his anthology of reporting, British scholar John Carey explains the power of the specific and concrete: "A distinguishing feature of good reportage is that it combats this inevitable and planned retreat of language from the real. However good it is, good reportage cannot, of course, get beyond language, because it is language itself. It is an axiom of modern critical theory that there are no accessible 'realities,' only texts that relate to one another intertextually. But even if he believes this, the good reporter must do everything in his power to counteract it, struggling to isolate the singularities that will make his account real for his readers—not just something written, but something seen."[2]

The goal for the reporter is not unlike the one Joseph Conrad described for the artist: "My task," writes Conrad, "which I am trying to achieve is, by the power of the written word to make you hear, to make you feel—it is, before all, to make you see. That—and no more, and it is everything. If

I succeed, you shall find there according to your deserts: encouragement, consolation, fear, charm—all you demand—and, perhaps, also that glimpse of truth for which you have forgotten to ask."[3]

In his anthology, Carey traces this linguistic imperative back to the earliest collected examples of reportage:

> This book is (and is meant to be) full of unusual or indecorous or incidental images that imprint themselves scaldingly on the mind's eye: the ambassador peering down the front of Queen Elizabeth I's dress and noting the wrinkles; Joe Louis's nostrils like a double-barreled shotgun; Mata Hari drawing on her filmy stockings on the morning of her execution; the Tamil looter at the fall of Kuala Lumpur upending a carton of snowy Slazenger tennis balls; Richard Hillary closing one eye to see his lips like motor tyres; . . . the assassin Booth catching his boot-heel in the drapery round Lincoln's box; Pliny watching people with cushions on their heads against the ash from the volcano; Mary, Queen of Scots, suddenly aged in death, with her pet dog cowering among her skirts and her head held on by one recalcitrant piece of gristle; the starving Irish with their mouths green from their diet of grass.[4]

What was the name of Queen Mary's dog?

No Passives Allowed

The language of journalism is active. I mean this syntactically, but in a larger sense as well. The best-written journalism comes from direct observation or eyewitness accounts of people in action.

The big story of the day, on Thursday, January 28, 1993, for the *St. Petersburg Times* appeared on page one with the headline "Man kills three in Tampa café." These six words, stark as a haiku, reveal the language of journalism. Three words: *Man kills three*. Subject, active verb, direct object order. Two more words—*in Tampa*—to reveal the *where*: close to home. One word at the end for emphasis—*café*—a homey word for dramatic contrast with the alliterative *kill*.

The blurb, or story summary, specifies the action: "Paul Calden calmly walked into the Island Center building in Tampa on Wednesday and shot five of his former coworkers at Fireman's Fund Insurance Co. Three died. He had been fired." Four verbs, the first three active and the final one brilliantly passive, suggesting the killer's own pathological sense of victimization.

The body of the story retells the action in chronological narrative:

TAMPA—It was shortly before 1 p.m. Wednesday and the Island Center Cafe was bustling with a lunch crowd of about 30 people.

A white bulletin board to the right of the entrance advertised "Today's Specials": taco salad for $3.75 and turkey and Swiss pita with macaroni salad for $3.50. Beer cheese and chicken noodle were the soups of the day.

But 33-year-old Paul L. Calden wasn't interested. Dressed in a business suit, Calden walked in through two glass front doors, went to the food counter and ordered a Diet Coke.

Then he walked toward a crowded table and pulled a 9mm semi-automatic handgun from beneath his suit jacket.

He quickly put it to the back of a customer's head and fired.

Within seconds, Calden had shot five people. All were high-ranking supervisors with Fireman's Fund Insurance Co., a company that had fired him eight months earlier. Calden reportedly was a claims manager for the company.

The room exploded into chaos.

"It was just bodies flying all over the place," said JoAnne McSorley, who was in the building at the time.

A 12-foot picture window behind the table where the victims were sitting was shattered. People scurried for cover, overturning tables. In her haste to flee, one woman left behind a pair of black high-heel shoes.

I never met a text I didn't feel like revising, this one included. James M. Cain could have written it better, as a cop story or a hard-boiled novel, but the elements are there: layers of detail that move from the mundane (the price of the taco salad) to the dangerous (the caliber of the gun) to the extraordinary (the abandoned high-heel shoes). By the way, always get the color of the abandoned high-heel shoes.

A seemingly extraneous detail (the two glass doors) foreshadows the violence, for gunshots will shatter a picture window. Another (the killer orders a Diet Coke) invites reflection on the nature of murderous and suicidal insanity. (Diets are for people with a future.)

The author could have done better than "The room exploded into chaos." That sentence, Orwell would say, has the look of something we've seen before. But its activity reflects the language of journalism. The murderer *walked* to the table and *pulled* a handgun. People *scurried* for cover, *overturning* tables.

Jacques Barzun has condemned such an approach to news telling as "irrelevant fiction-style."[5] In an essay published by the Freedom Forum, Barzun attacked what he called "the novelty" of using the techniques of fiction, such as scene setting, "to start a news report."

Barzun explains: "Now, I don't want to read that. I want the traditional, first-paragraph lead, which when well done is infinitely better prose than this feeble imitation of story openings in the *Saturday Evening Post*."

Barzun gets it wrong on two counts. The use of fictional techniques to tell news is not a "novelty." It is as old as reportage itself, as any exploration of historical anthologies will reveal. And although he condemns the use of fictional techniques as an expression of "the modern cult of art and complication," that is, elitism or putting on airs, Barzun may be guilty of the same sins.

Barzun doesn't need an experience of narrative from the press. Presumably he gets plenty of it from reading the traditional literary canon. But the newspaper has always played a role in America as the book of the masses. My grandfather, as far as I could tell, didn't read novels, nor books for that matter, but he read as many tabloid newspapers as New York City could offer, and he read them not just for the racing form or the straight news reports, but for stories, narratives of life in his city, written, at times, with the techniques of fiction.

On another tack, Barzun offers a persuasive criticism of the language of journalism, and, along the way, answers this important question: If the language of journalism is so active, concrete, and specific, why are so many pieces of journalism written in language that is passive, technical, and bureaucratic?

"It is a by-product of science and technology," argues Barzun, "which have made people want to sound expert, masters of some mysterious specialty endowed with a unique vocabulary. And since the technological is always progressing, the would-be smart and up-to-date have to keep inventing new ways of glorifying the commonplace with fancy new terms."

Orwell condemned such tendencies in his monumental 1946 essay "Politics and the English Language."[6] This essay inspired my move from English studies into journalism, and I have encountered other journalists, such as NPR's Margot Adler, who were similarly inspired.

"The inflated style," writes Orwell, "is itself a kind of euphemism. A mass of Latin words falls upon the facts like soft snow, blurring the outlines and covering up all the details. The great enemy of clear language is insincerity. When there is a gap between one's real and one's declared aims, one turns, as it were instinctively, to long words and exhausted idioms, like a cuttlefish squirting out ink."

The corruption of language, that is, bad or insincere writing, is a tool of tyranny. "In our time," writes Orwell, "political speech and writing are largely the defense of the indefensible. Things like the continuance of British rule in India, the Russian purges and deportations, the dropping of the atom bombs on Japan, can indeed be defended, but only by arguments which are too brutal for most people to face, and which do not square with the professed aims of political parties. Thus political language has to consist largely of euphemism, question-begging, and sheer cloudy vagueness."

Following Orwell's line of thinking, the job of the political reporter can be said to be, in large measure, a linguistic one: translating the evasive passive ("mistakes were made") into the accountable active ("The mayor knew of the plan and agreed to it").

Branch to the Right

The language of journalism is front-loaded or top-heavy or, if you prefer my neologism, front-heavy. On the level of stories, this is made emblematic by a narrative structure known as the inverted pyramid. But it operates on the sentence and paragraph level, too, even when the writer chooses an alternative narrative form to the wobbly pyramid.

Remember the old cigarette ad: "It's what's up front that counts"? That could serve well as the slogan for sentences in news stories.

"WASHINGTON—President Clinton will announce today he is lifting the 50-year ban on gays in the military, but the change will not occur immediately."

This standard news lead is direct, clear, and comprehensible. It achieves the effect described by Don Fry as "steady advance." The writer creates meaning by beginning a sentence with subject and verb.

Noam Chomsky taught us that in the deep structure of every sentence is a subject and verb.[7] That simple rule generates an infinite number of sentences, of such astonishing variety, that it is rare for an author, who is not self-plagiarizing, to repeat a sentence in a lifetime.

If meaning is created by subject and verb, then a sentence that begins with subject and verb *makes meaning early*.

I will use a technical term of textual linguistics to elaborate on this crucially important effect. Imagine each sentence you write printed on an infinitely wide piece of paper. Each sentence stretches from left to right.

A reporter writes a sentence with subject and verb at the beginning, followed by other subordinate elements, creating what scholars of writing call a "right-branching sentence."

I just created one. Subject and verb of the main clause are on the left ("A reporter writes") and all other elements branch off to the right. Many writers, John McPhee and John Steinbeck come to mind, create page after page of right-branching sentences, but with such variety in length and subordination that the effect is almost invisible.

The right-branching sentence is the staple of effective journalism in the modern era. It was not always the case. Traditional English prose favored a different style, with long introductory passages, the main clause discovered somewhere in the middle, or even near the period. You will recognize the style in Robert Burton's *The Anatomy of Melancholy:* "When Hippocrates heard these words so readily uttered without premeditation to declare the world's vanity, full of ridiculous contrariety, he made answer that necessity compelled men to many such actions and divers wills ensuing from divine permission, that we might not be idle, being nothing so odious to them as sloth and negligence."[8]

A rule of thumb: If you are ever called upon to diagram a sentence, avoid those written in the seventeenth century.

This tendency toward elaborate introduction, throat clearing, if you will, found its way into the sports reporting of the first half of this century. That's when writers like Grantland Rice and a young Red Smith inflated their prose and puffed up their sentences on the way to what Stanley Woodward described as "God-ing up the athletes." That's how Granny Rice could see Notre Dame's Four Horsemen "outlined against a blue-grey October sky," even though he was probably sitting in the press box.

Red Smith acknowledged the excesses of his youthful craft and explained that his goal, later in his career, was to purify and clarify his prose. Smith talked about the process: "In my later years I have sought to become simpler, straighter, and purer in my handling of the language. I've had many writing heroes, writers who have influenced me. Of the ones still alive, I can think of E. B. White. I certainly admire the pure, crystal stream of his prose. When I was very young as a sportswriter I knowingly and unashamedly imitated others. I had a series of heroes who would delight me for a while and I'd imitate them. . . . But slowly, by what process I have no idea, your own writing tends to crystallize, to take shape. Yet you've learned some moves from all these guys and they are somehow incorporated into your own style. Pretty soon you're not imitating any longer."[9]

Journalism scholar Dennis Jackson was intrigued by Smith's description of his style with its evolution toward clarity. Jackson pored over Smith's stories and columns from the 1930s through the 1970s, searching for specific, measurable differences. His conclusion: The older Red Smith, striving for clarity, stopped clearing his throat and wrote many more right-branching sentences.[10]

One of the last Red Smith stories to appear in the *New York Times* was his obituary of former heavyweight boxing champion Jack Dempsey. It was published in 1983, more than a year after Smith's own death.

> Jack Dempsey was one of the last of a dwindling company whose exploits distinguished the 1920s as "the golden age of sports."
>
> His contemporaries were Babe Ruth in baseball, Red Grange and the Four Horsemen of Notre Dame in football, Bobby Jones and Walter Hagen in golf, Bill Tilden, Helen Wills Moody and Suzanne Lenglen in tennis, Johnny Weissmuller and Gertrude Ederle in swimming, Paavo Nurmi in track, Man o' War, the racehorse, and Earl Sande, the jockey. But none of the others enjoyed more lasting popularity than the man who ruled boxing between 1919 and 1926.[11]

Three sentences, all right-branching, but splendidly different. Smith uses the verb *to be* to good effect, especially in the second sentence. The epic flow of that right branch carries a glorious list of names, rivaling Homer's naming of the ships. This is the secret of the right-branch sentence: It helps the writer create sentences of infinite length that are equally clear (if we could live that long). It also makes "calculating machines" like the Flesch test and the Gunning Fog Index go haywire by proving that comprehensibility is not necessarily a function of sentence length or syllable count.[12]

Literacy scholar Frank Smith tells us that all language is conventional. Reading, learning, and comprehension are all based on prediction, that is, the ability to predict the outcome of a sentence by understanding its linguistic grammar and a story by understanding its story grammar.[13]

But we know that pleasure also derives from surprise and variation. Because good journalistic sentences tend to be front-loaded, the writer can use the endings of sentences in powerful ways. Note that Red Smith concludes his lead with the powerful phrase "the golden age of sports."

William Strunk advised students to "place the emphatic words of a sentence at the end," an example of its own rule.[14] Many powerful sentences in journalism come out this way: with the meaning made clear at the beginning, and a memorable word or image near the period.

E Pluribus Verbum

The language of journalism, described by Hugh Kenner as the "plain style" is, in various senses, democratic. When used powerfully, it flows from democratic impulses and creates a model for public discourse.

"Plain style is a populist style," he writes, "and one that suited writers like Swift, Mencken, and Orwell. Homely diction is its hallmark, also one-two-three syntax, the show of candor and the artifice of seeming to be grounded outside language in what is called fact—the domain where a condemned man can be observed as he silently avoids a puddle and your prose will report the observation and no one will doubt it. Such prose simulates the words anyone who was there and awake might later have spoken spontaneously. On a written page . . . the spontaneous can only be a contrivance."[15]

An American aesthetic of plainness is articulated early and often in the creation of a canon of literature we used to call American. "I am glad you think my style plain," wrote Nathaniel Hawthorne to an editor in 1851. (One wonders whether the editor was praising or condemning the author.) "I never, in any one page or paragraph, aimed at making it anything else, or giving it any other merit—and I wish people would leave off talking about its beauty. . . . The greatest possible merit of style is, of course, to make the words absolutely disappear into the thought."[16]

Orwell puts this sentiment more plainly, despite the help of a simile: "Good prose is like a window pane." The reader notices, not the writing, but the world. This value, he believes, grows out of his political motivation: "Looking back through my work, I see that it is invariably where I lacked a political purpose that I wrote lifeless books and was betrayed into purple passages, sentences without meaning, decorative adjectives and humbug generally."[17]

One wonders then, whether the plain style as expressed in journalism was created by American democracy and, in turn, helped create the discourse of its public life. Evidence must be gathered, as usual, from Alexis de Tocqueville, who argued that Americans had no literature, and might never have one, not because of the plain style, but the inflated one: "I have frequently remarked," writes the Frenchman, "that the Americans, who generally treat of business in clear, plain language, devoid of all ornament, and so extremely simple as to be often coarse, are apt to become inflated as soon as they attempt a more poetical diction. They then vent their pomposity from one end of a harangue to the other; and to hear them lavish imagery on every occasion, one might fancy that they never spoke of anything with simplicity."[18]

Tocqueville cites one exception: "The inhabitants of the United States have then, at present, properly speaking, no literature. The only authors whom I acknowledge as American are the journalists. They indeed are not great writers, but they speak the language of their country, and make themselves heard."

What conditions led the journalists to this power to speak the language of their country? Tocqueville doesn't say, but at one point describes these practitioners of the plain style this way: "The journalists of the United States are generally in a very humble position, with a scanty education and a vulgar turn of mind."

Has the professionalization of journalists (including their professional education) led to the demise of the plain style, if it is possible to talk about language in terms of a demise?

William Zinsser might think so. This influential editor and teacher has preached the virtue of simplicity in his popular book *On Writing Well*. "Clutter is the disease of American writing," he argues. "We are a society strangling in unnecessary words, circular constructions, pompous frills, and meaningless jargon."[19]

His search for useless words in his own writing is relentless, as he demonstrates in his revision of his own manuscript. His passion for simplicity is reminiscent of E. B. White's description of William Strunk's classroom lesson on brevity: "When he delivered his oration on brevity to the class, he leaned forward over his desk, grasped his coat lapels in his hands, and in a husky, conspiratorial voice said, 'Rule Thirteen. Omit needless words! Omit needless words! Omit needless words!'"[20]

One hears echoes of Thoreau here and the stylistic imperative which he applied more broadly to American life: "Simplify, simplify." He also makes a connection between style and lifestyle that journalists and journalism scholars of the modern era might heed: "The scholar may be sure that he writes the tougher truth for the calluses on his palms. They give firmness to the sentence. Indeed, the mind never makes a great and successful effort, without a corresponding energy of the body. We are often struck by the force and precision of style to which hard-working men, unpracticed in writing, easily attain when required to make the effort. As if plainness and vigor and sincerity, the ornaments of style, were better learned on the farm and in the workshop than in the schools. The sentences written by such rude hands are nervous and tough, like hardened thongs, the sinews of the deer, or the roots of the pine."[21]

The toughness of those similes anticipates the style of tough-guy American practitioners of plainness, from Ernest Hemingway to Norman Mailer to Joan Didion to Edna Buchanan (tough guys come in either sex). Plainness and toughness and muscularity in prose come from an attitude William Blundell describes as "meanness":

> The mean writer is always a lean writer. He can't help it. [Notice the *he* throughout. There are no feminine referents in Blundell's work.] By meanness I don't refer to a harsh quality in his copy but to his attitude toward himself as he works. You may think it strange to cite an attitude as a consideration in good writing, but often it's the only thing separating the work of two equally talented people. The one turning out fat, flaccid, talky stories is not being tough enough on himself.
>
> The mean storyteller becomes two people, acting alternately as he works. The first is the sensitive artist-creator, the second a savage critic who eradicates every weakness in the creation. He's cruel, derisive and obsessively demanding. He hoots at the writer's affectations and pretty turns of phrase, blisters him for cowardice when he uses soft, passive constructions or hedges on conclusions, challenges every point of logic, demands sound reasons for the presence of every character and fact, and above all flagellates his victim for wordiness. He is a rotten S.O.B., worse than any editor who ever drew breath, and he is the artist's best friend.[22]

There is an almost priapic quality to Blundell's language here: prettiness and softness are bad; cruelty and hardness are good. That said, it also embodies, magnificently, the aesthetic of the plain style.

Lewis H. Lapham puts it this way:

> Before 1960 most of the writers and editors working on newspapers in New York understood that they had more in common with carpenters or stone-masons than they did with diplomats or poets. Many of them were self-educated, and they hired themselves out as journeymen, not as immortal artists. Having come of age in the 1930s and '40s, they were schooled in the lessons of poverty, and they tended to identify with the crowd in the bleachers rather than with the swells in the box seats. If asked to state their occupation, they would have said "reporter" or "newspaperman" (the term

"journalist" pertained only to Englishmen and fops), and they sought to write a simple and translucent prose, the idea being to make more clearly visible the subject of the story.[23]

The American Conversation

The language of journalism is concrete and specific; it is active and filled with people in action; the important things come first so that meaning is clear; it is democratic, and, as a result, tough and plain. So we must conclude that the language of journalism is nothing like human speech at all.

Speech rambles and turns back on itself; it stumbles and repeats; it stops and leaves gaps; it connects the disconnected; it uses strange pauses and odd sounds. How then can we explain Tocqueville's metaphor of speech when describing early America's journalists: "They speak the language of their country, and make themselves heard"?

He is not writing here of broadcast journalists, such as Paul Harvey or Charles Kuralt. He is reading authors and "hearing" them. In that sense he understands that illusion of speech in prose that writing scholars and teachers call *voice*.

The voice of most news stories is neutral and authoritative. Editorials are often written in institutional voices. Columnists, critics, and sportswriters often develop distinctive voices that readers seek out over their breakfast cereal and interact with in an imagined form of conversation.

The language of journalism is not like speech, but it is closer to speech than most other forms of writing. This is what Kenner means in describing it as "populist." It also explains the journalistic obsession with quoting, the attempts to represent speech in prose. Too often, especially in government stories, this means experts speaking in code or in meaningless sound bites.

But when eyewitnesses, especially everyday folks, are given their voices in print, the effect can be powerful, moving, puzzling, funny, or outrageous. These effects are best accomplished, in my opinion, on public radio where voices can be heard with full flavor of dialect and nuance of expression. But a good quote high in the story can also enhance the drama or sharpen a point. Remember JoAnne McSorley's words in the Tampa killing story: "It was just bodies flying all over the place." Not "There were bodies flying all over the place," but the more conversational, urgent, and human "It was just bodies."

The voices in American journalism for too long have been too monotone and monochromatic, coming most often from white male authority figures. The language of journalism has the flexibility to be more inclusive if journalists will expand their reporting strategies and let the voices of the young and the poor and the old be heard. I agree here with Jay Rosen.[24] A goal of journalism must be to improve the nature of public conversation on issues of concern, to define problems, sharpen arguments, and seek common ground. The adaptation of traditional forms (such as oral history) and the creation of new ones (edited transcripts of town meetings) will model modes of public discourse that will revitalize democratic feelings and impulses.

Never Too Clear

The most valued quality of the language of journalism is clarity, and its most desired effect is comprehensibility. Many poets, lawyers, and diplomats value clarity within their discourse communities, but, unlike the journalist, exalt ambiguity, ambivalence, subtext, and even paradox. These have their uses. The United States Supreme Court ordered that American public schools must be desegregated "with all deliberate speed," and with that intentional ambiguity tried to effect dramatic social change without inviting chaos.

As Stuart Adam has noted, all journalism exists on a spectrum that curves from the civic to the literary, that is, from information and announcements about hurricane preparedness to long, dramatic narratives about people facing the most dangerous hurricane in the nation's history.[25]

The qualities we most value in *literary* stories are narrative momentum, revealing scenes, sympathetic characters, and telling details. We conjure these qualities when we usually think of *good writing* or *the best writing* in journalism.

There grows a problem, and it buds out of Adam's use of the image of the spectrum. In journalism, the civic *is* literary. Just as plainness is achieved through craft and artifice, so is clarity of explanation. When the civic becomes literary, the language of journalism is used for its highest purpose: to reveal how the world works to readers who are imagined, not as consumers or market shares, but as citizens.

Here broadcast journalism takes the lead. The craft of the writer must result, beyond all else, in comprehensibility. Journalists must not merely make information available to audiences, but truly in-form.

Or, as William Greider put it, journalists must begin to take responsibility for what audiences know and understand about the world.[26] To achieve this, journalists must think not of *the reader* but of *readers*, and must seek to bridge their intentions with the differing expectations and experiences of those who turn to the news.

This often involves a set of language skills more often associated with encyclopedia authors than journalists. If it's your job to write something about Einstein's theories that a 13-year-old can use in a term paper, you'd best take a radical view of clarity and comprehensibility. For journalists, such radical clarity means controlling the pace of information, translating technical language, knowing when to show and when to tell, creating analogies to help readers understand numbers, and, most difficult of all, knowing when to leave things out. Only skilled writers master these techniques.

Teaching the Language of Journalism

If we can agree that something called "the language of journalism" exists, and that, like pornography, we at least know it when we see it (or hear it), and if we have some strong feelings about its public purposes, what then can we say about the teaching of journalism, in both classroom and newsroom?

Let me offer a few brief thoughts:

• We have to understand and help students learn, through literary study, the grammar of stories, and what makes a story different from an article. Too few editors can recognize the unrealized potential in the working drafts of writers. This failure derives from too limited an understanding, in theory and practice, of story forms. Attention to narrative forms matters, in this context, because it influences the level of diction. Storytellers, not article writers, will use language at its most active, concrete, and specific.

• We need to reconsider the socialization and education of journalists as they come to form an even more professional caste. Exalted above what Tocqueville encountered, armed with M.B.A.'s and law degrees, they are more likely to imagine themselves as bureaucrats, technocrats, and middle managers than as watchdogs or spinners of yarns.

I'm on Thoreau's side here, arguing against my own professional preparation. We need to find ways to recruit journalists with calluses on their hands. And if they come to us with soft hands, we must find a way to get them out of the classroom and into workshops and onto farms.

• More simply: You can't learn the language of journalism by writing from fact sheets or just working the phone. Students need eyewitness experiences that become powerful narratives. They can't make us see until they see.

• At the risk of contradicting my Thoreauvian imperative, I favor much more careful study of language than most universities now require, or even offer. I want students to know enough about the language, for example, that they could study Orwell or Strunk and White, and put some of that advice to practical use. This means attention to grammar, usage, semantic change, dialect, sources of new words, connotation and denotation, slang, and word etymology. Students can choose a short Anglo-Saxon or Old French word (jail) over a longer Latin one (incarcerate) before they know the difference. But the goal is a thorough experience of what poet Donald Hall calls the "insides" of words to inspire accuracy and play.

• Finally, a mastery of the language of journalism requires the constant practice of literate behaviors: reading, writing, critical thinking, making predictions, and, most important, engaging in conversation, with a guiding teacher or editor, about how texts are made.

Have I made myself clear?

Notes

1. John Leo, "Journalese, or Why English Is the Second Language of the Fourth Estate," in *Book of American Humor,* ed. Russell Baker (New York: W. W. Norton, 1993), 405–13.

2. John Carey, *Eyewitness to History* (Cambridge, Mass: Harvard University Press, 1987), xxxii.

3. Joseph Conrad, "Preface" to *The Nigger of the Narcissus in Three Great Tales* (New York: Vintage Books, 1958), ix–x.

4. Carey, xxxii.

5. Jacques Barzun, "The Press and the Prose," *Occasional Paper No. 10* (New York: The Freedom Forum, March 1992), 3.

6. George Orwell, "Politics and the English Language," in *The Collected Essays, Journalism and Letters of George Orwell,* ed. Sonia Orwell and Ian Angus (New York: Harcourt Brace Jovanovich, 1968), 4, 127–40.

7. Noam Chomsky, *Syntactic Structures* (The Hague: Mouton, 1957).

8. In *Seventeenth Century Prose and Poetry,* ed. A. M. Witherspoon and Frank J. Warnke (New York: Harcourt, Brace & World, 1963), 149.

9. Quoted by Charles Kuralt in "The View from the Road," The Red Smith Lecture in Journalism (University of Notre Dame, 1986), 3.

10. Dennis Jackson, "Sportswriter Red Smith's 'Jousts with the Mother Tongue,'" *Style* (DeKalb, Ill.) (Fall 1982): 414–35.

11. Red Smith, "Jack Dempsey, Former Heavyweight Champion, Dies," *New York Times*, June 1, 1983.

12. E. B. White, "Calculating Machine," in *The Second Tree from the Corner* (New York: Harper & Row, 1951).

13. Frank Smith, *Understanding Reading* (Hillsdale, N.J.: Lawrence Erlbaum Associates, 1988), 13–15.

14. William Strunk, Jr. and E. B. White, *The Elements of Style* (New York: Macmillan, 1959), 26.

15. Hugh Kenner, "The Politics of the Plain Style," in *Literary Journalism in the Twentieth Century*, ed. Norman Sims (New York: Oxford University Press, 1990), 187.

16. Quoted in *Themes in American Literature*, ed. Philip McFarland and others (Boston: Houghton Mifflin, 1975), 187.

17. Orwell, "Why I Write," *Collected Essays*, 1, 7.

18. Alexis de Tocqueville, *Democracy in America*, ed. Richard D. Heffner (New York: New American Library, 1956), 184.

19. William Zinsser, *On Writing Well* (New York: Harper & Row, 1985), 7.

20. Strunk and White, viii.

21. Henry David Thoreau, "A Week on the Concord and Merrimack Rivers," quoted in *Stylists on Style* (New York: Charles Scribner's Sons, 1969), 315.

22. William E. Blundell, *The Art and Craft of Feature Writing* (New York: New American Library, 1988), 160.

23. Lewis H. Lapham, "Advertisements for Themselves: A Letter from Lewis Lapham," *New York Times Book Review*, October 24, 1993, 3.

24. Jay Rosen, "Community Connectedness: Passwords for Public Journalism," in this volume.

25. G. Stuart Adam in *Journalism, Communication and the Law*, ed. G. Stuart Adam, (Scarborough: Prentice-Hall, 1976), 3–22.

26. From a seminar transcript quoted in *Making Sense of the News* (St. Petersburg, Fla.: Modern Media Institute, 1983), 6.

3

Journalism Enlarged

Stuff That Matters

Cole C. Campbell

On January 4, 1939, Henry Luce, the founder of *Time*, gave a talk titled "How I Make My Living" to the Women's Club of Stamford, Conn., just down the road from his home in Greenwich. He ended by reflecting on the larger social role of journalism:

> If people of all classes are far better informed than they used to be, then why is it that we seem to be making just as much of a mess of our world as ever our ancestors made in the days of their unenlightenment? I will leave the question with you—as perhaps the ultimate indictment of journalism and of a great deal else in the modern world. But leaving it with you, I also take it with me—for in it lies the doubt which too faithfully assails every responsible journalist. I will say only this—that just as the answer to the failure and befuddlements of democracy is more democracy, not less, so perhaps the answer to the unfruitfulness of journalism is more journalism, not less. And by more journalism I do not mean more of the same, but rather that journalism must enlarge its field, it must probe deeper, it must and will find a way to deal with those matters which lie most deeply in the nature and will and conscience of men and will make of them great matters, not private whisperings but great public arguments. There are more things in heaven and earth, O Journalist, than are included in your philosophy—or your craftsmanship.[1]

In this grandiloquent blend of Jefferson, Shakespeare, and his own contemplation, Luce offers more than the ultimate indictment of journalism. He also suggests the ultimate response. And in one brief passage, he puts into deep relief much of today's discussion about journalism among journalists.

Luce does not reflexively dismiss the "unfruitfulness of journalism" critique as an illegitimate intrusion into newsroom prerogatives. He neither excuses journalism as the overwhelmed servant of a too-demanding public nor damns the public as too flighty to deserve more than it gets. Nor does he suggest that journalists are caught up in a deterministic world beyond their grasp or influence—or responsibility. Nor does he assert that the very answer we hunger for is alive and well in better newsrooms but just requires a tad more patience, a bit more money, and stricter adherence to past standards.

Instead, he engages the critique as a responsible journalist assailed by doubt. He offers up the powerful injunction that journalism cannot simply do more of the same but must "enlarge its field . . . probe deeper . . . find a way" to transform essential matters of nature, will, and conscience into "great public arguments." In sum, he calls upon us journalists to transcend the limits of our current philosophy and craftsmanship. As the twenty-first century begins, how might we respond to Luce's call?

Enlarging the Field

When the twentieth century was young, Joseph Pulitzer, founder of the *St. Louis Post-Dispatch* and transformer of the *New York World*, spelled out his more expansive vision of journalism in a declaration now known as the Post-Dispatch Platform. The platform still runs every day on the newspaper's editorial page. It is mostly a recitation of the best crusading instincts of a journalist who came to prominence (and prosperity) fighting the barons of the Gilded Age. But tucked among its calls for progress and reform is a purely journalistic order: "Never be satisfied with merely printing news."

Pulitzer was not simply saying "news" should become "news, information, and entertainment," the triumvirate that now reigns over technological convergence and proliferating product portfolios. Pulitzer's newspapers had plenty of information and entertainment alongside and suffusing news stories. What Pulitzer was driving at is the essence of what Luce later suggests—that journalism is about more than recounting the day's events or passing along the latest police-blotter entry, legislative maneuvering, or political sideshow. Both Pulitzer and Luce directly challenge the notion that journalism is simply information craftily compiled for consumption.

"I want it perfectly understood," Pulitzer wrote his son's tutor, "that I want the boy to be a publicist, not merely a journalist. I want him to be a degree higher. I want him to be interested in public questions, public causes, public welfare, public good. . . . The paper I regard as a public institution."[2]

Pulitzer worked hard to connect his readers to what was happening in the real world—through his crusades, human interest stories, and direct-action projects such as raising from readers the money to build a pediment upon which the Statue of Liberty, languishing in a warehouse, could be erected.

Not long after Pulitzer promulgated his platform in 1912, such populist impulses were pooh-poohed by the Progressive movement (and later by its heirs). Instead of working with the people, progressives and the rising professional classes began to think of themselves as working *for* the people—a crucial prepositional and propositional shift. Professionals and experts began driving ordinary citizens out of many endeavors, perhaps none more noticeable than politics and public life. In this, they were abetted by journalists—who also were becoming increasingly professionalized (in part, ironically, a legacy of Pulitzer's insisting on a School of Journalism at Columbia University). Walter Lippmann, as an influential editor, author and political insider, laid the intellectual foundations for modern journalism in his works devaluing public opinion. He cast the role of journalists essentially as chroniclers orbiting elites, beaming back news of their doings to the common people, and offering "the hot glare of publicity" as a check against any particular powerful person becoming too self-serving. Dubious of ordinary people's competence as citizens, Lippmann described their role as limited to that of voters, with only one real option in public life—to, on occasion, vote the rascals out. That worldview, James Carey of Columbia University argues, permeates contemporary journalism and has debased, rather than enlarged, the craft.[3]

By mid-century, citizens were increasingly alienated from the larger world—and then condemned by professionals for their "apathy" or called upon to prove their political worthiness as "informed citizens."[4] Sociologist C. Wright Mills of Columbia University, who eventually was reviled as a pariah by establishment colleagues and revered as a patron saint by intellectual insurgents, documented this estrangement in a series of books on laboring classes, the power elite, and social scientists.

"Nowadays men often feel that their private lives are a series of traps. They sense that within their everyday worlds, they cannot overcome their troubles," Mills wrote in 1959. Outside the realm of job, family, and neighborhood, "they move vicariously and remain spectators."[5]

Piling on more "news, information, and entertainment" can reinforce citizens' standing as passive onlookers and make matters worse. As Mills notes:

> It is not only information that they need—in this Age of Fact, information often dominates their attention and overwhelms their capacities to assimilate it. It is not only the skills of reason that they need—although their struggles to acquire these often exhaust their limited moral energy. What they need, and what they feel they need, is a quality of mind that will help them to use information and to develop reason in order to achieve lucid summations of what is going on in the world and of what may be happening within themselves. It is this quality, I am going to contend, that journalists and scholars, artists and publics, scientists and editors are coming to expect of what may be called the sociological imagination.[6]

In contrast to Lippmann, Mills attributes the missing "quality of mind" not to people's limited capacity and inherent incompetence, but to social scientists and "literary men" failing to help people pay attention and act on information. If we take Mills' view, we journalists have a great opportunity to develop "the journalistic imagination" to better connect what happens in the larger world to the troubles in people's private lives.

Many precepts embraced by journalists are necessary but not sufficient to make such connections. Journalism is necessarily about distributing information and claiming attention, but it also must address how to increase attentiveness among overtaxed readers, viewers, listeners, and browsers. Journalism must be interesting, important, and credible (usually as defined by journalists), but it also must be engaging, meaningful, and authentic (as defined by users). Journalism is necessarily about finding and testing facts, but it also must identify and test the frames used to give meaning to those facts. We journalists are comfortable demanding accountability of the few, but we also must explore the responsibility of the many. We need to be detached observers in the sense of standing apart from what we witness in order to evaluate it dispassionately. But we also must—in the lovely phrase of Gil Thelen, executive editor of the *Tampa Tribune*—be committed observers, who choose to witness, and to sustain our vigils beyond the draw of novelty, because we care passionately about the well-being of our communities.[7]

We have a great opportunity to create—borrowing from scholar Ann Oakley's aspiration for social science—an "emancipatory journalism" that addresses

> how to develop the most reliable and democratic ways of knowing, both in order to bridge the gap between ourselves and others, and to ensure that those who intervene in other people's lives do so with the most benefit and the least harm. . . . The goal of would-be knowers is the elimination of as much bias or distortion as is possible in what it is that counts as knowledge. This means a meticulous, systematic, transparent, sensitive striving for descriptions of "reality" that satisfy not primarily knowers' needs for professional and scientific recognition, but the much more generous task of helping human beings to make informed decisions about how best to lead their lives.[8]

To develop the journalistic imagination and more democratic ways of knowing, we need to address some central questions:

How can citizens best understand "reality" with the least distortion? How do we journalists know what we know, and can we know it better in order to better describe reality?

How can citizens connect the troubles in their lives with the issues in the larger public sphere? How can journalists help citizens develop more capacity to use information and reason to create meaning, explore values, and "achieve lucid summations of what is going on in the world and of what may be happening within themselves"?

How can citizens and institutions create robust democratic practices that help them imagine and make the best choices in an ever-changing world? How can journalists contribute to this work?

"We are drowning in information and starving for wisdom," biologist E. O. Wilson writes. "The world henceforth will be run by synthesizers, people able to put together the right information at the right time, think critically about it, and make important choices wisely."[9]

A democratic society, then, needs more than the free flow of information. It also needs citizens who have the ability to synthesize that information and to make important choices wisely. Like unequal access to information, unequal opportunities to synthesize and absorb information can lead to political inequality. The work of keeping information flowing, of spreading the capacity to synthesize, of helping people make wise choices has never belonged to journalists alone. But we have a great opportunity to help people move from a state of distraction and information overload to a state of attentiveness and information synthesis. We must enlarge our conception of journalism beyond merely printing news to helping people make sense of their lives and their times. To do that, we must hone our minds and our methods in order to probe deeper.

Probing Deeper

Davis "Buzz" Merritt, longtime editor of the *Wichita Eagle,* has offered this instructive formulation: A successful community is one whose members know what is happening and take responsibility for it.[10] Journalists understand the first criterion for success—knowing what's happening—in terms of standard reporting. But we don't quite fathom the second—taking responsibility for what's happening. An expanded conception of journalism suggests we can do more to help the communities we serve succeed.

In constructing our pictures of reality, we can borrow more from other fields of inquiry just as we have lifted from computerdom the tools for computer-assisted reporting and database analysis. We can tap a variety of social sciences to hone our investigative, interpretative, and explanatory skills in something that J. T. Johnson of San Francisco State University has dubbed "analytic journalism."[11]

We need to consider not only new methods for procuring new facts—where to get them, how to test their accuracy. We also need to examine the way we, or our sources or our subjects, frame those facts. "There is no way of perceiving and making sense of social reality except through a frame," Donald A. Schon and Martin Rein of MIT write, "for the very task of making sense of complex, information-rich situations requires an operation of selectivity and organization, which is what 'framing' means."[12]

Frames are the only way that facts make sense. Every news story has a frame. But many of our frames are tacit or unconscious. We use them reflexively. We don't consider the many ways we might frame any given story. When we use the right frame, we can move through information efficiently. Physicist David Deutsch says many astronomers understand the motions of the planets not because anyone can memorize all observational data about them but because "understanding does not depend on knowing a lot of facts as such, but on having the right concepts, explanations, and theories."[13] When we use the wrong frame, we can get into trouble. "Faulty beliefs, both conscious and unconscious, rather than limited information, explain most poor decisions and misguided action," writes Alfred R. Oxenfeldt of Columbia University. "Facts alone usually are ambiguous and bewildering."[14]

When we let one frame dominate our view of a news event, we can become blind to other, more productive ways of seeing that event. The archetypal example is the horse-race frame that dominates election coverage and reduces discussion of the issues to their attractiveness to voting blocs. Jay Rosen of New York University says this frame connects us "to the inside story of the campaign, which actually is about winning. The press does less well in connecting the country to its candidates, linking politics to governing, and getting answers to our deeper questions."[15] Thus Green Party candidate Ralph Nader complained in 2000 "that the news media had covered his campaign only in terms of its effect on the Gore-Bush race. Although he raised issues, like lobbyists' dominance in Washington, that had been explored by serious newspapers, 'I was not asked any questions about any of the substance,' he said. 'It was all horse race.'"[16]

In addition to helping people know what's going on in their communities, how can journalists help them take responsibility for it? We know that news consumption is an indicator of a community's social capital—its capacity to build trust, distribute authority, and resolve disputes. We need to test whether different kinds of news reports produce stronger kinds of social capital. A good place to begin is Luce's charge that we tackle matters "which lie most deeply in the nature and will and conscience of men" and "make of them great matters, not private whisperings but great public arguments."

Making Great Public Arguments

Christopher Lasch, the late historian and cultural critic, picks up Luce's argument on behalf of argument:

> What democracy needs is vigorous public debate, not information. Of course, it needs information too, but the kind of information it needs can be generated only by debate. We do not know what we need to know until we ask the right questions, and we can identify the right questions only by subjecting our own ideas about the world to the test of public controversy. Information, usually seen as the precondition of debate, is better understood as its by-product. When we get into arguments that focus and fully engage our attention, we become avid seekers of relevant information. Otherwise we take in information passively—if we take it in at all.[17]

Unfortunately, Lasch continues,

Increasingly information is generated by those who wish to promote something or someone—a product, a cause, a political candidate, or officeholder—without arguing their case on its merits or explicitly advertising it as self-interested material either. Much of the press, in its eagerness to inform the public, has become a conduit for the equivalent of junk mail. Like the post office . . . it now delivers an abundance of useless, indigestible information that nobody wants.[18]

The result, James Carey of Columbia writes, is "more like observing talk-show gossip and petty manipulation than like bearing witness to the truth. It is a journalism of fact without regard to understanding."[19]

E. J. Dionne of the *Washington Post* calls upon journalism to "do far better than it does now in demonstrating the connections among facts, arguments and political action. . . . What is needed is what might be called an investigative reporting of ideas. . . . Journalists would examine not simply what a particular proposal might do to individuals or particular groups, but also how various proposals fit into a politician's long-term goals for the society. The key is to understand how a set of proposals are linked to a set of ideas, and how those ideas would shape the day-to-day lives of citizens."[20]

John Schwartz, Dionne's colleague, reports on the innovative online work of Rob Malda and Jeff Bates, the 23-year-old entrepreneurial editors of Slashdot.org:

> Part online newsletter, part fanzine, part town hall meeting, Slashdot represents a startling experiment in journalism. Its motto says it all: "News for nerds. Stuff that matters." . . . Articles on Slashdot are often little more than simple links to a report or announcement from some other news or corporate site on the Web, accompanied by a brief commentary from Bates, Malda, or any of the hundreds of regular Slashdot contributors. Then the real fun begins: Dozens or even hundreds of other contributors chime in, adding commentary and more information of their own, often arguing with one another in a rich braid of digital conversation. . . . Put it all together and you get a textured discussion that helps readers sort truth from fiction, fact from paranoid fantasy. Slashdotters truth-squad one another. . . . News on Slashdot is always an open process.[21]

This model dates back to Addison and Steele in eighteenth-century England. Their *Tatler* and *Spectator* made no distinction between writer and reader in publishing essays by, about, and for the denizens of London coffeehouses. "In danger of running out of material, Steele at one point warns his audience that unless they write in the journal, it will have to close," critic Terry Eagleton reports, later adding: "If Addison and Steele mark the moment of bourgeois respectability, they also signify the point at which the hitherto disreputable genre of journalism becomes legitimate."[22]

Now that journalism is once again held by many Americans to be a tad disreputable, perhaps we can reclaim some legitimacy by making our news coverage "always an open process," treating citizens as our partners and not merely passive consumers in making the connections between public affairs and private troubles. That will require us to become a lot more open to learning from others than we now are.

Finding a Way

The spine and spirit of Luce's charge to enlarge journalism, to probe deeper, and to initiate great public debate is a call for journalists to escape the limits of our current philosophy and craftsmanship. To do this, we need to become better learners and more daring experimenters. Unfortunately, our culture values reflex over reflection. Most journalists are intelligent people drawn to the work because it rewards brainpower. But many believe that journalism has little time or need for reflection. They pride themselves on their news judgment, the wisdom (and power) accumulated like tree rings through years of instantaneous decisions. They laud street smarts and Rolodexes of ready-to-be-quoted experts and insiders. They prefer categorical thinking—Who's the victim? Who's the villain?—to expansive thinking that leads to new categories and fresh perspectives. Like the French, they would rather starve their idiom (and thus keep it theirs) than nourish it with concepts and terms borrowed from neighboring disciplines of inquiry.[23]

Betty Medsger, a reporter-turned-journalism educator, refers to journalists as "thinkers without thoughts"—people with "significant intellectual powers" who "have spent so much time on automatic pilot that their powers of reflection have been impaired."[24] Phil Meyer, another journalist-turned-scholar, ties this to our conception of journalism as more craft than profession. "A craft is learned by emulation: watching a master perform and then imitating that person," Meyer writes. "A profession is learned from first principles so that when things change, the professional understands the changes and adjusts techniques to it."[25]

Tom Wicker of the *New York Times* agrees that journalism needs a more solid grounding in the world of ideas. "We need a print press with an intellectual orientation, rather than focused on events and personalities," Wicker said in a lecture at Northwestern University. "Is that kind of a press really possible in this country? I don't know, but I think we should find out. That's the only kind of print press that's going to survive."[26]

There is much work to be done to re-orient news organizations toward ideas and learning. The Readership Institute commissioned by the Newspaper Association of America and the American Society of Newspaper Editors included a study of newspaper cultures. That study concludes that most newspaper companies have defensive cultures, marked by perfectionistic obsessions and oppositional styles. In other words, those of us who work at newspapers lose sight of overall goals, get lost in details, coordinate little with others and have unproductive conflicts that result in safe but ineffectual decisions. And we don't know how to deliberate and solve problems in group settings. These cultural attributes are the antithesis of a constructive learning culture.

"Having a strongly constructive culture is what it takes to deal with rising competition and change," according to a summary produced by the Readership Institute's overseers at Northwestern's Media Management Center. "There is a big gap between the present newspaper culture and what your colleagues or the research says it should be."[27]

We need to transform our newsrooms into open cultures—open to learning from citizens, communities, our colleagues in other parts of the organization. If we don't, we will never find a way to enlarge journalism, probe deeper, and initiate great arguments.

Putting Information in Its Place

The travertine marble walls of Col. Robert R. McCormick's Tribune Tower in downtown Chicago are inscribed with stirring quotations from the Western canon about the role and responsibility of a free press.[28] My favorite, chosen in 1997 by McCormick's successors, is on the north wall of the Nathan Hale Lobby, near the elevators that serve the newsroom. It comes from Arthur Miller, the playwright best known for *Death of a Salesman* and *The Crucible*: "A good newspaper, I suppose, is a nation talking to itself."

In his understated way, Miller picks up a thread spun by John Dewey, the University of Chicago educator and philosopher who took on Walter Lippmann, his contemporary, by defending the collective wisdom of ordinary people engaged with public life. It is only when people talk to each other, Dewey said, that they fully come to understand their own minds, build a stronger shared intelligence, and give life to society. To fault citizenry because of the limitations of individual citizens misses the point of a democratic society that transforms individual wisdom, aspirations, and experience into what Dewey calls "pragmatic intelligence."[29]

We can learn by connecting the insights of historically significant figures in journalism and public life to our own experience and the ideas of contemporary thinkers. Pulitzer and Luce both ground the field of journalism in its purpose, in the ways it can promote the public good and help people make less a mess of the world. Mills and Oakley suggest we need to find better ways to connect lives and events, to more democratically decide what's worth knowing. Lasch and Dionne, echoing Dewey and Luce and Arthur Miller, urge us to connect journalism more directly to public debate. Malda and Bates, like Addison and Steele, offer a model for reconnecting readers to journalism by focusing on "stuff that matters" and treating citizen-contributors as collaborators in describing the world.

What's most important is that we learn and act on what we discover. Henry Luce's analysis of the challenge facing journalism has lost none of its potency over time. In a reprise of Luce's critique, Neil Postman, the prolific and incisive cultural critic who teaches at New York University, raises almost exactly the same issues sixty years later—and points us back to the age of Addison and Steele to begin our search for answers:

> If there are people starving in the world—and there are—it is not caused by insufficient information. If crime is rampant in the streets, it is not caused by insufficient information. If children are abused and wives are battered, that has nothing to do with insufficient information. If our schools are not working and democratic principles are losing their force, that too has nothing to do with insufficient information. If we are plagued by such problems, it is because something else is missing. That is to say, several things are missing. And one of them is some way to put information in its place, to give it a useful epistemological frame.
>
> In the eighteenth century, the newspaper provided such a frame, and given the present information flood, it may be the only medium capable of doing something like that for our use in the century ahead.[30]

This generation of journalists can respond to Luce's, and Postman's, ultimate indictment—and prospectus for ultimate exoneration—of journalism. We can enlarge the field of journalism. We can put information in its place by better framing "stuff that matters." We can help citizens, in Mills's phrase, achieve lucid summations of what is happening in the world and within their lives. To do so is our special opportunity and our certain obligation.

Notes

1. Henry Luce, "How I Make My Living" in *The Ideas of Henry Luce*, ed. John K. Jessup (New York: Atheneum, 1969), 53–54.

2. Daniel W. Pfaff, *Joseph Pulitzer II and the Post-Dispatch: A Newspaper Man's Life* (University Park: Pennsylvania State University Press, 1991), 31.

3. James Carey, *James Carey: A Critical Reader*, ed. Eve Stryker Munson and Catherine A. Warren (Minneapolis: University of Minnesota Press, 1997).

4. See especially Michael Schudson, *The Good Citizen: A History of American Civic Life* (Cambridge, Mass.: Harvard University Press, 1998).

5. C. Wright Mills, *The Sociological Imagination* (New York: Oxford University Press, 1959; Fortieth Anniversary Edition, 2000), 3–4.

6. Ibid., 5.

7. Jay Rosen, *What Are Journalists For?* (New Haven: Yale University Press, 1999), 264.

8. Ann Oakley, *Experiments in Knowing: Gender and Method in the Social Sciences* (New York: The New Press, 2000), 3–4.

9. Edward O. Wilson, *Consilience: The Unity of Knowledge* (New York: Alfred A. Knopf, 1998), 269.

10. This particular formulation is attributed to Merritt by David Mathews, president of the Kettering Foundation.

11. J. T. Johnson and Steven Ross, "Proposal for the Establishment of the Institute for Analytic Journalism" (unpublished, 1994).

12. Donald A. Schon and Martin Rein, *Frame Reflection: Toward the Resolution of Intractable Policy Controversies* (New York: Basic Books, 1994), 30.

13. David Deutsch, *The Fabric of Reality: The Science of Parallel Universes . . . and Its Implications* (New York and London: Penguin Press, 1997), 1–2.

14. Alfred R. Oxenfeldt, *Decision Economics* (Menlo Park, Calif.: Crisp, 1997), 17–18.

15. Jay Rosen, "The Master of Its Own Domain," *IntellectualCapital.com*, May 11, 2000. Available at http://www.intellectualcapital.com/issues/issue.373/item9296.asp.

16. Adam Clymer, "Nader Sees Greens Building Status as a Major Party," *New York Times*, November 18, 2000, A16.

17. Christopher Lasch, "The Lost Art of Argument," in *The Revolt of the Elites and the Betrayal of Democracy* (New York: W. W. Norton & Co., 1995), 162–63.

18. Ibid., 174.

19. Carey, 247.

20. E. J. Dionne, *They Only Look Dead: Why Progressives Will Dominate the Next Political Era* (New York: Simon & Schuster, 1996), 257–58.

21. John Schwartz, "Truth-Seeking Geeks Slice into a Web of Lies," *Washington Post*, May 10, 2000, C1.

22. Terry Eagleton, *The Function of Criticism* (London: Verso, 1984, 1996), 29–43.

23. For a thoughtful explanation—and defense—of this preference, see Roy Peter Clark, "The American Conversation and the Language of Journalism" in this volume. For a comparison of French and English as dynamic languages, see Robert McCrum, William Cran, and Robert MacNeil, *The Story of English* (New York: Viking, 1986), 19–48.

24. Betty Medsger, "Thinkers Without Thoughts," *American Journalism Review* (March 1999): 64–65.

25. Phil Meyer, "Why Journalism Needs Ph.D.s," *The American Editor* (September 1996): 10–11.

26. "Wicker: Newspapers Must Give Depth," a report published on the Medill School of Journalism website dated November 3, 1999. Available at http://www.medill.northwestern.edu/inside/99wicker110199.html.

27. John Lavin, presentation to the Marketing and Circulation Committee of the American Society of Newspaper Editors, Media Management Center, Northwestern University, October 8, 2000.

28. The complete list is in *Tribune Tower: American Landmark* (Chicago: Tribune Co., 1968, 2000).

29. I know Dewey primarily through his commentators. See Carey, above at note 3, and William R. Caspary, *Dewey on Democracy* (Ithaca, N.Y.: Cornell University Press, 2000).

30. Neil Postman, *Building a Bridge to the Eighteenth Century: How the Past Can Improve Our Future* (New York: Alfred A. Knopf, 1999), 89–90.

Part II

Media Leadership

In 1947 the Hutchins Commission argued that freedom of the press was in jeopardy for three reasons: (1) because the media were not providing citizens with what they needed to make informed decisions; (2) because some members of the media engaged in irresponsible practices; and (3) because pluralism was being lost within an environment of increasingly concentrated media ownership. The failure of the media to regulate themselves, the commission warned, could lead to citizen protest and eventual government control.

If we could transport Robert Maynard Hutchins and his colleagues a half century into the future, into our own time, imagine their exploration of the current media landscape. The concentration of ownership would have intensified and the size of media companies grown beyond their imaginations. New media—from television to cable to the Internet—would have created a 24–hour news cycle that increased their sense of the importance of the media as a democratic institution. They would find public confidence in the media at a low point. They would probably be astonished by an America that was more prosperous, more diverse, more powerful, and more confused than at many moments in its history.

On January 29, 1992, a group of twenty media leaders gathered at The Poynter Institute to begin a conversation about media leadership and ownership that continues to this day. Over three days, they expressed a sense of urgency, described as "a time of trouble for American journalism and the public it serves," and issued "A Call to Leadership" (1992) to the owners and managers of media companies, and to "all who treasure the news business."

For the rest of the 1990s, the arguments among journalists and media leaders became more heated, dividing parties into what amounted to a cultural war. Control of newspaper resources turned more and more to the business side, which demanded greater efficiency, cost control, and higher profit margins. Acquisitions and mergers created long-term debt and absentee ownership. Journalism, in some cases, lost its central role in the development of huge, diversified companies. The influence of Wall Street investors waxed. The influence of news managers waned. The morale of rank-and-file journalists plummeted.

Bob Steele, who directs Poynter's ethics program, adds another dimension to the conversation about media leadership, arguing that "The Principled and Skilled Leader" (2000) has a responsibility to move "beyond good intentions." Steele's contribution is that moral leadership requires more than a virtuous pre-disposition. It involves sets of skills that can be learned and developed. It requires anticipatory instincts and behaviors. It means green-light, not just red-light, responses. And it concerns all members of the media enterprise, from reporters, to editors, to business leaders, to owners.

Paula Bock, a reporter from the *Seattle Times*, offers a ground-level view of media. Inspired by an invitation from The Poynter Institute in 2000, Bock begins her personal journey in rich conversation about mission and purpose with her colleagues in Seattle. This leads her to a deep contemplation on her role as a journalist, and the themes that inspire and motivate her: peace, human dignity, and social justice.

4

A Call to Leadership

Roy Peter Clark

This call to leadership is written at a time of trouble for American journalism and the public it serves.

- Profits from the news business, while high compared to other industries, are down.
- A corporate culture has superseded a journalistic one.
- Absentee owners and investors lack a passion for local communities.
- Goals and standards are set by business managers without the understanding or participation of the people who work for them.
- Short-term financial interests and burdensome debt threaten the long-term health of the news business.

All around us, the forces of social, technological, and economic change challenge traditional modes of thinking, production, and delivery. Some of the conditions facing news organizations are, no doubt, cyclical and will ameliorate with an upturn in the economy. But others are clearly structural—they will change us forever—and demand new kinds of leadership.

A great irony results from the combination of these forces: Never has the quality of journalism been so high, yet the morale of journalists so low. Reporters are suspicious of the motives of their editors. The editors worry about the values of business managers. Some news organizations are in turmoil, fighting what amounts to a cultural cold war over values and resources.

In the face of these disturbing trends, we search for roads that lead to a bright future for journalism. Such a future depends on courage, the centrality of journalistic values, a new level of discourse and understanding among all levels in news organizations, and the articulation of a common mission and purpose.

How do we produce newspapers and newscasts that people need, want, and value; that help build community and preserve democracy; that inspire; and that make a fair profit across good times and bad?

What follows is a blueprint for leadership. It respects the most sacred principles of journalism, but challenges stale thinking and cloudy vision.

A failure to act now threatens the news business with obsolescence or, worse, irrelevance. Determined, high-minded, and inspirational leadership is the best hope for our franchise, our profession, and the citizens we serve.

Sink Roots into Communities

- Accept ownership and leadership of a news organization as a public trust that results in great journalism to serve the public interest.
- To do that, insist that news staffs understand their towns. Encourage the hiring of people who are passionate about their ideas and committed to improving their communities.
- Create career tracks and incentives to make the local executive function as owner. End the concept that one must move away to move up.
- Invest a meaningful share of your profits to improve the quality of the news product.
- Reject the pressure for short-term profits that impair community service and that will damage the business in the long run.
- Take the long view, invest in community, and let local executives create a sense of family—these measures will reduce financial risk and produce a more consistent, reliable rate of return.

Share Power

- Share financial and strategic information, including profit margins, revenues, and budgets, with everyone in the organization. Create a shared vision and build trust through full disclosure.
- Listen to the voices of editors, other journalists, and people in all departments as they help you set goals and allocate resources. Do not fear the younger, junior people who work for you. Seek out their concerns. Encourage them to challenge your assumptions, as you challenge theirs. Invite them to your "high table." Encourage debate, dissent, negotiation, compromise.

- Help news people learn about the business side. Make yourself a shrewd student of journalism. News people and business people must find a common language to understand their shared purposes and reconcile their conflicting values.
- Abandon the command and control style of management. Build consensus. Remove barriers created by hierarchy. Favor participation, collaboration, and teamwork.

Embrace Change

- Help create a company that thrives in an environment of relentless change. Be agile and responsive to new technologies and demographic shifts.
- Seize the initiative. Invest in research and development. Take advantage of technologies created by other industries or companies.
- Imagine new levels of cooperation, even joint ventures, with industries and companies you once considered dangerous competitors. Profit from new markets with innovative forms of journalism.
- Develop new products and services to match our changing audiences. Involve in decision making members of groups you want to serve. Let them help you reach their peers.
- Form partnerships with special interest media, community news organs, and alternative publications to expand your influence without diluting precious resources.
- Create environments where new journalistic forms will emerge and compete in the marketplace of ideas.

Inspire the Next Generation

- Invest in human beings.
- Commit yourself to their ongoing education and create a learning workplace where they can grow and prosper over time.
- Set high and consistent standards. Reward risk taking and innovation. Share expectations and responsibilities. Honor accountability. Encourage diversity in people and ideas. Create a workplace where people have fun and are proud to work for your news organization.
- Expect executives to create newsrooms where people read and discuss important ideas, where they develop interests both deep and broad, where they can renew themselves to avoid burnout and dead ends.

- Continue to raise entry-level salaries to attract the best and the brightest into the news business.

Build Our Common Public Life

- Never forget what business you're in. Provide a forum for public discussion to preserve and enhance democratic society.
- Reaffirm the enduring requirements of free and responsible journalism, such as those articulated by the Hutchins Commission in 1947:

    ~A truthful, comprehensive, and intelligent account of the day's events in a context which gives them meaning.

    ~A forum for the exchange of comment and criticism.

    ~The projection of a representative picture of the constituent groups in the society.

    ~The presentation and clarification of the goals and values of the society.

    ~Full access to the day's intelligence.

- Open new channels of communication, giving access to the various voices within communities.
- Encourage the development of courageous and compassionate editorial voices that challenge the community, crusade for reform, and urge action and change.
- Help the public set and act on its agendas. Keep the community in conversation with itself. Celebrate its accomplishments.
- Deserve the First Amendment.

5

The Principled and Skilled Leader

Beyond Good Intentions

Bob Steele

"The best time to deal with an ethical issue is before *it becomes a problem."*

When I came across these cogent words a number of years ago, I wrote the sentence down and posted it above my phone. This simple, yet profound, fifteen-word statement serves as the cornerstone of my advice to journalists and newsroom leaders on the subject of ethics. I use this sentence as a mantra of sorts, whether I'm teaching in workshops or advising someone over the phone on a real-time ethical dilemma. It's a touchstone phrase, raising warning while urging wisdom.

I've found that the best of editors and news directors are skilled in applying this "before it becomes a problem" philosophy in their daily work. These leaders address issues early. They are clear in their guiding principles, strong in their core values, and skilled at what I call "front-end ethical decision making."

I've observed Sandy Rowe, editor of the *Oregonian* in Portland, Oregon, practice these qualities on a regular basis. Whether she's leading her staff on a major project or calling me to discuss a thorny ethical issue, Rowe grounds her thinking in the core values that undergird what she and her newspaper stand for. She's reflective and reasoned without abandoning her aggressiveness. She's a model of what we call the "green-light" journalist—someone who moves ahead on important stories based on professionalism and principles.

I've observed these same qualities in John Lansing, a veteran local television news director and general manager in Minneapolis, Chicago, Detroit, and Cleveland, and now a corporate executive for Scripps Howard

Broadcasting. He practices strong leadership by blending solid journalism and ethical standards. He leads by example. He demonstrates the confidence and competence that translate into public service reporting.

To be sure, Rowe and Lansing don't head off every ethical issue *before* it becomes a problem. They've called me, on occasion, when they've found themselves well down a road filled with potholes; but they are wise enough to know how to seek guidance even while gripping the steering wheel. I've observed such qualities in other leaders from newsrooms of all sizes. I gain insight into their strengths only because of their willingness to expose their thinking and to admit they don't have simple answers to tough issues.

Skip Foster, editor of the *Shelby Star* in North Carolina, and Maria Barrs, news director at KDFW-TV in Dallas, keep their moral compass in hand to gauge where they are heading, even while ringing me up for some outside perspective on a tough call.

Forrest Carr, news director of KGUN-TV in Tucson, Arizona, and Rich Oppel, editor of the *Austin American-Statesman,* employ their strong moral gyroscopes to provide leadership stability and connect to their core values while also bouncing ethics issues my way for additional thoughts.

Scott Libin, news director at KSTP-TV in St. Paul, is a master at identifying stakeholders in ethical issues and leading productive ethics discussions based on alternative solutions. His competence and confidence allow him to check his thinking with an outside voice when wrestling with thorny issues on investigative reporting or conflicts of interest.

Chris Peck, editor of the *Spokane Spokesman-Review* in Washington, is another leader who brings strong principles and a solid decision-making process to his daily work. His effectiveness with his staff and his readers is enhanced by his willingness to reveal the *how* and *why* of his decision making, especially when making tough calls.

I cite these individual leaders, not because they are perfect in their craft or ethics, but because they embrace their leadership roles and their professional obligations. They demonstrate both good intentions and the ability to carry them out. Those dual qualities are essential given the profound challenges newsroom leaders face.

A Troubling Landscape

I have a special and, at times, disquieting listening post for assessing the good, the bad, and the ugly of American journalism. I also have a fascinating and disconcerting vantage point for observing the range of news content presented to the public—from the brilliant to the banal.

I've been wearing multiple hats the last decade as director of Poynter's ethics program. I'm sometimes the "rabbi" to journalists and newsroom leaders seeking guidance as they search for the ethical high road. At other times I'm asked to "judge" those who are under suspicion of making wrong turns. And, at times, I'm called upon to be the "prosecutor" of those who clearly have veered recklessly off course.

To be sure, I'm often conflicted by my competing roles of "saving souls," "weighing evidence," "assigning guilt," or, to some, "shooting the wounded."

From my listening post, I hear, in one ear, the voices of sincere reporters, editors, news directors, producers, and visual journalists trying their best while working in a minefield of explosive issues. In the other ear, I hear questions from reporters writing stories about other journalists and news organizations being scrutinized for apparent or alleged professional indiscretions and big-time ethical failures.

From my lookout, I can see many newsroom leaders and journalists trying to do the right thing in difficult circumstances. They are struggling to be ethical while conducting high-stakes investigative reporting; to be effective in holding powerful elected officials accountable; to be sensitive while reporting on victims in the wake of tragedy. These journalists carry their idealism to the battleground. They want to make a difference. Some succeed.

Yet I can also see journalists rushing to the battlefield and, in their haste, setting off ethical land mines. I see the resulting harm to themselves, their news organizations, the profession of journalism, and to any source unlucky enough to be caught in the shrapnel. The failures become legend, and the consequences are costly to journalism's credibility and to the journalist's reputation.

From Good Intentions to Capacity

These conflicting impressions draw me to a perspective on ethics articulated by Barbara Toffler in her book *Doing Ethics: Managers Talk Ethics*. While not referring directly to journalism, Toffler makes a useful distinction between what she calls "ethical intention" and "ethical capacity." "Intention," she says, "is only a trigger to action." Intention speaks of the desire to do well and do right. Toffler says "implementation of action requires another ingredient—capacity—the ability to carry out an intention."

In other words, the *desire* to do the right thing is not enough. Good purpose is disarmed without the proficiency to follow through. Individuals must have the skill to carry out their aim. Intention is empty without capacity.

Toffler develops this argument by challenging managers to be leaders who put their values to work and their ethical decision-making skills into play. "The capacity power inherent in high position is enormous," she says. "In the case of ethical dilemmas, it does not provide the answer to 'what is right?' but once the decision on 'right' is made, capacity power makes doing *right* probable."

I can attest to the great importance of "capacity power." It's clear to me that those editors, news directors, and other newsroom leaders who are skilled at carrying out their good intentions are the most successful in the practice of journalism. They are the leaders who convert their principles and core values into sound ethical decisions and actions.

Connecting Leadership, Craft, Ethics, and Culture

Editors and news directors spend a great deal of time guiding their news teams in the practice of journalism skills: researching, reporting, interviewing, photographing, writing, editing, designing, producing. Leaders and their subordinates help journalists hone their craft so individuals are competent enough to measure up at the toughest of times.

Yet some leaders hold the faulty assumption that journalists come to the newsroom with fully formed values, strong moral reasoning, and critical thinking skills. We know, from observation and from research, that this is not the case. Most journalists are still sorting out their ethical beliefs and struggling with the competing values of their profession. Many admit they lack competence and confidence in their ethical decision-making skills. Many say they want more training.

Some newsroom bosses become so immersed in production that they fail to prepare for the tough calls. These leaders may be good managers at running the assembly line, but they are not good leaders on core values and critical thinking. They don't develop their teams to anticipate, identify, and resolve ethical challenges.

Some editors and news directors don't see a connection between the craft elements of journalism—the writing process, for instance—and the craftsmanship of ethical decision making. Both writing and ethical decision making are based on logical steps—collaboration between individuals, time-honored protocols for checks and balances, and oversight by assigned leaders. Leaders who don't cultivate reflective processes—including ethical decision making—within their organizational culture are inviting trouble.

Finally, some newsroom managers don't emphasize ethical decision making as a developmental skill because they see themselves as weak in that category. They don't have the confidence or competence to be effective leaders.

From Captain to Coach

For newsroom leaders, the capacity to carry out good intentions depends upon a combination of strong guiding principles, expertise in the skill of ethical decision making, and the ability to pass both the principles and processes on to others.

Successful leaders employ a range of techniques for inspiring, motivating, and training staff. They use the right leadership style at the right moment to produce excellent products.

They know when to be the *captain* and make a tough decision, often on deadline, based on their official role and responsibility. Their hand is on the tiller, they steer with confidence, and they make decisions with firmness.

Successful leaders must be *experts* at times. They bring their professional experience, knowledge, and personal skills to the decision-making process. They take action to solve an ethical problem or, better yet, to avoid one.

At times, successful newsroom leaders step into other roles. They are *Socrates*, influencing the decision-making process by asking the hard questions, challenging staff members to anchor thoughts in reason, not just emotion. They are *Aristotle*, influencing the process in a systematic and analytical style. They draw on deductive reasoning and search for good alternative solutions, rejecting polarized extremes.

Successful leaders act as *guides*, directing a process that values openness, tolerance, and counterintuition. They embrace complexity and resist simple answers. They value the collective strength of the group.

The most successful newsroom leaders are strong *coaches*, modeling principles and demonstrating values through their own behavior. They build capacity in the newsroom by sharing responsibility. They work one-on-one with subordinates and staff, developing ethical decision-making skills and allowing others to learn from both struggle and success.

On a continuing basis, successful leaders blend these styles and approaches in the quest for excellence. They know how to be effective coaches and guides, and they put those styles to work. When situations demand, they switch to being the captain or the expert.

They are clear in what they and their organizations stand for. Their clarity becomes commitment. They build it into competence and confidence. Their good intentions are connected to their capacity to carry them out.

Lessons Learned When Leaders Fail

To be sure, there have been achievements to celebrate in American journalism in the last few years. We must not ignore the examples of excellent, courageous reporting that measure up to the highest standards of our profession. It's essential to recognize how often we do things well, how frequently we serve the public interest and democracy with meaningful, high quality, ethical journalism.

Just as we judge our physicians and our accountants, our architects and our teachers, and all other professionals by the full scope of their work, not just by their successful moments, we must hold ourselves accountable on the full range of *our* work as journalists and leaders.

We must probe the cases where something went wrong. We must explore why we failed in our ethics. We must perform postmortems on the cases that shattered our confidence and rocked our foundation. We must figure out how to minimize the problems that erode our quality, corrode our credibility, and devalue the role journalism plays in our society.

We can learn a great deal by looking back on a landscape littered with notorious cases, often so familiar that they are known by just a word or two, though they signify something much larger. Chiquita. Staples. Tailwind. Dark Alliance. The Unabomber. Food Lion. Richard Jewell. Kevorkian. Monicagate. Elián. Wen Ho Lee. McVeigh. O.J.

On other fronts, we learned hard lessons from how we covered the bloodshed at schools in Jonesboro, Paducah, Pearl, Springfield, and beyond, improving in some ways when we faced the profound challenges of covering the massacre at Columbine High.

We stumbled in our awe of celebrity in covering the deaths of John Kennedy, Jr., and Princess Diana. We searched for elusive truth in reporting the deaths of hundreds of less-famous people when TWA 800, Alaska Airlines 261, and Egypt Air 990 went down.

To be sure, these high-profile cases are not alone in the instances that have troubled journalism professionals and the public. Sometimes, the ethics questions surface even when the journalism is applauded. That's what happened with the "Orphans of Addiction" project in the *Los Angeles Times*. Reporter Sonia Nazario used fly-on-the-wall reporting techniques for several months to observe and report the plight of children trapped in their families' cycle of alcohol, drugs, and disease. Despite accolades for the stories, Nazario admits that her reporting was ethically problematic. She says she would have taken other steps to protect the vulnerable children during the reporting process and during the two months it took her to write and publish the story.

"I was so immersed that I became somewhat desensitized," she says. In hindsight, Nazario says she would have better anticipated possible ethical dilemmas and used outside child-abuse experts "to make sure I wasn't clearly off line."

There's a lesson in leadership in that case. Editors at the *Times* had great responsibility for guidance and oversight, especially on the ethics issues. The leaders had an obligation to help Nazario anticipate the danger spots and to consider alternative approaches to minimize harm. The newspaper's editors had an obligation to figure out a faster way to turn the reporting into a published story.

The editors and staff at the *News & Observer* in Raleigh, North Carolina, learned important lessons after publishing a story on the influx of Hispanics to North Carolina. Their well-intentioned effort created a strong backlash when the paper's profile of one Mexican immigrant led to his apprehension by Immigration and Naturalization Service officials and his eventual deportation.

Editor Anders Gyllenhaal reflected on lessons learned in a column to readers. "One of [the lessons] is whether the *N&O*, with its eyes on the universal themes of this story, failed to think enough about the impact on this one, largely powerless, fairly ordinary young Mexican. . . . We'd approach this story somewhat differently if we had to do it over."

Then there was the case of KENS-TV and KSAT-TV in San Antonio, two local stations that seriously misused their tools by erroneously reporting that shots were fired and children were injured at a local elementary school. These stations got caught up in the misguided, breaking news-live coverage mentality that put speed before accuracy. They failed to verify facts, misinterpreted the situation, and hyped the story, scaring many parents and other residents. The leaders at these two television stations had not developed the guidelines and decision-making protocols that could have changed the way the reporting played out.

Let me suggest that in case after case the underlying problem was not one of bad intentions but of failed capacity. I believe that, for the most part, good people in these newsrooms wanted to do the right thing. To varying degrees, they veered off course because good intention was not connected to solid capacity. Principles and core values were abandoned. Leaders did not prepare their staffs. Journalists did not make competent ethical decisions at key points. Mistakes were compounded. Quality suffered. Credibility was eroded.

Why Systems Fail

Taken as a whole, these cases reveal that our systems for newsgathering, editing, and delivering news under pressure are not strong enough:

- Our checks and balances fail when put to the test. Important questions are not asked. The right people are not included in the conversation at key points. Decisions are made in haste and without reflection.
- Our veterans, and sometimes our super-stars, are as prone to hitting ethical land mines as our rookies, and maybe more so. Their tunnel vision impairs their logic and skill. They overrely on their gut and overemphasize their autonomy. Their inflated egos expose an Achilles' heel.
- Our talented leaders get complacent, overconfident, or inattentive. Then they get trapped, making decisions from a restricted range of less-than-ideal choices. They manage by assumptions that prove false. They don't anticipate danger points. They overuse their official and expert styles and misinterpret nuances in the newsroom culture. They don't connect with their journalists as a thoughtful guide and an effective coach. They fail to prosecute stories to ensure factual accuracy and contextual authenticity.

Conflicts of Journalism and Business Values

Editors and news directors face ethical challenges produced by the decisions made not in the newsroom but in the boardroom. These issues often emerge at the intersection of business and journalism values.

In an era where live shots, "lede graphs," and links will all emerge from a converged newsroom, the minute-by-minute, second-by-second reporting plays out in a mixed-media maelstrom. High-stakes competition influences the economics of the business. Even in those organizations where convergence has not arrived, the pressures to grow the bottom line are intensified by the demands for top-line, revenue-enhancing creativity. Given those dynamics, it's no surprise that some recent ethical explosions are connected to misguided priorities and misplaced values.

The news executives at CBS News were using dull ethics tools when they made the decision to digitally alter reality in the now-infamous Millennium New Year's Eve newscast from Times Square. Viewers of the *CBS Evening News* broadcast saw Dan Rather in front of a billboard touting CBS. The technology wizards digitally removed a giant logo of the competing NBC network as well as an ad for Budweiser from the video image of Times Square, replacing them with their own CBS corporate logo. It was clever marketing, but outright deception and dishonesty, technological expertise trumping ethical principles.

Then there is the case of the *Los Angeles Times* and the explosion produced by a volatile mixture of misguided business motives and tainted journalism product. The paper got itself into a questionable partnership with the Staples Center sports arena that compromised the newspaper's journalistic credibility. That arrangement involved sharing advertising profits from an issue of the *Times*'s Sunday magazine entirely devoted to coverage of the Staples Center itself. Despite concerns expressed at various stages by some news editors and other managers, the top executives at the paper kept building a lucrative house of cards that was bound to collapse under the weight of conflicts of interest.

The aftermath was significant. There was great turbulence in the newsroom of the *Times* and considerable agitation among journalists nationwide. In the wake of significant negative publicity, the newspaper's publisher, Kathryn Downing, admitted to her own "fundamental misunderstanding" of editorial principles. Editor Michael Parks acknowledged that poor decisions were made. And Mark Willes, chairman and CEO of the paper's parent company, Times Mirror, and the architect of the plan to "blow up" the wall between the paper's editorial and business departments, conceded he "didn't realize it was wrong."

None of these leaders is in the same job today.

What Do You Stand For?

When I lead ethics seminars, I start out by asking the participants, "What do you stand for?" I ask them, "What are the ethical principles and values that guide you?"

That "What do you stand for?" question takes us to the core of who we are and what we are about, whether we are reporters covering stories, editors responsible for oversight, or leaders in charge of the business operation. If we can't answer that question with precision and conviction, then we find ourselves troubled by the state of ethics in our profession. Our compass gets knocked out of whack, and our gyroscope wobbles.

The role of journalists is to serve citizens by disseminating information that helps them function well in a democracy. They also provide other forms of information that help people lead their lives.

It's the journalists' duty to help us understand what is going on at city hall, at the state capital, and in the halls of Congress, even when what is happening in a governmental arena seems routine and mundane.

It's the journalists' duty to help us grapple with the contention and discomfort surrounding race relations and to struggle with the public policy issues embedded in our views on abortion.

It's the journalists' duty to help us make sense of the important issues surrounding DNA, HIV, HMOs, and IPOs, as well as keeping track of the FBI and the CIA.

It's the journalists' duty to help citizens weave through the rhetoric on the political campaign trail; to give us more issues and less horse race; to probe the positions of candidates and hold them accountable when they are elected.

It's the journalists' responsibility to provide the public with meaningful information about the decrease of violent crime in America and the increase of suicide among teens and the elderly. It's the journalists' responsibility to report meaningful statistics about housing and jobs and the gross national product, and tell us about trends in religion, faith, and spirituality. It's the journalists' responsibility to help us understand the difference between a true medical breakthrough and incremental progress, between proven scientific fact and laboratory hypothesis.

Of course, journalists must also offer us the other slices of daily life, as we know it, from the ball scores to the weather forecast to the school honor rolls. And, to be sure, journalists should give us some of that good news about triumphs and heroism, to balance all the coverage of tribulations and horror in our world.

Whether on the front page or in the perspective section, whether in the lead story, the newscast, or a feature at the end, journalism is storytelling about the people and places, the issues and the events in our small communities, our metroplexes, and a much larger world beyond our borders. Journalism is storytelling about education and health care and public safety; about transportation and energy and politics; about religion, the environment, and the economy. At least journalism should be about those things.

Profound Professional Obligations

The journalists' duty in our society is both special and essential. Nobody else does what journalists do. Not doctors nor teachers, not lawyers nor judges, not bakers nor architects, not airline pilots nor police officers.

Because of that singular role, journalists have a profound responsibility to be very good at what they do, to strive for excellence every day in every byline, every photograph, and every newscast.

At the seminars I lead at The Poynter Institute and in newsrooms across the country, I stress that point. The most significant ethical responsibility for a journalist is to strive for excellence. That's not to diminish the values of truth-telling and fairness, for instance, but to embed them within the application of the craft itself. Accuracy, independence, compassion, and other ethical values infuse the many craft skills journalists must practice every day.

Perhaps the greatest weakness in American journalism is that we are not good enough at what we do. That may be our greatest ethical failing. We are not good enough at ferreting out important stories about chicanery in the halls of government; not good enough at revealing racial discrimination in major corporations; not good enough at providing the context on complex technology stories; not good enough at connecting important international issues to our communities; not good enough at making the routine around the corner important enough for us to pay attention to.

Journalists should be faulted for not reporting more meaningful stories about children and senior citizens; for not writing clearly about economics, medicine, and science; for missing stories about successful local businesses, innovative teachers, and hard-working firefighters.

When we fail to measure up in our work, when we are not good enough as journalists, that is an ethical failure. When our professional skills and competence are not what they should be, that is an ethical failure. When we miss important stories from down the block, across the nation, or around the world, that is an ethical failure.

Ethics and Excellence

Journalism ethics is about the essential role of the press. Journalism ethics is about truth-telling, the duty to inform the public in a compelling way on significant issues. Journalism ethics is about independence, our responsibility to guard the stewardship role of a free press in an open and democratic society.

When individual journalists, newsroom leaders, and news organizations fulfill these responsibilities and duties, they act ethically. They honor the principles and values at the core of professional, principled behavior.

When KHOU-TV in Houston documents multiple cases of Ford Explorers crashing after their Firestone tires fell apart, and that reporting leads to a recall of millions of potentially defective tires, *that* is principled and professional journalism. KHOU news director Mike Devlin said his journalists deserve great credit for their reporting. "It's not the act itself that's so impressive, but the commitment." Devlin says his team members were obsessed with researching and reporting, continually asking each other, "What are we doing? What's the story?"

When the *Portland Press-Herald/Maine Sunday Telegram* publishes a series of insightful articles on teenagers largely based on the voices of the teens themselves, *that* is value-based journalism. Barbara Walsh's award-winning reporting gave adults an intriguing look into the world of teenagers and connected teens with each other in ways seldom accomplished by journalists. "In reporting and writing 'On the Verge,' I had to ignore a lot of my journalistic training," Walsh wrote. "Instead of focusing on the extreme culture, looking for kids who did really bad things or towns where pregnancy rates were higher than normal, I searched for ordinary teens struggling with everyday problems, fears, pressures."

Editor Jeannine Guttman told readers the reporting used "civic journalism reporting models, where stories are framed from the experiences of regular people rather than always relying on the voices of 'experts' and public officials. . . . Whenever we use this new model, we find that readers react much differently to the stories."

When the *News & Observer* publishes stories revealing the failure of state government to properly regulate the hog processing industry and the resulting environmental dangers, *that* is professional and principled journalism.

When National Public Radio takes us to Rwanda, East Timor, Yugoslavia, Chechnya, and other killing grounds to hear the agonizing sounds of genocide, *that* is powerful and principled journalism.

When the *New York Times* publishes its continuing series of stories on the scourge of AIDS in Africa, helping us understand the dimensions of this global issue, *that* is compelling and principled journalism.

When the *Spokane Spokesman-Review* in Washington reframes its editorial page into an interactive forum, prompting more voices from the community and better opportunity for readers to listen to other views, *that* is principled, civic-minded journalism.

When WBUR-FM reporter Jason Beaubien gives his public radio listeners in Boston a comprehensive story on life inside one inner-city elementary school, *that* is principled and important journalism.

When the *Winston-Salem Journal* in North Carolina tackles one of the most complex and contentious issues of all—race relations—and publishes an eight-part series that informs and educates its readers, *that* is excellent and ethical journalism. The *Journal's* series, "Dividing Lines: Race Relations in Forsyth County," tackled race relations through the long lens of history and the microscope of daily life in schools, businesses, and community gathering places. That series, like others in recent years by the New Orleans *Times-Picayune* and the *Akron Beacon Journal* in Ohio, and, most recently, the *New York Times,* accomplished many things, including sparking a lively conversation among citizens and within a community.

Consider the probing medical reporting of Laurie Garrett at *Newsday.* The thoughtful coverage of migrant workers by Anne Hull for the *St. Petersburg Times.* The precise business and economics coverage by Mike Jensen of NBC News. The compelling photography of Clarence Williams of the *Los Angeles Times.* The artful storytelling by Bartholomew Sullivan of the *Commercial Appeal* in Memphis as he weaves stories about the trials of Ku Klux Klan wizards and the deaths of country music legends. The evocative writing on poverty and children by Isabel Wilkerson and Jason DeParle of the *New York Times.* The authoritative reporting on national security issues by Jack McWethy of ABC News. The insightful political commentary of syndicated columnist David Broder.

Leaders and the Culture They Create

To be sure, these journalists, and many others across the land, deserve great credit for their fine work. But they and their colleagues work within news organizations led by women and men who create an environment where excellence is expected, valued, and recognized.

The excellent journalism is a product of good intentions *and* strong capacity. The leaders pay attention to the newsroom culture. They create and constantly emphasize strong principles and core values, outstanding journalistic skills, and high-quality ethical decision making.

Ethicist Barbara Toffler addressed this issue of organizational culture: "The values and operating style of an organization (the culture) have a potent effect on what managers identify as ethical concerns in their work and how they go about handling those concerns."

I've seen how cultural factors play out in newsrooms, including instances where poor leadership produces serious problems. I've seen:

- Managers who fail to identify the core values that should underpin their organization's commitment to the role of journalism in communities and society.
- Managers focused on the assembly line and unaware of the journalistic and ethical weaknesses that can erode product quality and corrode credibility.
- Managers who are rooted in their command-and-control model and don't respect the concerns of others.
- Managers who overemphasize the bottom line to the detriment of journalistic duty, whose short-term thinking undermines their ability to honor legitimate economic goals.
- Managers who discount contrarian voices in their newsrooms, stifling meaningful discussion and creative thinking.
- Managers who think they have all the answers because they have stripes on their sleeves or experience under their belt.
- Managers who see ethical issues in absolutes, failing to help their staffs recognize and sort through the gray area that is part of almost every ethical dilemma.

Principled and Skilled Leaders

To the contrary, strong leaders are much more than product managers. They focus on both short-term demands and long-term goals. Their mission and vision reflect noble ideals and good intentions.

They build capacity in themselves and their people and apply it to the obligations of journalism. They prepare themselves and their newsrooms for the range of professional, business, and ethical challenges they face.

These are the principled and skilled leaders who

- Are clear in what they and their news organizations stand for. They support their core values with meaningful, practical guidelines and functional decision-making protocols that clarify roles and responsibilities.
- Are sure their systems are sound and well lubricated. They develop effective processes that guarantee conversation and oversight. They prepare, practice, and learn. They anticipate the unexpected.
- Are reflective. They listen to their gut, but they don't just blindly trust it. They value and practice reasoned decision making.
- Are sharpening their own skills so they can make good calls on complex issues and, when necessary, on deadline.
- Are adept at coaching their subordinates and staff in their decision-making skills. They build capacity in others.

Capacity, Competence, and Confidence

Skilled and principled leaders are the champions of learning in their organization. They provide the incentive, opportunities, and resources for individual growth and organizational development. They accept responsibility for all decisions while sharing recognition for good decisions by others.

Good leaders see a correlation between their skills and the mission of journalism. Leaders who have the capacity to carry out their good intentions can be courageous and assertive. They and their staffs can be aggressive in gathering information and bold in what they report to the public.

These principled, skilled leaders have the professional and ethical competence that produces justifiable confidence. That confidence in oneself and the organization refuels the capacity, which in turn empowers hard-hitting, compelling journalism that is ethically sound, which in turn earns the confidence of the public.

6

One Journalist's Sense of Mission and Purpose

Paula Bock

In the summer of 2000, The Poynter Institute asked me to speak to a seminar on the mission and purpose of journalism, from one writer's perspective. To prepare, I plunged into the Deep.

Mission. Purpose. Meaning. The big *whys*—in journalism and in life.

Before surfacing, I would relive a bittersweet sunset in a charred refugee camp; realize why I hate talking to strangers on airplanes; and deepen my respect for the peasant woman who decided not to bind my grandmother's feet. But all that comes later.

My journey of discovery began at the *Seattle Times*, where I gathered wisdom from colleagues whom I admire for their passion. Like the best writers and editors in any newsroom, they know what they want to do, they're good at it, doors swing open as they pass by. I wondered, sometimes, if they were born that way.

I learned, instead, even the best stumble. The secret is that they've figured out—for themselves—what's important. So work leads beyond pay checks or pats on the back. And when the stumbling gets rough, there's a reason to keep going.

Knowing what you want to do, and why, can steady you in a newsroom of competing agendas. It can help you weed out what's irrelevant among the daily tangle. It can give you courage and strength.

After all, there's only so much time in a day, in a journalism career, in your life. Might as well do something, in your heart, that matters.

Florangela Davila, reporter, race and class team:

> We have the most privileged profession. I still think that. You have the privilege of stepping into worlds and places and meeting people and delving into that honesty, that sphere of vulnerability that a lot

of people hide. You talk to people about death, or people who have new babies. You get to do the whole range of emotions. That's what I like. You get to make it known that people aren't alone. That basically everyone is human. It's a vehicle to bring humanity back to day-to-day living. You produce a daily product and you remind people of what's important.

David Boardman, assistant managing editor, directed numerous Pulitzer-winning investigative and public service projects:

For me, it didn't start out with that public service drive.

I was more motivated by love for writing, and then over time I found I had a real passion for politics. Journalism seemed like a place to bring those two things together.

The greatest piece of the passion is moving the rock of society. Really making a difference. I've tended to think of making the difference on more of a macro level, not just in a person's life as they read the paper. Righting wrongs and fixing things. I feel we have an obligation, this sacred trust. If we pursue this, in a best-case scenario, will it have any impact? If not, maybe we need to turn to something else that will have an impact because there are so many things that need addressing. From an investigative editor or writer's point of view, there's this whole playground of wrongdoing.

Suki Dardarian, assistant managing editor, metro and enterprise news:

The little things make you feel proud.

You get payback when you see a reporter commit a great act of journalism. When you see an editor commit a great act of journalism. When you hear Chris Solomon jumped on his bike to get to the I-90 bridge when a tanker spilled and mountain bike was the only way to get there.

When I was a reporter, I used to see the pod of editors in the middle of the room and think: what a horrible existence. They're yelled at by upper management, yelled at by defensive reporters who don't want to listen, and then get second-guessed by everybody, including readers.

When I got into it, I found out it was totally the opposite. It's an opportunity to take competing visions and meld them, always keeping in mind, what does the reader need? Are we doing that? Then there's the thrill of getting it into the paper and saying, "Damn, that was good."

Tyrone Beason, business reporter specializing in biotechnology:

I'm much more of a teacher, a describer, as opposed to a watchdog, an enforcer. Some people are good at investigative scoops, the gotcha journalism. I'm fascinated with the process of learning about the world, about advancements, about change. To pick up on the rhythms of life. How things evolve—whether it's a community, a family, a drug company. You get to connect dots for people who weren't there or who don't have the time to pay attention themselves.

Lily Eng, editor of Weekend:

I've had four or five young reporters straight off the bat. Part of my job is getting them into the field. Making sure they're getting all the basics and making sure they're reaching for higher ground. When I see them get it, that's when I realize I'm getting it, too.

The other day, I had a conversation with a veteran reporter about story ideas. It was supposed to be a fifteen-minute conversation; an hour later, we were still talking about these wonderful story ideas. I was able to help her story ideas bloom. To take a germ of an idea and make it come alive—that's thrilling.

If you're a reporter, you have to be a storyteller. If you're an editor, you want to hear a good story. You're a story listener.

Kathy Andrisevic, editor, *Pacific Northwest*, the Sunday magazine:

It's moment to moment, you know. When everything's coming together in that Zen sort of way, and a story takes a curve or a turn that's unexpected and new and brilliant—that's what I live for. It doesn't happen every week.

[The magazine] should be a leisurely read. It gives you a chance to explore all those things you're frantically doing and re-evaluate your posture toward those things. . . . It needs to be this rough coming together and saying, "This is what we are at this time." . . . And over time, what are we saying about how we live?

You create an environment where people have control of their time. People who own their own time make things happen. Then you sit back, and if someone threatens that, you beat them off with a stick. I believe that's what a good editor does: Keeps the philistines at bay.

Betty Udesen, photojournalist:

We're not just validating writing. Hopefully, we are giving another layer of information to the reader. Also, we're representing the community. Hopefully, when you look back, you'll be able to flip through the paper and say, yeah, that was really the community.

Sometimes I feel like we're able to take a picture that enables people to stare at people they'd usually turn away from on the street. They can take a closer look, and if they can't stomach it, they can turn the page.

People often turn past a story if they think, "That person is nothing like me, it has nothing to do with my life, why should I read that story?" So you have to connect. Sometimes it's the look in their eye, the way they hold their hand, or something they have on the wall in their kitchen.

Sometimes I'm looking to be direct. Sometimes our pictures are just to add a little fun. Sometimes I'm looking at a situation to find out what's surprising to me and that's what I want to bring back. Usually, I treat the story like it's a neighborhood and I'm trying to find the relationships. I want to show the humanity of the situation.

It's not that we change a situation with our photography, but we document a situation and bring it to the reader and let them grow.

Rick Zahler, associate editor, *Pacific Northwest*:

Work, for a lot of people, especially when they are new in their career, is motivated by fear and worry and insecurity. You do things because you're worried if you screw up, something bad will happen to you. But it's not good for sustained motivation and not very positive.

So what are the positive things? Take those qualities that you naturally gravitate to, that make you comfortable, secure, fulfilled. What do you need to get out of work? What would that look like?

I had an illuminating conversation with Alex Tizon, a Pulitzer Prize-winning reporter who writes about social issues.

He told me he was miserable his first decade at the *Seattle Times*. Then, after several years of groping, talking with friends and colleagues, and reading about work and meaning, he realized certain big themes and questions kept popping up in his life, and he could use the newspaper to explore them. It was a small shift in imagination that made a huge difference. His misery index plummeted; his work (already primo) soared. Alex challenged me to figure out my themes. This turns out to be harder than it sounds, to step back from the daily rush to see the larger landscape.

One place I rediscover my own sense of mission and purpose is at a free clinic on the Thai-Burma border, where I volunteer during winter vacations. Every year, I bring home a gift from the war zone, an understanding that life is precious and fragile. We get to be here for a while and then we move on.

I also searched for clues to my own themes in stories I'd written over the past decade. I flipped through the dusty stacks and picked five that resonated most. Then I asked myself: Why these stories? What common themes run through them?

After several Diet Cokes, here's what I came up with:

My first theme is *peace*. Peace on a macro level in a society. And peace on a personal level, the inner peace that people seek and find for themselves.

I've had the opportunity to wade through the aftermath of conflicts in Vietnam, Cambodia, Kosovo, Somalia, and Burma. For a long time, I thought I was writing about war. Really, I was writing about peace.

I realized the victors were actually victims—of greed, of hate, of history, of all sorts of demons that would return to haunt them in temporal and visceral ways. And the conquered? They so often showed strength and courage that continues to astonish and comfort me.

One such story was about Amerasian children, the offspring of American soldiers in Vietnam. They were hated in Vietnam because they were living evidence of consorting with the enemy.

On the streets of Ho Chi Minh City, Dam was a wild, illiterate buffalo boy, shunned even more than other Amerasians because he was black. When he came to Seattle, he was kicked out of school, out of his adopted family, and then out of the city. Still he makes his peace. Here's part of his story.

After a full year at Sharples High School, Dam can read only two words on the washing machine. COLD. HOT. He points to START. "Wash?" he asks. He does not attempt PERM PRESS. He squints at the letters and shrugs. Dam puts his hand on the dryer's glass porthole, feeling its warmth like a belly. The laundry tumbles out soft and clingy.

"When I grow up, I have to have a family, because family life tends to support each other. I want to have a boy, to look like me. I have to play the role of a father, support the boy, send him to school, provide food for him. I'll read to him before sleep. Tell him stories. I will tell him what was going on in my life. Let him know. The children will ask me about Grandpa and Grandma. I won't hide anything."

Outside the laundry, Dam stares at Seattle's skyline with empty eyes. Puget Sound and the Columbia Seafirst Tower are blurred. All his shirts are in the wash, and his Goodwill raincoat feels clammy next to his skin. A bus rumbles past. Construction workers jackhammer the ground, shaking emotion to the surface. Dam puts his face in his hands. Life in an American city will go on without him.

"I receive whatever God gives me. I like my life. The thing I like from God is he gives me the chance to stay in school, to learn some skills, to get a job."

Dam, who started life in a Catholic orphanage, has retained a reverence for the forces that control his destiny. He has accepted a fate that others would fight—and lose. That is his saving grace. A small gold pendant hangs from a chain around Dam's neck. It is not a cross. It is the word B-R-A-T spelled out in gold letters. He found the charm on the street and doesn't know what it means.

There's also personal peace. Not peace of passivity or contentedness. Peace of survival. Of strength. Meet Henrietta, the Hat Lady. She is a modern-day milliner who began stitching her own hats—and dignity—in Texas in the 1960s, when African Americans were not allowed to try on clothes in department stores.

Now she has a small pink shop in drip-dry Seattle. Henrietta's story took an unexpected turn when her husband died while I was profiling her. The Hat Lady found solace and peace in her hats.

Henrietta has been "going through," as she puts it. They were together 35 years; four months apart has seemed an eternity. These days, Henrietta tucks wads of Kleenex into her purse along with her usual lace-edged handkerchief.

"I'm trying to get my life back together," she says. "It seems he loved me so long ago! I'm trying not to feel sorry for myself, but sometimes I get an unconscious remembering. Breakfast is not the same. The elegance of him always giving me breakfast and coffee in bed! I am trying to keep the early morning special. God is good, giving me that man."

Oh, Baby, he'd say when they'd browse in department stores. Try that on. That'd look nice on you, Baby! The bodice of the lime-green suit was embroidered with glass bugle beads that cascaded toward a fitted waist and sleek skirt. Lime is not a color Henrietta would ordinarily choose for herself, but her husband insisted. "He liked how it looked on me," she says. "We'd always browse."

My second theme involves *humanity*. I love to write about relationships between people, especially friendship.

Without friends, life would crumble.

Friends are what keep us going day to day. The lucky among us make friends for life. And then, there are Delmar and Dallas. Here's part of their story.

To Dallas Dodd, there are two things most beautiful in the world. The first is the sight of just about any crop when it is still green and flexible, shimmering in the wind, seed pods swollen but not headed out. The second is the flash of the silvery steelhead in a jump three feet off the Grande Ronde River. The 47-year-old farmer is also fond of his wife, Dianne; his aging German Shepherd, God, country, Tom Clancy novels, hunting and ketchup. He treasures his many friends, especially 76-year-old Delmar McMillan. When they are not in the fields or down by the river, Dallas and Delmar can often be found at the Anatone Café, where a poster above the door is testimony to their friendship. "Delmar and Dallas," someone wrote in red felt-tip on a picture of two oblivious fishermen about to be swallowed by a humongous bass. "Who has to buy tonight? Watch out for the big one."

Later in the story, seventy-six-year-old Delmar has acute heart problems in addition to his usual woman problems; Dallas's brother, Donald, is dying of cancer; and to top it off, the USDA deputy secretary of agriculture casually mentions that tight grain supplies might prevent the United States from selling much wheat to China this year.

In the café, Dallas's hands clenched around his coffee cup because up here on the plateau, the farmers grow mostly soft white wheat, the kind China and Japan buy to make noodles. What good is putting all that work into a crop if the market is cut out?

"Calm down, Dallas," Delmar always tells him. "It's not the end of the world."

The end of the world almost came in 1987, the year Dallas's older brother, Donald, was dying from cancer. Suddenly, a two-brother farm became a one-person farm, and even working 14 hours a day, 182 days in a row without once going fishing, Dallas didn't know if he had what it took to bring the crops to fruition. Too much time on the tractor for thinking. Didn't matter if the tractor radio was tuned to NPR or Rush Limbaugh or nostalgic tunes from the '50s. Nothing could drive away the looming possibility that he might fail the family farm. "Don't be so hard on yourself," Delmar would tell him.

Delmar retired from the fertilizer company and started coming around more and more to help till and seed and work the 90-foot sprayer. Dallas's nephew Ron helped drive the tractor and fix machinery. Harvest time, neighbors rounded up 14 combines to help cut the grain. Donald died a year later.

The day of his funeral, the half-harvested fields of Anatone were quiet, all the combines stilled, only grasshoppers jumping.

Delmar took Dallas fishing. Cast, drift, trawl, strip it in, cast again. Donald's name surfaced a couple times, but really they didn't talk much. It was a good day. They reeled 50 bronze and green smallmouth bass to the bank, eased out the hooks and watched the fish swim off through the eddies.

My third theme is a little messy. For lack of a better term, I'll call it the *Little Brown People*. By that, I mean all those people you read about en masse on page A13, in a war, or a famine, or as "labor" on the business pages. They are people you diminish and dismiss because you don't identify with them; they don't seem real. Your eyes glaze and skitter away.

I'd put Delmar and Dallas in the LBP category, even though they're not little and they're certainly not brown. Here's why. To me, before I got to know them, they were just farmers. No, worse. Agricultural subsidies. A paragraph of print. No heart. No brain. No soul.

I don't embrace the term *Little Brown People*, but I recognize the notion is out there, and as a journalist, I must take some responsibility. I realize that every time I write about people in a way that renders them less than human, I have made it that much easier for others to treat them in ways inhumane.

Recently I was flipping through the United Nations Millennium Report; released by Kofi Annan in September 2000. I came across some startling passages.

> Let us imagine, for a moment, that the world really is a "Global Village." Say this village has 1,000 individuals, with all the characteristics of today's human race distributed in exactly the same proportions.
>
> What would it look like? What would we see as its main challenges?
>
> Some 150 of the inhabitants live in an affluent area of the village, about 780 in poorer districts. Another 70 or so live in a neighborhood that is in transition. The average income per person is $6,000 a year, and there are more middle income families than in the past. But just 200 people dispose of 86 percent of all the wealth, while nearly half of the villagers are eking out an existence on less than $2 a day.
>
> Men outnumber women by a small margin, but women make up a majority of those who live in poverty. Adult Literacy has been increasing. Still, some 220 villagers—two-thirds of them women—are illiterate. Of the 390 inhabitants under 20 years of age, three-fourths live in the poorer districts and many are looking desperately for jobs that do not exist.
>
> Fewer than 60 people own a computer and only 24 have access to the Internet. More than half have never made or received a telephone call.

There are six billion people in the world. Most of them are little brown people. Not movers or shakers or Microsoft millionaires.

On one of my flights from Seattle, I sat next to a woman wearing a paisley scarf. She looked over as I was typing on my iBook, and asked: Where was I going? What was I doing? Where did I go to college? Did I get to travel a lot for my job? Who did I write about?

I dread those questions. And I realized this time, as I was answering, why they make me cringe. Because I'm hearing this voice saying, "Oh yes, journalism conference, Harvard, yeah, some faraway places, fascinating people." But you know what?

Inside, I'm really a little brown person.

If I weren't standing here right now, I'd be squatting in some rice paddy in China. My grandmother's grandmother was the fourth wife of an almost-wealthy landowner. He provided for her and his other wives, and in return, they granted him certain favors and bore his children.

Except my grandmother's grandmother, to whom no children came. So she adopted a foundling baby boy. She ended up raising his daughter, my grandmother.

She made three decisions that have everything to do with my life today: First, she did not bind my grandmother's feet. If my grandmother's feet had been bound, she wouldn't have been able to walk far or work hard and may never have crossed the Pacific. Second, she had an old retired army general teach my grandmother and some other village girls to read and write. This had never been done before. Third, she sent my grandmother to America, at seventeen, in an arranged marriage with a Chinese laundryman in Baltimore.

How easily I could have been a little brown peasant girl, one of the many women in our global village who can't read—let alone write.

I remember one afternoon in Huay Kaloke refugee camp on the border between Burma and Thailand. I was on assignment for the *Seattle Times* with photographer Tom Reese. The camp had been attacked and burned to the ground. Seven thousand refugees lived under blue plastic tarps with no toilets and only one medic.

We're doing rounds with the medic, himself a refugee, as he walks, in flip-flops, over charred and steaming mud.

Then we come to a newborn swaddled in white muslin. The baby in the shroud. The infant is frail, wizened, smaller than my notebook, lighter than Tom's camera, so weak he cannot suck. "This baby will die. Serious malnutrition," Than Hlaing says, using his shadow to shield the infant's face from the sun. The baby drags his left eyelid open and struggles to smile on one side of his face. The furrows deepen around his dry mouth. It is unbearable, really, watching this doomed child smile.

For a long time, I thought the saddest scenes were those of total devastation. I now understand that flickers of spirit are what rip the soul most. All around, all the time in Huay Kaloke, we hear the constant pounding of people rebuilding their homes, digging post holes with tin cans, lashing together green bamboo that is too skinny, too soft, too young to last long in a place attackers have threatened they'll burn again.

We walk past scattered plumes of smoke rising from hundreds of cooking fires and we spot a little girl washing her baby brother in an aluminum rice pot. They are beautiful in the heavy glow of supper hour, gold sun clinging to wet skin. The girl dips her small hands into the pot, forming a cup. She lets the water slither down her brother's shoulders, rubs her fingers along his toasty back, feels it glisten.

Then comes something that completely shakes me. The children's mother looks up from where she squats, stirring fish paste, and asks, "Please, won't you join us for dinner?" I am overwhelmed by her kindness. I am afraid to accept even one grain of rice from a family that has so little. I am appalled at my hunger to absorb her spirit, ashamed I will take more of it than I could ever give back. I am angry that we can only do so much, and that what we can do is not nearly enough for all these families cooking supper and the babies about to die.

Just one more scene. It's a moment imprinted deeply in my mind. We're melting, plastered to hard benches during a graduation ceremony for refugee medics trained by Dr. Cynthia, the Mother Teresa of the Thai-Burma border. The ceiling fan is broken. The graduation drones on and on. French, British, and Australian donors make long speeches that are laboriously translated into several languages.

Then a woman from the International Rescue Committee stands up. She holds up her two hands. She says: "Everybody has two hands, but not everybody can use their hands to help other people. If you are lucky and have hands that can help, you must use them." Then she sits back down.

Here's my last theme: We are all lucky to have two hands.

Part III

Community

The presidential election of 1988, in which George Bush defeated Michael Dukakis, engendered a good deal of soul-searching among journalists about the health of American democracy, the nature of public life, and the role of the media. Throughout the 1990s, a group of practical scholars and reflective practitioners began a conversation in which they reimagined how journalism could create a support system for civic life. The conversation turned into a movement, called either "civic" or "public" journalism, and that movement ignited a fiery debate that created heat, light, and a good deal of acrid smoke.

Jay Rosen, a brilliant scholar from NYU, challenged journalists to re-examine their political role, asking, again and again, "What are journalists for?" He clearly savored the delicious ambiguity of that question (which became the title of his book on the subject). At one level, the question had to do with the utility of journalists: what do we need them for? At another, it demanded a search for purpose: what do journalists stand for?

An early version of these ideas appeared in "Community Connectedness: Passwords for Public Journalism" (1993). In this essay, Rosen invites conversation on how journalists can reinvent their work as a support system for public life; how they can improve the quality of public conversation in a community; and what changes are possible in the culture of newsrooms that would help inspire such reforms.

Over the course of the decade, Poynter positioned itself as one of the few neutral brokers in the argument surrounding the civic journalism movement. Rather than become an advocate for one side or another,

Poynter preferred to study, test, and promote useful tools for journalistic thinking and practice, wherever they might be found.

In her essay "Blacked Out: Local Television and Community Coverage" (2000), Jill Geisler reports on the neglect of traditional government reporting by local news stations and its negative consequences for communities and citizens. If we have abandoned our sentry and listening posts, she argues, perhaps it is our duty to claim them back.

Keith Woods, Geisler's colleague at Poynter, begins this section with a powerful case that excellent journalism must include many different expressions of community. Rather than describe these with the overburdened word *diversity*, Woods posits a new theorem (2001), a formula for enriching our work by first understanding ourselves. That process will help us understand our communities.

7

The Woods Theorem

A New Formula for Diversity in American News Organizations

Keith Woods

Ever since the ninth grade, when I struggled for a C in Mrs. Chighizola's algebra class, I've questioned the premise that there would ever be a real-world reason to add and multiply letters of the alphabet. And though I dodged those critical-thinking classes by bailing out of business courses in college and graduate school, algebra has haunted me well into adulthood.

My daughter needed help with it in eighth grade. My son, in seventh grade. By the time my stepdaughter was puzzling over integers in the third grade, algebra had seeped so pervasively into my life that I was using the distributive property to balance the checkbook.

So it was that I found myself in the summer of 2000 contemplating an algebraic interpretation of diversity in daily journalism. It looks like this:

$$E = w\ (y + c + f)$$

Journalism excellence (E) is equal to the amount of work (w) you do on improving yourself (y), your craft (c), and your story frames (f). Call it the Woods Theorem. Call it Mrs. Chighizola's revenge.

Defining Diversity

The astute reader might notice right away that there is no D (diversity) in that formula. There are a couple of reasons. The biggest problem with the word *diversity* is that it means too much to mean anything. Depending upon where you stand in the country, the company or the newsroom, diversity's definition can range from the euphoric to the euphemistic. We could be talking about the maximum inclusion of all races, ethnicities, voices, perspectives, experiences, and cultures, or we could be talking about black people. We could be talking about everyone of every class, gender, and sexual sort, or we could be talking about everybody but straight white men.

A smart newsroom manager might test this theory in a meeting by saying, "We could use more diversity around here," then polling people about what they heard. If one person hears "more black people," and another hears "affirmative action," and another hears "tokenism," and yet another hears the ubiquitous and squishy "people of diverse perspectives," then there's work to be done on definitions.

Add to that the suspicion, sometimes justified, that this diversity business is all a bunch of feel-good social engineering with little if anything to do with journalism, and you have good reason to banish the word forever from staff meetings and spell-check. Better, then, that we get away from the dysfunctional, one-noun-fits-all trap and use more words in the name of less confusion. Better that we say what we mean. That, after all, is what good journalism does.

$$E = w (y + c + f)$$

It's About Excellence

The other reason the D isn't in the formula is that what we're talking about here is bigger than that. We're talking about living up to the principles of excellent, ethical journalism. That's the E. Ask journalists what those principles are, ask them anywhere in this country or any other place where the press is free, and the answers will be the same: they stand for truth, accuracy, fairness, courage, precision, comprehensiveness, independence, giving voice to the voiceless, holding the powerful accountable, informing, educating, taking people where they can't or won't go. The best among us treat that list as a recipe, not a buffet. Leave out too many of the ingredients, too many of the principles, and credibility collapses like a bad soufflé.

That's what happens for many people who see themselves rarely reflected in the mythical mirror journalism holds up to the world each day. Their voices are often muted, their stories untold or poorly told. Their communities are alien territory to many in the working press. Their images are distorted by journalism that fails, time and again, to capture the depth and complexity that would make their stories truer, more accurate, fairer, more complete.

In the not-so-distant past of U.S. journalism, that monumental failure of mission was intentional. The distorting effects linger today, and the knowledge and understanding gulf between the newsroom and whole communities remains wide enough to render our journalism suspect.

It's not all neglect, superficiality, and stereotypes, but too much of it still comes out that way.

Excellence is what happens when the principles upon which journalists stand are applied to everyone, every community, every class and kind with the same passion. That's the work (w) in this formula. That's what diversity can do.

$$E = w (Y + c + f)$$

It Starts with You

Whether you're trying to manage a workforce, interview a source, or craft a sentence, the biggest hurdle to greater, fairer journalism most often resides in you. When diversity is defined as hiring people of color, as it often is, many say that better coverage will flow only when the newsroom "reflects the community it serves." It's true that change, welcome change, happens when racial diversity increases. At the least, it means the effects of historic exclusion are being addressed.

But that definition of diversity fails to take into account the fact that the most racially diverse newsroom will still find itself with atheists covering Christians and black people covering American Indians. No matter how diverse the newsroom, there will still be journalists reporting on people unlike themselves. So there is always work to be done, and that work begins with you:

- Listen to yourself—Know your biases and fears. Where don't you want to go and why not? How is that affecting your journalism?
- Challenge your assumptions—Do you figure some people won't talk to you, so why bother? Do you think you already know what sort of story you'll get from some folks or some places? How are your preconceptions subverting otherwise trustworthy journalistic instincts?
- Educate yourself—Read a book. Pick up a newspaper. Tune in to community radio and public service TV. Invite a neighborhood historian to lunch. Ask yourself regularly, "What have I done lately to learn more?"
- Act—Once you've discovered new truths about yourself, your community, or your profession, change something. It's too easy to fall back into comfortable stereotypes and familiar ways of doing things.

Take those guidelines and apply them to the newsroom, and the foundation can be laid for substantive change in the way undercovered people, neighborhoods, and issues are handled. The heterosexual reporter who wants to report past his discomfort with gay men might come to better understand the difference between sexual orientation and sexual preference. He might learn to pay greater attention to the meanings of words in stories about sexuality.

A reporter who tunes in to her belief that people who live in trailer parks fit the stereotype of being unsophisticated "trash" might spend time meeting people where they live, expanding her understanding, deepening her knowledge, and bringing greater depth and context to her storytelling.

That sort of introspection becomes important when a manager, reporter, or producer is trying to assign, investigate, or write a story. It makes it more possible to take the next step up in making excellence possible.

Next Step Up: Talking

Before each seminar on diversity or covering race relations, journalists are asked to write about how comfortable they feel discussing difference. Some say they're just fine with it, and they'd be even better if their coworkers or bosses would stop beating around the bush and deal with the issues straight on.

Many others, though, say they are afraid that they'll be misunderstood, that their ignorance will show, that they'll be called "racist" or accused of "playing the race card," that they'll inadvertently hurt someone's feelings, that they'll start an argument or end a friendship. "Whenever race comes up in my newsroom," a TV reporter in Virginia said at a Columbia University workshop in the summer of 2000, "fear comes after."

Considering all the things that can go wrong and the great personal stake people think they wager on the conversation, avoidance seems like a reasonable human response.

The problem, of course, is that it's not a particularly good journalistic response. Ignorance unchallenged perpetuates itself and fuels fear. Fear leaves doors unopened, questions unasked, claims uncontested. Stories never get fully discussed or adequately critiqued. Coverage decisions go unexamined. In the end, that leaves people uninformed or underinformed, and that falls well short of journalistic excellence. The interpersonal skills that are necessary to move past fear and ignorance, then, become an integral part of responsible, ethical journalism. Avoidance is not an option.

Perhaps the greatest paradox, the one that journalists rediscover every time they decide to tackle diversity of one sort or another, is that there is a tremendous appetite out there for the very conversations we're so deftly avoiding. Without some conscious attention to the things that inspire fear, though, silence reigns and journalism suffers. Here are the things people most often say they need in order to move past their worries and have a productive conversation across difference:

- Be honest—It's almost always among the first five things people say. For some, that means what it says: render your opinion truthfully. Others are suspicious of those who use too many euphemisms or otherwise muddy up the opinion they're trying to express. Say what you mean and say it clearly.
- Seek clarification—Those who worry about being misunderstood want others to give them and their ideas the benefit of the doubt. Suspend judgment long enough to ask at least one question. The most effective tool a journalist has is the question, "What do you mean?"
- Be respectful—How you say it is as important as what you say. Sarcasm, derision, name calling, finger pointing—all scare people away from the table. Challenge ideas with passion, not poison.
- Be willing to change—Practice the skill of truly considering another's way of seeing things. Be open to being wrong. You don't have to change your mind. Just make sure it's possible.
- Stay in the room—A difficult debate between a man and woman about how a breast cancer story played; a tough discussion across race about the use of a racial epithet in a headline; an unsettling admission of anti-gay bias from one of your colleagues. All could end the conversation permanently. The toughest thing to do when something is uncomfortable or painful is to keep doing it. But the cure for the pain, a wise man once said, is in the pain.

There are more things people frequently ask others to bring to the conversation across difference: a sense of humor, knowledge about others, a sense of history, humility, forbearance, the willingness to take a risk. Those qualities are keys that open up the conversation to greater depth and breadth.

Journalism gets done every day without some or all of those qualities present. But if the goal is to change the sound of radio news or the look of the morning paper and the 10 o'clock show, then journalists will have to work on shoring up the bedrock of our craft: communication.

$$E = w (y + C + f)$$

In Other Words . . .

Can the inner city encompass the suburbs? Is it possible to be both black and blue collar? How does an Asian person look? If a gay man is attacked "because he is gay," wouldn't he get attacked all the time?

Precision is an essential ingredient of excellent journalism. It removes doubt and confusion, not just clutter. When we're talking about issues of race, class, faith, sexuality, gender—any of the areas that have proven explosive or underexplored, the need for concise reporting and writing is magnified. Asking good questions and interrogating your copy in search of meaning are two ways to work on the *c*—craft—in the diversity equation.

As with the word *diversity*, the language of journalists who deal with such matters is littered with overburdened adjectives and nouns, each asked to carry around meanings well beyond the definitions you'll find in the dictionary. *Blue collar*, an economic term, doubles as a synonym for *white*. *Inner city* is a geographic term, but it is often asked to convey race (black or brown) and class (probably poor). How often have such words as *suburban*, *urban*, or *mainstream* been used to connote race? How often is *fundamentalist* employed as a clever cover for religious "wacko"?

Euphemisms engender mistrust, because the careful reader will understand both what you're saying and what you're hiding. Better to just come clean with what you mean.

It's critical for a journalist trying to raise his level of craft to scrutinize the meanings behind things. Ask clarifying questions of a source who uses euphemisms and coded language—especially when you feel sure you know what the source meant. Too often, journalists will simply report the euphemisms, leaving the reader, listener, or viewer to do the decoding. That's not precision journalism.

Another tendency when dealing with these things we call diversity is to assume the passive voice when talking about conflict. That runs contrary to some fundamental journalistic teachings, but it's more than just weak sentences. It has more insidious consequences. Consider this common phrasing that appeared in newspapers across the country after the 1998 beating death of Wyoming college student Matthew Shepard:

"Police said robbery was the main motive for the attack but that Shepard apparently was chosen in part because he was gay."

The writer uses a verb (was chosen) in the passive voice and attributes the cause of the action—the beating—to the victim, not the perpetrator.

The fact is that Shepard was gay every other day of the week and was not murdered. What changed? The motives and actions of his assailants.

In the language of difference, the distinction between one sentence structure and another is huge. In sentences structured like the one above, the motives of the actor become secondary to a personal characteristic—race, ethnicity, gender, faith, sexual orientation—that the victim cannot, or would not, change. The cause of action (the blame?) rests with the victim:

"He was arrested because he is black."

"She was attacked because she is Jewish."

Make the sentence active, and watch how the information changes:

"Police said the men beat Shepard because they hated gay men."

"The attack was driven by the suspect's anti-Semitic beliefs."

"He said police arrested him because they are suspicious of all black people."

Those are true causal relationships. In the latter structure, the cause of the action rests on the shoulders of the actors. If a reporter can't write the sentence in the active voice, placing the action where it belongs, chances are he doesn't have enough information to write a sentence at all.

Identifying Problems

The reasons for taking such care with identifying people by characteristics of their difference are rooted in history and ethics. Racial identification offers a powerful example. Until the early 1970s, many U. S. news organizations routinely identified racial and ethnic minorities, particularly black people, by their race, no matter what the story was about.

The practice accomplished several things, none of them journalistic. It helped maintain the sense that U. S. society was first a white society, with others regarded as interlopers. It sought to prove, with selective reporting, that those who were not white were the source of society's many problems. And it contributed to the problem of stereotyping that is as old as humanity and entered the new millennium with a new name: racial profiling.

It is into that historical and influential context that an identification by race falls. So when race is included in a story it takes on power beyond the average adjective. It is no more an innocuous word than "fire" when yelled in a crowded theater. In that way, the issue is one of ethics. Along with the power of the reported word comes responsibility to use the language with courage, purpose, and an awareness of the harm it may cause. Those who have been historically singled out to their detriment—this includes religious groups, women, gays and lesbians, poor people—are particularly vulnerable to harm by journalists who give too little thought to the matter. Singling them out without reason unnecessarily perpetuates their *otherness*.

As with much of what goes awry with reporting on difference, though, holding true to sound journalistic practice can solve a lot of the problem. Facts should be relevant, and their relevance should be clear. Specific is better than general.

A story reporting that police are seeking a "Hispanic" man fails those tests. What does it mean to be Hispanic? Do Mexicans and Puerto Ricans and Nicaraguans and Dominicans share a common look as well as a common language? An identification by ethnicity or race only sounds specific. It isn't. It doesn't tell you what the nose looks like, or the eyes, or the hair, or even the tint of the skin. It provides no real information, unless the characteristics of a group are so similar that, in essence, they all look alike.

There are features that are common within most ethnic groups. The pale skin and red hair of the Irish. The dark hair and swarthy complexion of Italians. The wide nose and tightly curled hair of black people. But when was the last time you saw a story that said police were searching for a five-foot-ten Italian? Or, "The suspect appeared to be Jewish"? It's easy to see how ridiculous those descriptions are when considering the huge range of images people are likely to conjure from those descriptions. It is just as ridiculous to describe someone as Asian.

Color is specific. Eye shapes and ear sizes are specific. Race and ethnicity are not. If a person has mahogany skin, it doesn't matter if he regards himself as Asian, Indian, Arab, or African American. His skin is still mahogany.

Race and ethnicity are relevant and specific when the story is about race or ethnicity. Stories about the emerging Hmong population in Minnesota or the thriving Arab communities of greater Detroit are about ethnicity. A melee between white parents and black parents at a Long Island park is about race, and it doesn't matter what shade of skin the combatants have. But if you're trying to describe the combatants so detectives can find them, neither black nor white describes anything but heritage.

Journalists must ask the question of relevance before any racial reference appears in a story. Even then, the reason for the reference should be explicit in the story. Every fact in a story should hold up to that test.

$$E = w (y + c + F)$$

Reframing the Picture

Though it seems most journalists dismiss the notion of objectivity as a noble myth, many in the profession also bristle at the suggestion that they engage in *framing* when they conceive and carry off story ideas. The reality, of course, is that preconceptions about stories, issues, people, and communities are constantly influencing—framing—everything from the first interview to the last edit. Those preconceptions are formed by who we are, what we've learned, seen, read, heard, believed. They become part of the frames within which stories take form.

Understanding and challenging those frames is a critical piece of striving for excellence. The insight will help journalists freshen old frames, create new ones, break out of reporting habits that lead to predictable coverage, and recognize the cliché-laden language that fits so comfortably into the stories framed as *diversity*.

The word itself has framing power. For many, it means *soft feature*. It's often interpreted as a story about what makes people different. It vacillates between positive news and angst. A good example of that can be found in the coverage of immigrants. The most frequent frames journalists use for telling those stories are the *new arrivals* frame (sometimes employed belatedly for newly discovered arrivals) and the *problem people* frame. Both are legitimate. Both are overused.

The new arrivals frame chronicles the changing face of America, documenting demographic shifts and often emphasizing the challenges created and encountered by the new immigrants. That segues smoothly into the problem people frame, in which even upbeat stories are told through the prism of social pathologies. Lost are the stories that would transform the new arrivals into people living ordinary lives. Each stage of the writing process—coming up with ideas, collecting information, focusing, writing, and editing—can lead to that result.

In the late 1990s, two reporters were dispatched to learn about the burgeoning Mexican and Central American groups moving into the suburbs of a large southern city. Their approach was informed, thoughtful, thorough. One of them signed up for a Spanish class, and both sought out a listening post, an intersection where many of the city's newest citizens might meet. They landed upon a social services center, a rich fount of contacts and stories.

What they discovered fairly quickly, though, was that they wound up telling most of their stories from the problem-people perspective, largely because that sort of story flows easily from a place teeming with people in need of one thing or the other. Those are often good, important stories. But not when they dominate coverage. If the frame is familiar—and it is, given the media's history of covering immigrants as victims or sources of problems—then it's hardest to see.

In this case, the reporters would have to consciously go after stories that don't hinge on problems. That sort of thing will only happen if journalists first adjust their eyes to see the frames that are out there. Start by re-framing the definition of diversity. It is not simply a minority story or a victim story or a brown face in a white crowd. In reporting and writing, it means many things at once:

Inclusion

Include in your coverage those who have frequently been left out of the news, particularly black people, Asians, Latinos, Native Americans, white women, gays, lesbians, and poor people of all races. Show them in their *ordinariness* by including them in stories and images about things other than race, class, gender, sexuality, and social pathology. Use them as mean-ingful sources; as parents, business owners, rocket scientists, pollsters, etc.

Covering the Undercovered

Find the people whose stories aren't being told and tell them. Find people where they live, learn, play, pray, and work. Get to know the listening posts in your community so you can locate stories that help your readers understand the people and the world around them. Discover the universal stories of perseverance, heroism, humor, irony, love, loss, redemption—all the news values that guide daily coverage and resonate with the people you seek to serve.

Mitigating Bias and Prejudice

Strive to tell stories that are free of euphemisms and stereotypes. Examine the framing of stories for unchecked bias. Be ever conscious of the dangers inherent in juxtaposed words and pictures so that you avoid delivering unintended messages.

$$E = w (y + c + f)$$

The Equation's Secret

There is another way to write the equation: $E = D$. Excellence equals diversity. All of what precedes this paragraph can be translated into the language of excellent, ethical journalism without embellishing a single syllable.

Excellence is telling complete truths. It's fair and balanced reporting. It's pursuing accuracy and authenticity. Journalists who work on their own biases and fears ask better, more informed questions. When they step beyond the familiar, they discover more truths; they tell more accurate and complete stories.

When they elevate their craft toward excellence, they use language more precisely. They avoid euphemisms, eliminate superfluous facts, write in the active voice, minimize harm to vulnerable people. When they work on challenging and creating storytelling frames, they infuse their journalism with greater depth and breadth, and they paint a more authentic picture of the people, neighborhoods, and issues most in need of our excellence.

It's all about doing good journalism. $E = D$.

Were it that simple, though, I would have gotten better grades in algebra and there'd be no need for essays such as this one. Something has to change. Something fundamental. Just as a ninth-grader had to learn a new way of thinking before it was possible to find the value of x in an algebraic equation, journalists aspiring to excellence have to think differently about the value of D.

Treat diversity, in its many forms, as a synonym for accuracy or truth or clarity. Demand that reporting and writing reflect those high standards. It will mean more phone calls, more visits to unfamiliar places, more wrestling with new issues and ideas. It will feel like more work because for so many of us it is. But consider this: if getting to excellence means you've got to go an extra mile, then you've probably been stopping a mile too short.

That's an ageless journalistic truth, not new math.

8

Community Connectedness

Passwords for Public Journalism

Jay Rosen

Let us begin with some propositions about the task of a free press.

- If journalism can be described as a purposeful activity, then its ultimate purpose is to enhance democracy.
- Thus, democracy not only protects a free press, it demands a public-minded press.
- What democracy also demands is an active, engaged citizenry, willing to join in public debate and participate in civic affairs.
- No democracy—and thus, no journalist—can afford to be indifferent to trends in public (or private) life that either draw citizens toward the public sphere or repel them from it.
- Part of journalism's purpose, then, is to encourage civic participation, improve public debate, and enhance public life, without, of course, sacrificing the independence that a free press demands and deserves.

Taken together, these propositions amount to a revised public philosophy for daily journalism. Reporting fairly and accurately on the day's events, holding government accountable for its actions, analyzing and commenting on public affairs—to these traditional notions can be added a less familiar but equally important idea: that journalists must play an active role in supporting civic involvement, improving discourse and debate, and creating a climate in which the affairs of the community earn their claim on the citizen's time and attention. This expanded notion of press responsibility—the press as a support system for public life—is the idea behind a small but growing movement in daily journalism known as community connectedness.

The aim of this short paper is to describe what this movement is about, and to sketch its significance in a wider frame: the sense of purpose that motivates journalism professionals and animates most discussions of a free press.

In February 1990, James K. Batten, chief executive of Knight-Ridder, Inc., gave a lecture at the University of Kansas emphasizing the importance to newspapers of "community spirit"—by which he meant "the willingness of people to care about where they live and to wade in to help solve its problems."

Batten advanced the belief (confirmed, he said, by research) that those "who feel a real sense of connection to the places they live" are more likely to become newspaper readers. This sense of connection was eroding, he observed, pointing to "millions of our fellow citizens" who "feel little interest in—or responsibility for—their communities," and thus avoid not only the newspaper but the whole sphere of politics and public affairs. Noting "the sluggish state of civic health in many communities in the 1990s," Batten asked his audience to consider: "If communities continue to erode, how can we expect newspapers to continue to prosper, over the long term?"

Community connectedness begins, in effect, with Batten's question. At its core is the concern that millions of Americans are somehow withdrawing from public life, at both the local and national levels. Along with this creeping trend toward disengagement has come, of course, the steady decline in newspaper readership. The suggestion Batten sought to advance was that these two developments might be related. It is one of the thoughts that gave birth to community connectedness.

Equally important, however, is the dawning perception that the press as an institution cannot maintain its standing if the withdrawal from public life continues apace. Journalists, accustomed to seeing themselves as adversaries and opponents of government, may overlook the dangers of a rising disgust with public institutions. They may unwittingly contribute to their own demise by turning people off to politics and public affairs, or by failing to realize their own contributions to politics-as-usual. They may fail to see that the troubles with America's political system implicate them, along with everyone else.

These, then, are the dual origins of community connectedness as a current of thought. One worries about the fate of the newspaper as a viable business, and locates the prospects for that business in the sense of connection people feel to the places where they live. The other worries about the authority and influence of journalism as a profession, and links the standing of that profession to the health of the political system as a whole—in particular, to the willing engagement of citizens in politics and public life. Community connectedness points with alarm to our growing sense of dislocation from the communities where we live, and from the wider political community we inhabit as citizens of the world's oldest democracy. It also takes what had earlier been a premise of the daily newspaper—the existence of a public attuned to public affairs—and makes that the newspaper's project. Thus, community connectedness is about helping to form as well as inform "the public."

A month after Batten's address, Burl Osborne, editor of the *Dallas Morning News*, gave an interview as the incoming president of the American Society of Newspaper Editors. Osborne noted the "extent to which people are isolated from public life, from the self-governing process, and from the source of our public institutions." He called on newspapers to "encourage people back into the streets," as it were.

In January 1990, David Broder of the *Washington Post*, perhaps the most respected political reporter in America, published a series of columns urging his colleagues to take more responsibility for the deteriorating quality of political discourse. Broder wrote, "We cannot allow the 1990 election to become another exercise in public disillusionment and political cynicism. It is time for those of us in the world's freest press to become activists, not on behalf of a particular party or politician, but on behalf of the process of self-government." Broder added, "We have to help reconnect politics and government—what happens in the campaign and what happens afterward in public policy—if we are to have accountability and genuine democracy in this country."

Thus, from a chief executive (Batten), a leading editor (Osborne), and a prominent reporter (Broder) came a similar message to journalists: it was time to do something about the withdrawal and disengagement of citizens, and the press would have to be the do-er. Clearly, there was something in the air in the early months of 1990. But it was not only words. There were also deeds to contemplate, most notably the actions of the *Columbus* (Ga.) *Ledger-Enquirer*, a Knight-Ridder newspaper then engaged in a bold experiment.

In 1988 the *Ledger-Enquirer* had published a series of articles detailing a host of long-term problems the city had yet to face. Nothing came of the series, so the editors decided to take a stronger step. They organized a public meeting where residents could discuss the future of their city and the problems they wanted to see addressed. Off the response to that meeting, a new civic movement was born, United Beyond 2000, in which the editor of the newspaper, Jack Swift, was a leading figure.

The purpose of the group was not to lobby for specific policies, but to get public dialogue working again, so that those who wanted to see something done about the city's problems would not feel so alone. The group sponsored other public forums and backyard barbecues where residents could trade views and discover common interests. Meanwhile, the *Ledger-Enquirer* continued to pound away in its news columns and editorial pages at the lack of vision and long-term planning in city government. In a presentation to Knight-Ridder editors, Swift described the goals of his paper's experiment: "We're trying to find every way we can to help citizens empower themselves, get involved in their community, work together on mutual concerns, and make a difference."

Swift and his colleagues at the *Ledger-Enquirer* made the cover of Knight-Ridder's 1989 annual report, and Swift was named the winner of the company's yearly excellence award. This gave the corporate stamp of approval to the newspaper's risky step into community activism. As might be expected, the *Ledger-Enquirer*'s initiative proved controversial within the profession (even more so after Swift's tragic suicide in 1990 left some with the impression that he had taken too many risks). The grounds for the controversy are real—the paper's project was risky—but the Columbus project can be seen as the first in a wave of newspaper experiments that tried to put the words of Batten, Osborne, and Broder into practice. Consider the following developments.

- The *Sun* in Bremerton, Washington (a Scripps-Howard paper) sparked community interest in preserving open space with an editorial about the threatening consequences of unplanned development in the region. The newspaper then convened a steering committee of 150 community leaders, and conducted some fifty public forums about open-space preservation throughout Kitsap County. Inspired by the discussions, citizens nominated parcels of land to be designated "open space" and gathered signatures to put a bond issue on the ballot to purchase the space. (The measure later failed.) A new civic group, Friends of Open Space, was born out of the process, and it continues to seek ways of financing the preservation of open space. The paper also cosponsored an Economic Diversification Summit that brought together 250 community leaders to discuss the county's economic future. The summit was preceded by a *Sun* series examining how other regions had coped with overreliance on military spending.
- The *Wichita Eagle* (Knight-Ridder) adopted an activist approach to election coverage with the explicit aim of improving voter participa-

tion and strengthening political debate. The *Eagle* selected ten key issues it determined were important in a 1990 statewide election and focused continuing coverage around them, with the announced intention of engaging readers and forcing the leading candidates to respond. It also conducted a sustained effort explaining why the election mattered to citizens, encouraging them to vote, and providing user-friendly guides to participating in the election.

• In a bolder step, called "The People Project," the *Wichita Eagle* undertook a cooperative campaign to encourage residents to rethink their own approach to the city's most serious problems: education, crime, political gridlock, and stresses on the family. Enlisting as partners a local TV and radio station, the *Eagle* presented readers with the information and opportunity to get involved and meet others seeking solutions to the city's problems. The People Project included three community-wide "opportunity fairs," where citizens with common interests could come into contact, exchange ideas, and begin to work together for change.

• Taking a cue from both Wichita and Broder's columns, the *Charlotte Observer*, (Knight-Ridder) in cooperation with The Poynter Institute and WSOC-TV, the local ABC affiliate, pledged to give up the horse race approach to the 1992 campaign and to focus reporting on what residents said mattered to them. A *voters' agenda* was created out of interviews with readers. Follow-up surveys and meetings with citizens were planned to help the *Observer* keep its focus on the public's concerns, rather than machinations of campaign insiders. The *Observer*'s approach won wide notice among campaign reporters and editors for being more in tune with the serious mood of voters in the 1992 election.

• The *Star-Tribune* in Minneapolis (then Cowles Media) invited readers to join in a continuing series of more than 130 neighborhood roundtables organized at the initiative of the newspaper. The purpose of the roundtables was to bring residents together to discuss public questions of current concern, including health care, race relations, and the economy. The newspaper made available briefing books to aid in the discussions, and encouraged interested citizens to become discussion leaders and roundtable hosts. An estimated 1,500 residents responded to the initial call for participants, and the roundtables have continued under a variety of formats at locations throughout the metropolitan area. Pleased with the response, the paper went on to create one and a half new editorial staff positions with responsibility to design and implement projects that, in the paper's words, "enable our readers to reconnect with their newspaper, their political system, their communities, and each other."

- *The Portland* (Maine) *Press Herald* (then Guy Gannett Publishing) assigned a reporter to thoroughly understand the problems in the state's system of workers' compensation, which had become a public disaster, bankrupting businesses with huge insurance costs, failing to protect workers from serious injury, and paralyzing state politics. The paper's four-part series (in which the reporter was urged to draw strong conclusions) ended with a recommendation for a complete overhaul of the system. When the series drew a large public response, the paper gathered together the major players in the controversy and encouraged them to deal with the issue—and each other— for the first time in years. The meeting helped break the logjam on the issue and begin the process of reform.

At first glance, many of these initiatives may seem like a revival of the old-fashioned newspaper crusade. And they do borrow some of the spirit of an earlier era, when activism and journalism weren't seen as opposites. But what distinguishes community connectedness from simple crusading is the emphasis on public discussion and civic involvement. The experiments outlined above put the authority of the newspaper behind a simple but powerful proposition: that politics and public life ought to address the community's deepest concerns, and ought to engage citizens in the process.

The *ought* is essential, for community connectedness has a prominent moral dimension. It prescribes for any community a preferred state of affairs by stressing action over drift, engagement over withdrawal, deliberation and debate over silence and denial. The journalists who are pushing the movement forward have declared an end to their neutrality on these questions. More than any pet project or chosen solution, then, the agenda behind community connectedness is simply that public life should work—it should solve problems, engage citizens, and produce a useful discussion. To advance such an agenda implies a rethinking of the journalist's task, and this, ultimately, is what the movement is about—the very different view of responsibility represented by the experiments in community connectedness.

Of course, this wider responsibility—to offer a support system for public life—can never be journalism's alone. No newspaper has the resources or influence to reshape the public climate or to revive civic participation by itself. Nor would many communities want such a powerful agency in their midst. So connections are frequently made between the newspaper and other agencies—foundations, broadcasters, universities, civic groups. In working with such partners, the goal is to create a plurality of public spaces where citizens can engage with the affairs of the community. To sense the connection between this plurality of spaces, on the one hand, and the singular space of the newspaper, on the other, is the leap of logic that community connectedness proposes to take.

If public spaces alive with activity are essential to a healthy democracy, then so too is the existence of what we might call "public time." Public time is a condition we may or may not achieve, depending on the performance of our institutions and our own attitudes as citizens. A community lives in public time when it recognizes and debates publicly those things it must recognize, must debate, if its future is to be decided through rational and democratic means. Public time involves a certain orientation to the present, in which distraction, drift, and the dispersal of attention are overcome so that a community can collectively grapple with what it is collectively becoming. Among the propositions journalism stands for is that we ought to live in public time, and this *we* and this *ought* are two of the moral claims behind community connectedness.

Finally, community connectedness upends the usual view of credibility in journalism. Credibility has traditionally been associated with distance and detachment. In this view, a newspaper remains credible by separating itself from those who might seek to influence the news or compromise the journalist's independence. In the new view, represented by community connectedness, credibility begins with concern. A newspaper becomes credible by demonstrating that it cares about the quality of the public lives we lead, about the health of the political sphere in a particular community, about the demand democracy makes on all of us to dwell in public time.

Credibility as care and concern doesn't refute the importance of distance and detachment, which are rooted, after all, in a genuine concern for truth. But the new view of credibility recognizes an even deeper truth: that journalism cannot remain valuable unless public life remains viable. That's a notion worth buzzing about, in newsrooms and all the other spaces where journalists gather and gather their thoughts.

9

Blacked Out

Local Television and Community Coverage

Jill Geisler

Imagine that the history of local TV news was on a videotape, and you could rewind that tape, say, twenty years. You'd see local newscasts that resembled mini-C-SPANs. Stories told start to finish in meetings. Abundant video of white guys in ties, seated around tables. Reporters delivering standups from outside the government buildings where those meetings took place.

Now fast-forward to today. The meeting footage has for the most part gone away.

But so has some important newsgathering.

Don't look for an academic study to chart local broadcast journalism's drift away from the halls of government. Such a widespread, far-reaching survey doesn't exist. But talk to veterans of local TV news who have lived through it. Most peg the shift as beginning in the early to mid-'80s: driven by research, consultants, technology—even a desire to do more creative storytelling.

Lucy Himstedt remembers how it was. She was a reporter and producer at KTHV-TV in Little Rock, Arkansas, from 1979 to 1990. In her early years there, several reporters would make daily checks at the Capitol. "It didn't matter whether anything was going on or not. If the Legislature was in session, that was the lead story in the newscast," she recalls. But then things changed, around the early '80s, says Himstedt, now vice president and general manager of WFIE-TV in Evansville, Indiana. "We were told by consultants and research that government and politics is boring," she says. Indeed, at times those TV segments could be drearily dull.

Himstedt isn't a consultant basher. Yet she knows that, at stations across the country, the message that "government is boring" transformed the way stations shaped their newscasts. Today, there is less coverage of the people who are elected, appointed, or hired to serve the public. Less attention to the process of decision and deal making. Fewer chances for the public to see city hall—even if it is just through the lens of the evening news.

Brian Trauring, news director at WATE-TV in Knoxville, Tennessee, is concerned about where that leaves broadcast news today. "Issues such as taxes, road repair, and garbage collection are often ignored because they lack an emotional element," he says. "Reporters and producers are not fully aware of local legislative procedures and naturally shy away from generating story ideas involving local government."

Technology may have played a part in TV's move away from city hall coverage. Electronic newsgathering—live cameras—emerged in the mid-1970s and proliferated in the '80s. "Why have a boring package at city hall when you can have a live reporter on a street corner with a fire behind him?" asks Doug Fox, who's covered politics at WFAA-TV in Dallas for twenty-six years.

Fox, whose station still invests in political and government coverage, sees fewer stations making the commitment his does, and fewer young reporters interested in his job. It's not easy to cover city hall in a way that will engage readers and satisfy the bosses. "I'm beginning to feel like an endangered species," Fox says.

We may have to rely on the recollections of experienced journalists to confirm that government meetings used to be a staple of local TV news. But there are hard data confirming how little attention is paid to the subject today.

In 1997, a group of journalism professors from several universities released what it called "the first known attempt to sample the news content of television newscasts on a national scale." Professors participating in the Consortium for Local Television Surveys taped newscasts in eight cities—in November of 1996 and January, February, and April of 1997—and analyzed the content. Their findings? Crime and criminal justice stories took up nearly 30 percent of the local news time (more than any other topic), while government and politics accounted for only half as much—about 15 percent. Natural disasters and calamities took up 10 percent, education coverage 2 percent. In releasing the data, project director Joseph Angotti, then a professor at the University of Miami and a former vice president of NBC News, called the sparse coverage of government affairs perhaps "the most disturbing news to come out of the survey."

COLTS professors still analyze local news, although the group's membership has changed and cities have been added to and subtracted from the survey. Their preliminary findings from newscast samples taken in nine cities from January through May 1999 show a story similar to 1996–97's: Crime and criminal justice took up nearly twice as much airtime as government and political coverage—23 percent to just under 12 percent. Calamities took up a bit more than 11 percent, education about 5 percent.

Survey coordinator David Kurpius, a professor at the Manship School of Mass Communication at Louisiana State University and a former local TV news director, is reluctant to make year-to-year comparisons because the cities in the sample have changed. (Los Angeles and Miami are not included in figures compiled in 1998 and '99, as they were in 1996–97.) But he sees the overall story as one of misguided choices: "Are stations just covering what's cheap and easy, like crime and criminal justice, or are they covering stories that help citizens and communities make decisions and play a part in the democracy? We're finding they're doing crime . . . which should be obvious to anyone who watches TV news."

An even larger-scale study found much the same. The Project for Excellence in Journalism, funded by the Pew Charitable Trusts, last year vetted nearly 600 newscasts and 8,000 stories from nineteen markets. Its findings: Crime coverage was tops, taking up 22 percent of news time, followed by human interest (11 percent), education/welfare/society (10 percent), science/health/technology (9 percent), and politics (9 percent). "Coverage of the political process in general in local news is nothing to be proud of," says the project's deputy director, Carl Gottlieb, who spent twenty-two years in TV news. But it's not just the scant amount of time television devotes to the topic that concerns him. It's also the kind of government stories on which the stations focus: "Not process, but scandal; not real issues, but personalities"—story treatments that "reduce substantive issues to nothing more than a game."

Government coverage was hardly a game to Valerie Hyman when she was urging stations to change their approach to storytelling. In the late 1980s, Hyman was the director of news development for ten TV stations of the then-Gillett group. She was an award-winning investigative reporter, fresh from a Nieman fellowship at Harvard, passionate about quality journalism. Part of her job was to help reporters become better storytellers. I know. I was a Gillett news director whose staff she coached at WITI-TV in Milwaukee.

Hyman issued a challenge to us: ban video of meetings from all our newscasts for a month. Get it off the air. Break our reporters' dependence on those predictable pictures that fail to tell the deeper stories of government decision making. She urged our reporters to go to the meetings and gather the facts, but then to get out of the marble halls and into neighborhoods, to tell government stories through the lives of citizens. Her mantra: "The meeting is not the news; the meeting is about the news."

Doing it Hyman's way meant more work for news crews accustomed to finding and telling their stories in a kind of one-stop-shopping at city hall. Going to meetings was merely Step One. Finding the places and showing the faces affected by the meetings added significantly more steps. But the effort paid off in stories with greater dimension. Our coach was pleased.

Today, more than ten years later, Hyman sees an ugly mutation of her message when she watches local newscasts. It seems that the part of her advice that's really stuck is the part about getting out of the marble halls. Step One—going to the meeting—is often skipped. "In too many cases," she says, "stations have abandoned meeting coverage altogether, and by missing the meetings, they are missing important news."

What's behind the abandonment? Hyman says stations have added newscasts without adding sufficient staff; news consultants have pushed for higher story counts; and news directors are being told to develop stories that appeal to "target demographics." She is in a position to know. Not long after her Gillett work in Milwaukee, she signed on with The Poynter Institute in St. Petersburg, Florida, to direct its broadcast programs. For ten years, until 1999, she taught Poynter seminars on TV reporting and producing, visited stations and reviewed newscasts. She sadly reports that, over time, she witnessed a decline in coverage of institutions—less news from state capitols, city halls, and school boards. "It is not good for citizens," the trainer says flatly.

Citizens. In the business of television, not all citizens are created equal. Some are more valuable than others: the so-called target audience. Advertisers want to reach them; certain TV content is said to attract them. "You really want adults twenty-five to fifty-four," says Matthew Zelkind, news director of WKRN-TV in Nashville. Zelkind talks candidly about the business of news, not just the journalism. "We look at who are our viewers, and who we want them to be. You have to craft your product to who your viewers are."

He adds: "Government many times is complex and doesn't allow us to tell it in small doses. It may not be completely relevant to large numbers of people." So his station dedicates resources elsewhere, especially to breaking news and weather. He hasn't abandoned government coverage but is selective about the stories his station covers. "Many of the issues that are important to government aren't important to people on a day-to-day basis," he says.

But what about the journalists' challenge to be the daily eyes and ears of the public, the watchdog on government? How can that happen if reporters aren't regularly assigned to the beat? Marion Just, professor of political science at Wellesley College, is part of the scholar team on the Project for Excellence in Journalism's local TV research project. She says television's selective coverage of government contributes to public cynicism. "If you don't cover what government does, but you cover its mistakes, then you aren't going to create the kinds of citizens who want to take an active role in the political process," she says.

Zelkind won't go so far as to argue that his approach to covering government—small doses of selected stories—is everything viewers need. But, he says pragmatically: "The very unfortunate reality is that it is a big business. A TV station is absolutely there to inform, to give issues and community service. But without ratings, there would be lots of unemployed [TV] people."

Ratings come from people making conscious choices about news and where to get it. And research shows that for Americans, television is their top choice. In a March 1998 Gallup survey, local television news surpassed local newspapers in both trust and frequency of use. Doesn't that mean viewers are satisfied with the news coverage that television provides? Maybe not.

TV news viewership—local and national—has been eroding. The Radio and Television News Directors Foundation, concerned about declining interest in local news, commissioned a study in 1998 that compared the opinions of the general public with those of local TV news directors. The directors were asked to predict the public's interest in various story types. They had a pretty good handle on crime: They estimated 67 percent of the public would be very interested in "crimes that happen in your area." The general public's response was 65 percent.

But when it came to the public's interest in state and local government news, the news directors estimated only 23 percent would be very interested. The public's response: 41 percent. That suggests an interest TV news may not be serving.

Lewis Friedland, associate professor of journalism and mass communications at the University of Wisconsin, believes well-executed government coverage can attract viewers to TV news. He's done five years of field research that looks at some of the country's best and worst TV news coverage of government and civic life for his book *Civic Innovation in America*. "TV stations, for the most part, are shooting themselves in the foot—giving people more and more information they don't need,"

Friedland says. "I have no doubt in my mind that people want more than they're getting."

From in-depth interviews he's done with viewers, he's concluded, "Many people positively dislike TV news." They tell him local news fails to show true pictures of things that matter to them. They see body bags and beauty tips, house fires and health hints, and say that's not enough. They tell him they want information about their parks, their garbage pickup, their property taxes, their schools—the kind of information reporters develop from nosing around at meetings, given the opportunity.

Is coverage uniformly bad? No, Friedland says. "Some stations take a serious, long-term approach, not whipsawed by consultant-driven gimmicks. They do day-in, day-out coverage of civic life." Those that do, he says, tend to be market leaders.

But even news directors who have enjoyed ratings success are concerned. Stuart Zanger, the former news director of WCPO-TV in Cincinnati, left TV news in 1999 to teach. Zanger's station helped build its ratings and reputation by acting as a government watchdog. It won a George Foster Peabody Award and the 1999 Society of Professional Journalists' award for public service in journalism, earning the honors by keeping local government under a microscope. The station's investigative team spent months looking into the construction of two new sports stadiums in his town, projects using nearly a billion dollars of taxpayer money. WCPO uncovered crony contracts, wasted dollars, and broken promises to minority and women contractors. The series led to changes in the way the stadium building business is conducted in Cincinnati.

Zanger is proud of that series and his former station but hardly satisfied with broadcast journalism's approach to covering government. He says it is rarely done daily or in depth. "We're not set up anymore, in most newsrooms, to be able to report," he says.

He blames the industry's "money lust" for the staffing levels and content choices in local newsrooms. "We devote a person to health and one to consumer [issues], because the consultant tells us that's what people want. But how many people do we have that we can send out on the street—to go out and find stories?"

He thinks many of those stories can be found in and around the meetings television is missing. "People care about government stories. They're not boring. But they have to be well researched and well written and about issues that are important." He says that kind of reporting runs afoul of resource allocations in today's cost-conscious newsrooms.

Plenty of news directors agree with Zanger. As part of the Project for

Excellence in Journalism's 1999 review of TV news content, researchers surveyed news directors at fifty-nine stations and got responses from forty-six. Professor Just summarized the findings: The average profit margin of newsrooms responding to the survey exceeded 40 percent. Nearly three-quarters of the stations have added broadcast hours in the last three years, a demand that has generally matched or overwhelmed any budget increases. News directors widely agree on what constitutes quality local TV but say lack of staffing and time and budget pressures get in the way.

In fact, nearly eight in ten news directors said staff size was a problem. Seventy percent of stations required reporters to produce a story a day. Thirty percent required more.

Enterprise reporting, the kind that comes from digging for information and developing sources, is difficult for reporters to produce when they must turn in a story every day. Fox, WFAA's political reporter, feels the pressure to feed the news machine daily. "I'm doing my first NFT—not for today—story since February," he said to me. It was November 10.

Even TV news consultants are concerned about staffing levels at stations they visit. They insist lack of human resources, not consultants' advice, is keeping stations from meaningful government coverage. Audience Research & Development's Phyllis Slocum, a news consultant with fifteen years of experience, says, "We've never told people not to cover government, because government is the source of economic, cultural, and even moral legislation." But, Slocum says, this coverage "takes a lot of work. . . . You cover government by thinking, by spending some time."

She echoed the concerns of the news directors in the PEJ survey. "There's been a proliferation of newscasts and no corresponding rise in bodies," she says, ticking off the time periods in which stations have added or lengthened newscasts in the past ten years: mornings, weekend mornings, and early evenings.

Joe Rovitto concurs. He's been advising stations for six years. Before that, he was a TV news director for seventeen. His firm, Clemensen and Rovitto, of Redding, Connecticut, handles research and consulting for twenty stations around the country. He, too, insists he's "never advised against covering government." But has he lobbied for it? Rovitto says he's more likely to encourage issue coverage than to press for general coverage of the political process. However, in two markets where his stations are located in state capitals, he says his research showed high viewer interest in the legislature, and he advocated beefed-up coverage of the lawmakers.

But Rovitto also added his voice to the chorus of those concerned about the ability of news staffs to produce fresh, meaningful material each day.

"The pressure to fill newscasts is immense," he says. "Very few staffs have the time to go to meetings. They hit the door, the assignment editor gives them a piece of paper, and they go" to whatever story the assignment desk has selected. Then, he says, the crews are expected to turn the story in for the 5 P.M. and 5:30 P.M. news and re-cut it for the 6 P.M. and the late news. That leads to what Rovitto calls "short-cut journalism"—a triage in which newsrooms select stories that are easy to find, easy to tell. They can't afford those that take too much digging and might not make deadline for that day's shows. "You simply have to make a choice. If you know you can't cover a story properly, you don't cover it at all."

That pressure, he says, is keeping stations from doing the very thing consultants are supposed to help them do: differentiate their newscasts from their competitors'.

Rovitto believes news directors want to aim higher. "I can honestly say to you there's not one single station I work with where the news director doesn't want to do it right. Their challenge is to find creative ways to give reporters time to find the relevant stories."

That challenge weighs heavily on those who run TV newsrooms. Journalism trainer Hyman says in the past few years, even TV station general managers and news directors have told her they watch less news in their own homes. They find it irrelevant, predictable, and boring. Reporters and photographers have told her this isn't the business they signed up for. Producers said they are padding newscasts with nonlocal, unimportant stories from feed services because there's too much time to fill and not enough staff to produce meaningful homegrown material. Hyman's conclusion: "The truth is, media corporations need to put more dollars back into their newsrooms." The money, she says, should go to staffing.

Hyman knows news audiences are eroding but holds out hope nonetheless. "We can bring people back to their sets with compelling, engaging coverage of what's really going on in their communities. It's local coverage people want; distilled versions of the ongoing news of the day, told in a way that makes people want to watch."

And she knows where reporters can go—right now—to find those stories. Back to the meetings.

Author's note: This essay first appeared in the *American Journalism Review* (May 2000) and is reprinted with permission.

Part IV

Craft

No teacher of journalism has taken the work of journalists more seriously than Melvin Mencher, who trained a generation of reporters at the Columbia Graduate School of Journalism. Over the years, Mencher encapsulated his values in a set of aphorisms, published by Poynter as "The Sayings of Chairman Mel" (1997). These survive, not just in this book, but in the nerve endings of reporters trained by Mencher, especially his final challenge: "It is immoral not to be excellent in your craft."

That reconciliation of ethics and craft rests at the heart of Poynter pedagogy over the decade. No teacher or thinker has had more influence on the teaching of craft at Poynter than Donald M. Murray, a Pulitzer Prize–winning journalist and a founding parent of the writing process movement. A powerful expression of Murray's teaching can be found in his essay "Writer in the Newsroom" (1995). Murray honors the eyes of the reporter and the soul of the writer, challenging editors to make room for the narrative visions that only writers can see.

Karen Brown Dunlap, dean of the Poynter faculty, teams up with Foster Davis to reveal how the effective editor helps a news organization fulfill its mission through the exercise of many roles, from coach, to captain, to news leader (2000). Pegie Stark Adam and G. Stuart Adam, who met and married at Poynter, reveal the power of WED, not just in their personal lives, but in the integrated critical energy of "Writing, Editing, Design" (2000). Judging and presenting the news are acts of skilled professionals, not mired in the limitations of their separate disciplines, nor stuck in an antique assembly line model of production, but liberated and informed by consultation and collaboration.

Another fusion of craft and ethics is expressed by Kenneth Irby, one of America's most influential leaders in the field of photojournalism. Along with revealing the practical power of digital photography, Irby warns journalists to be vigilant of its misuse, to develop protocols that will create "Credible Photojournalism in a Credulous Age" (2001). Irby's work has profound implications for understanding the relationship between journalism and society. As Americans have witnessed with greater frequency, the old saw "seeing is believing" has been inverted. High-profile cases, such as those involving O. J. Simpson or Elián González, reveal how citizens bring their life experiences and biases to the viewing and interpretation of an image.

The development of new media has challenged Poynter, and all schools and news organizations, to rethink issues of craft, values, community, leadership, and culture. A wonderfully versatile journalist and advocate for new media, Mike Wendland, turns the table on himself. His essay "Reading the News in the Inkless World of Cyberspace" (2000) describes an experiment in news deprivation and offers perspective on how the special power of each news medium contributes to both personal insight and public conversation.

10

Writing, Editing, Design

G. Stuart Adam and Pegie Stark Adam

The term WED was expressed initially in 1987 in a conversation between Roy Peter Clark and Mario Garcia. The occasion, we have been told, was an ad hoc curriculum meeting at the Institute in which these two Poynter originals reflected on the changing formats and character of the newspaper and the forms of training and education these changes called for.

Some of the changes were the products of Mario's fecund imagination. His reputation as a publication designer was already established and growing. He had acted as a consultant to newspapers that, with his encouragement and intervention, had made substantial changes in design. Additionally, Roy was established as a master writing coach who was enriching the vocabularies and capacities of a generation of writers, long attached to limited notions of news leads and nut graphs, by showing how to speak a more literary language and deploy literary devices in journalism. So the collaboration foreshadowed by the term WED arose naturally out of their respective professional interests. Roy says that it was Mario who invented the term WED.

There were, of course, larger forces at work as WED and its operations were hatching. Television had created a powerful visual dimension to the experience of news; computer-based technologies were revolutionizing newspaper production; USA Today, with its gaudy color palette and ambitious graphics, was a success; and newspapers generally were becoming more colorful and distinctive. It was as if managing editors and publishers were awakening to an idea George Orwell mooted in his essay "Why I Write." There he said plainly that "above the level of a railway guide, no book [or, for that matter, newspaper] is quite free from aesthetic considerations."[1] It seems that the Mac, its cousins, and their software were liberating aesthetic impulses in newspaper editors akin to those that mark any medium or artifact in which makers seek to blend economy, functionality, and beauty. So WED was born into a congenial environment. It was bound to thrive. But what is WED? How do you make/become a WEDitor?

WED is an acronym for Writing, Editing, and Design. It refers to newspaper journalism that blends artfully the disciplines of writing, graphics, photography, and design so that pages provide a balanced and integrated relationship between visual and verbal elements. When WED works, individual stories convey a common meaning through a perfect integration of words, visuals, and design elements.[2]

So WED is a method that gives pride of place to the writer, the graphics artist, the page designer, the photographer, and the illustrator. It encourages collaboration among the crafts, and it requires the supervision and guidance of a WEDitor, an individual with reasonable fluency in the languages of journalism's several crafts. A WEDitor is someone who speaks, depending on how you view the matter, several languages or one comprehensive language—the language of WED. He or she is the master of WED applications, the critic who supervises and directs.

WED is also the subject of a continuing series of seminars, the first of which took place in 1989, at the Institute under Mario and Roy's direction. It is a subject in which we began to take an interest as teachers of journalism in 1991–92 when we departed on our own voyage through its various stations and headed toward a more or less final destination in 1996. With Mario and Roy in 1992, we co-directed a Poynter seminar called "Words and Visuals in the News." It turned out to be a reasonable success, although we concluded at the end of a very busy week that it needed to be more carefully organized. So we reorganized and reorganized it three more times.

In 1996, we directed the last of the four WED seminars in which we played a central role. This last seminar was called simply and directly, "Writing, Editing, and Design." By that time, we believed (modestly) that as teachers we had analyzed, unpacked, and, with the continuing help of Mario, Roy, and others,[3] had presented successfully a week of classes that conferred on the seminarians a viable understanding of WED. What follows is an account of the thinking that guided the development of the seminar and our vision of WED applications.

Barriers to WED

A movement or new school is normally born with an argument. Someone or something stands between the advocates and their goals. For WED advocates, aging templates and outdated practices had to be challenged.

We argued in our seminars that the barriers to the development and progress of WED were/are:

- industrial methods of editorial work and production that had persisted despite opportunities for change provided by the new technologies;
- fixed views of the hierarchy of journalism's several crafts;
- confusion about or ignorance of the natures of the collaborating crafts;
- and a lack of imagination.

The proposition that industrial methods of editorial work and production interfered with the new project was based on the observation that large newspapers had relied for decades on an intense division of labor. The crafts, although sharing common journalistic purposes, worked more or less in isolation. Writers occupied one silo; photographers another; graphics editors yet another. In the world of editorial production, there was little communication between the visual journalists and writers, and the process of integration and newspaper making was the achievement of editors to whom the work was handed off from individuals who worked more or less independently.

In this system, we argued, editors gave a privileged place to writers. They were the elite; the other crafts were subordinate with jobs conceived to provide support to a project belonging fundamentally to writers. So with the silos and the hierarchy went an unpolished and uncritical view of what the ancillary crafts could provide. We knew perfectly well there were exceptions in the world of publishing—*Life* magazine, in which the work of photographers was featured, comes to mind—but in mainstream newspapers throughout North America, the capacities of photographers, illustrators, graphic artists, and designers were underexploited. Creative possibilities were diminished by a relatively fixed and rigid view of visual elements. In a sense, creative impulses and imaginative possibilities were buried under the weight of ancient bureaucratic habits.

It is easy to explain why this method of production took hold and survived. In its way, the division of labor was an expression of the production techniques born in the Industrial Revolution. The result was a medium dominated by the view that the newspaper need only be read—not seen.

Removing the Barriers

To remove these barriers, we suggested that journalists start by visiting what we called WED galleries. In the first instance, we provided such a gallery by posting examples reflecting the standards we were promoting on the Institute walls. The gallery pages were from such papers as the *Orange County Register*, the *San Jose Mercury News*, the *St. Petersburg Times*, the *Philadelphia Inquirer*, and *Scotland on Sunday*. They were works of WED to behold and to emulate.

Then, in a series of lectures by specialists, we invited students to consider carefully the details and elements of each of the contributing crafts. This required, for example, that graphic artists give careful attention to news writing and scrutinize such items as news leads, sentence structures, the active voice, and metaphors. It required also that writers and editors examine with corresponding care the composition, lighting, and framing of the work of the best photographers. Illustrators and photographers were asked to write stories; writers were asked to draw or to think about how to use and construct items that called for bar charts, fever lines, timelines, and pie charts.

This is where notions of language and vocabulary entered the picture of WED. Two parallel notions were explored in the seminar sessions. The first involved the idea that WED is a language as well as a set of applications. In order to practice WED, it would be necessary first to learn its language(s). With that idea established, the seminar moved to a consideration of group dynamics and team work. We assumed that teamwork called for a new set of protocols that would diminish the impulse to divide the work and maintain the silos. The seminar culminated in a practicum in which teams were formed comprising writers, graphics artists, page editors, designers, and photographers so that each could apply—in a team—what we had been discussing in the sessions.

The Importance of Language(s)

But the foundation—or starting point—for the theory of WED derived from a simple theory of language. Language is a mysterious phenomenon. It springs from the depths of the mind and represents a unique and profoundly complex capacity of humans. But our use of the terms *language* and *vocabulary*, and the weight we gave to them in teaching WED, were relatively simple (although, we think, consistent with the theories of language and culture). By pointing to the languages of the crafts of journalism, we intended to point out, first, that languages give names to things, activities, and processes. Secondly, we were reminding everyone that people communicate and collaborate successfully when they use a common language. Thus, when we referred to the languages of journalism's crafts, we were encouraging potential WED practitioners to expand their vocabularies so that they could express more richly the vocabulary of their own craft and then incorporate, at the same time, the vocabularies of their working companions.

There was a third element to the part of WED theory derived from a simple theory of language. The vocabulary each journalist uses to refer exclusively to devices and tasks each alone uses and performs could fill a long book. But absorbing the vocabularies would not complete the task of those aspiring to practice WED. When we spoke of the languages of the WED crafts, we were referring also to the manner in which they are spoken and applied. Masters not only create and use a craft's vocabulary, but they speak it eloquently. So for all the crafts, we were referring to the manner in which the vocabulary is spoken and used by masters. Beyond the words of the masters are the applications and practices. In a world made by master craftsmen and artists, these applications and practices are, in one phrase, best practices.

The Languages and Roles of W and E

For writers in journalism, the journey into the language of craft starts in a familiar world of news leads and nut graphs—from the inverted pyramid and the active voice to briefs and project stories. It moves further through the technically eloquent reflections of William Strunk, Jr., for whom economy is a writer's principal virtue: "Vigorous writing is concise," he wrote. "A sentence should contain no unnecessary words, a paragraph no unnecessary sentences, for the same reason that a drawing should have no unnecessary lines and a machine no unnecessary parts. This requires not that the writer make all his sentences short, or that he avoid all detail and treat his subjects only in outline, but that every word tell."[4]

A practiced writer is likely to have seen this remarkable paragraph, but it is in the WED syllabus more for the sake of the illustrator, photographer, graphics editor, and designer than for the writer who may have missed it. It adds to their vocabularies just as Joan Didion's reflection on the experience of writing adds yet another dimension. Like Strunk, she links the visual to the verbal, but she adds a dimension to the process by conferring authority on the visual field and by saying, in effect, that the structure of her sentences follows strictly from what she sees. "Many people know about camera angles," she writes, "but not so many know about sentences. The arrangement of the words matters, and the arrangement you want can be found in the picture in your mind. The picture dictates whether this will be a sentence, long or short, active or passive. The picture tells you how to arrange the words and the arrangement of the words tells you, or tells me, what's going on in the picture."[5]

A serious editor of words, once he or she is past the judgment that an event is newsworthy or a phenomenon worthy of attention, is likely to think of Strunk's and Didion's observations and speak of propositions, arguments, syntax, analogies, metaphors, the active voice, the subjunctive, dangling participles, leads, focus, and narrative. He or she will ask, "Do the words work?" So will a good WEDitor, the individual who presides over the WED process, and so might the participants in the WED processes, though not writers, be obliged to understand what their collaborators are doing and what constitutes an acceptable standard of expression.

The Language and Role of *D*

The letter *D* refers to all the visual components of the paper—the work of photographers, graphic artists, illustrators, designers, and copy editors. In WED, visual decisions are inspired by the content of the story or the text itself. The *D* partner in the WED process must be engaged with the writer and editor to discuss in detail the meaning, mood, and angle of the story before making visual decisions. With such preparation, *D* partners can select just the right images—photos, illustrations, and graphics—with the appropriate size, shape, composition, color, and contrast to combine with the headline in a way that commands attention and engages the reader. They can select a typographic treatment with the appropriate style, size, and weight to reflect the mood and meaning of the headline. They can lift out essential quotes and readouts and display them in a voice reflected in a specific typeface and weight, and place them where they fit the narrative. They can choose a grid that establishes the underlying framework with its meticulous internal measures and appropriate pacing so that all the elements work in harmony. They can select from a variety of color palettes to promote further the emotion and tone of the story.

The *D* partner speaks the complex languages of the visual arts and uses that language to guide visual applications in subtle, but powerful, ways. Only through collaboration with the writer and editor can the *D* partner accomplish his or her goals, which are to engage the reader to enter the environment of the story, to help the reader navigate through a page and, in the end, to understand the full meaning of the story or stories.

Making WED Work

Learning how to speak the language(s) of WED constituted a foundation, or first step. So a considerable amount of time in the seminar was devoted to examining each of the WED crafts and learning their languages. The second step was to promote a conversation among potential collaborators who now would operate on a more even playing field.

The changes promoted by the new technologies and called for by WED required a reconsideration of the hierarchy of the crafts. The old way placed the writer at the top of a hierarchy. The old way put graphics editors, photographers, designers, and illustrators in the service of the writer and word editor. By contrast, WED put the writer at the center (rather than the top) of the process as it opened the door to collaborations and distributed the work more generously. In one kind of story (presented by example), the writer would be king (or queen), and the photographer would provide advice and his or her powers of observation. In another story, the photographer might be in charge and the writer would have provided his or her literary powers to provide carefully crafted cutlines and other enhancements. Sometimes the graphics editor, sometimes the illustrator, sometimes the photographer would make the crucial call on the shape the story would take. In the foreground would be the designer, working with typefaces, a color palette, and grids imagining the ways in which the item or items marking the news and feature pages should come together. So in its operations, WED is more egalitarian and collaborative. It calls for insight among all the practitioners into what each craft can contribute to showing and telling—to the project of providing artful representations of the news. WED, we argued, calls for team work.

This declaration led routinely to a comment: "It's a good idea to have everyone involved in the 'front end' before a word is written, but how realistic is this? On plan-ahead stories, maybe. On breaking news, hardly!" It turns out that in many papers, once the process is set up and put into practice, the process works surprisingly well on breaking news as well as features. Here's why: the front-end meetings where story ideas, concepts, and angles are discussed are sometimes held right in the newsroom and are very short and informal.

One paper, in particular, has incorporated this model of WED into its daily routine—the *Virginian-Pilot*. Although the following example was not available to us at the time of the original seminar, we can point to the *Virginian-Pilot* today as an example of the effective use of WED.

The *Virginian-Pilot* and WED

The following are the words of Denis Finley, deputy managing editor for presentation, on the WED process:

> After the morning budget meeting, which includes editors, photo and graphic representatives, and sometimes writers if they wish to attend, an inventory is established and the important stories for the day are identified. Reporters, editors, photo editors, and graphic artists work to put together packages that are as complete as possible in anticipation of the next two news meetings, which will take place in the newsroom around the A1 designer's work station.
>
> At the first meeting, which is held at 2:30 P.M., the designer collaborates with the various editors attending the meeting to get a working headline for the main front page story. She works with the graphics and photo people to discuss possible images. She begins sketching possible front pages on a Mac in the middle of the newsroom. Her computer monitor is available for everyone to see. Anyone can make a suggestion or comment, or give her updates on the story that she can incorporate. WED discussions are going on all day with the design person as the WED leader.
>
> At the next meeting (6 P.M.), also held at the designer's work station, everyone stands and discusses the way the stories of the day's events will be handled. When the front page goes to the press, everyone has had a say. This is WED team work in action.

Current Examples

The *Pilot* is especially keen on helping the reader understand a story in detail. On these three examples, note how labels and headlines speak directly to the reader, sometimes asking a question, always helping the reader navigate through the information and giving direction to what is inside the paper.

The *Virginian-Pilot*, May 30, 1997

The country didn't know whether Timothy McVeigh would be convicted. The package gives, in short summary points, the reasons on both sides of the case—why he will be convicted or why he will not.

Written by the writers and editors and designed by the photographer and designer, this package sets a mood with placement at the top of the page, and with color that drains from McVeigh's face on the "He is guilty, he will die" side. The story itself is broken apart and written into short, bulleted points to accompany the image and package treatment. There are more stories inside as the labels tell the reader, but the front page treatment enhances the true, intense, and frightening meaning of the story. It engages the reader, invites the reader in to read more and understand up close and in more detail about what this means to McVeigh and to those of his victims.

The *Virginian-Pilot*, June 14, 1997

McVeigh is condemned to death. The photo of relatives is powerfully moving (see p. 143). The story is displayed with facts of the case pointed out. The headline says it all in one word. And the headline is displayed in a tombstone-like way with every bombing victim listed. The guilty McVeigh sits in front—small, vulnerable, resting on his own tombstone.

The *Virginian-Pilot*, August 18, 1998

Clinton's speech was short (see p. 144). Everyone was watching. What better way to record the moment than to give the reader the entire text, word for word. We all saw Clinton on TV. No need to see him as the lead art again. His words become the art, the most powerful visual available to convey the importance and impact of the story. The decision was made based on discussions among the editors, writers, photo editor, and designer with their goal being to emphasize the importance of the historical moment and to give the reader the entirety of the script in the most dynamic way possible.

The WED Gallery

During our seminars we studied numerous papers from around the world, analyzing how WED was working or not working in the pages. We called this the gallery walk, a term Mario coined. We encouraged participants to do the same when they got back to their newsrooms. Here are two other recent examples of pages that we believe reflect successful WED thinking and packaging. They are from the *San Jose Mercury News* and the *Times Union* in Albany, New York. The cutlines reflect the kind of in-depth WED analyses we conducted in our gallery walks.

DEATH

Silent McVeigh handed his fate

WHAT'S NEXT

McVEIGH CAN APPEAL

He is expected to file a notice of intent to appeal within a month. He could challenge a range of issues, from the constitutionality of the federal death penalty to the rulings restricting the evidence his lawyers could introduce. The appeals could last for years.

WHAT IF HE DOESN'T APPEAL?

He could be executed in about a year. Some familiar with McVeigh's political views suggested he wants to be a martyr for the fringe groups that share his views.

HE ALSO FACES OTHER CHARGES

Prosecutors in Oklahoma City want to convict McVeigh of murder in state court and have him sentenced to death under state law as a safeguard against successful appeals in the federal case.

CO-DEFENDANT'S TRIAL

The date for Terry Nichols' trial on murder and conspiracy charges likely will be set after August.

Church bells toll as the news reaches Oklahoma

DENVER — A federal jury Friday condemned Timothy McVeigh to death for the 1995 bombing of a federal office building in Oklahoma City that killed 168 people, injured hundreds more, and shattered a nation's belief that the face of terrorism seldom before could come from America.

McVeigh, sitting with his elbows on the defense table and his hands clasped in front of his face, appeared absolutely unshaken as U.S. District Court Judge Richard P. Matsch announced the jury's recommendation that McVeigh should die. McVeigh didn't even blink the jury stared straight ahead.

■ The jury recommended a separate penalty for each charge.

■ Survivors' relationships that McVeigh's sensitivities weren't real and genuine.

Flashing numbness and cheeks reddened, jurors cried over each other's shoulders and held hands.

McVeigh's younger sister and niece wept as the verdict was read. McVeigh's father, William McVeigh, slumped in his seat, and his mother, Mildred Frazer, stared so deeply into the courtroom below that anguish peered outward.

As mourners streamed free from the courtroom, the 29-year-old Persian Gulf War veteran made a small, one-fingered wave to his parents, mouthed "It's OK," and bent inside the outer wave to his jury that condemned him, nodding his head up and down.

They stared blankly back.

The jury's death decision is binding. Matsch said he will formally sentence McVeigh to death by lethal injection. Court date was not set, after a July 1 deadline for motions and appeals.

McVeigh's lead defense attorney,

Please see **Death**, page **A6**

James Sheppard and his wife, Wilma, lost six family members in the 1995 blast at the Murrah federal building in Oklahoma City. Shortly after hearing that Timothy McVeigh had received the death penalty, the couple said they would pray for his family.

Base closures

House and Senate panels throw up road blocks to stop Clinton administration's plans for another round of base closings. **Story, A3**

Crop circles a hoax

The mystery of the crop circles on the Perquimans County wheat field was solved when the owner found a wooden plank nearby, convincing him that the pranksters were terrestrial, not celestial. **Story, B3**

Chicago Bulls win NBA title with 90-86 victory over Utah

Story, C1

TUESDAY
AUGUST 18, 1998
Made news, and hot,
high in the news 90s/80s

The Virginian-Pilot

SERVING HAMPTON ROADS SINCE 1865

CLINTON'S CONFESSION:

"I misled people."

Good evening. ■ This afternoon in this room, from this chair, I testified before the Office of Independent Counsel and the grand jury. ■ I answered their questions truthfully, including questions about my private life; questions no American citizen would ever want to answer. ■ Still, I must take complete responsibility for all my actions, both public and private. ■ And that is why I am speaking to you tonight. As you know, in a deposition in January, I was asked questions about my relationship with Monica Lewinsky. ■ While my answers were legally accurate, I did not volunteer information. ■ Indeed, I did have a relationship with Ms. Lewinsky that was not appropriate. ■ In fact, it was wrong. ■ It constituted a critical lapse in judgment and a personal failure on my part for which I am solely and completely responsible. ■ But I told the grand jury today and I say to you now that at no time did I ask anyone to lie, to hide or destroy evidence or to take any other unlawful action. ■ I know that my public comments and my silence about this matter gave a false impression. ■ I misled people. Including even my wife. I deeply regret that. ■ I can only tell you I was motivated by many factors. ■ First, by a desire to protect myself from the embarrassment of my own conduct. ■ I was also very concerned about protecting my family. ■ The fact that these questions were being asked in a politically inspired lawsuit, which has since been dismissed, was a consideration, too. ■ In addition, I had real and serious concerns about an independent counsel investigation that began with private business dealings 20 years ago — dealings, I might add, about which an independent federal agency found no evidence of any wrongdoing by me or my wife over two years ago. ■ The independent counsel investigation moved on to my staff and friends, then into my private life. ■ And now the investigation itself is under investigation. ■ This has gone on too long, cost too much and hurt too many innocent people. Now, this matter is between me, the two people I love most — my wife and our daughter — and our God. ■ I must put it right, and I am prepared to do whatever it takes to do so. ■ Nothing is more important to me personally. ■ But it is private, and I intend to reclaim my family life for my family. ■ It's nobody's business but ours. Even presidents have private lives. ■ It is time to stop the pursuit of personal destruction and the prying into private lives and get on with our national life. ■ Our country has been distracted by this matter for too long, and I take my responsibility for my part in all of this. ■ That is all I can do. ■ Now it is time — in fact, it is past time — to move on. ■ We have important work to do — real opportunities to solve, real problems to solve, real security matters to face. ■ And so tonight, I ask you to turn away from the spectacle of the past seven months, to repair the fabric of our national discourse, and to return our attention to all the challenges and all the promise of the next American century. ■ Thank you for watching. ■ And good night.

HE SAYS HIS PRIVATE LIFE IS "NOBODY'S BUSINESS"

FROM WIRE REPORTS

WASHINGTON — Resigned to be provocative and combtive for political forgiveness, President Clinton testified for more than four hours at the White House on Monday before admitting, in an extraordinary television address to the nation, that he had carried on a relationship with a former White House intern that he said was "not appropriate."

In his address, Clinton did not directly acknowledge a sexual affair with the intern, Monica Lewinsky, after seven months of emphatic denials. But he said, "I did have a relationship with Ms. Lewinsky that was not appropriate. In fact, it was wrong."

"I misled people. Including even my wife. I deeply regret that. Clinton told Americans in an evening address in which he criticized the independent counsel investigation for delving into financial matters in his private life.

Speaking to shore off morale imprisonment proceedings, Clinton said part of the reason he did not come forward earlier was to save himself from embarrassment because of his mistrust of Independent counsel Kenneth Starr's investigation.

"This has gone on too long and too much and hurt too many

Please see **Clinton,** *Page A16*

President Clinton admitted Monday to having a relationship with Monica Lewinsky that was "not appropriate."

NAVY BODY-FAT STANDARDS

A petty officer may be discharged for failing a body-fat test 3 times while a surgeon remains after failing 7 times.

BY TARA REDFIELD
STAFF WRITER

VIRGINIA BEACH — Petty Officer 1st Class Marlene O'Rance is a single mother with 2½ years left until retirement.

But her career may not last that long. She could be discharged any day because the Navy says she's too fat.

At 5-foot-3 and 174 pounds, O'Rance has exceeded the Navy's maximum permissible body fat — recently raised from 30 percent to 34 percent for women — three times in the past four years.

But her case isn't a simple matter of biceps and bellies.

O'Rance argues the Navy could have helped her meet the requirements had it given her breast reduction surgery, a procedure the service's own doctors recommended she have.

The Navy's fitness and body-fat standards, while intended to ensure that sailors can adequately do their jobs, may be inconsistently applied and could lead to the discharge of capable sailors.

And while she is being eyed for discharge — and the loss of $40,000 in severance pay and recently retirement checks — other sailors who exceed the Navy's body fat standards are being kept in uniform, particularly male officers.

One is Lt. Cmdr. Milan Pankratis, who has failed the body-fat test seven times in a row but is holding on to his job as an assistant

Please see **Bodyfat,** *Page A16*

Petty Officer 1st Class Marlene O'Rance may be discharged because of her body fat. She says a double standard exists in the Navy.

Use state's $150 million surplus to hire teachers, Gilmore says

BY WARREN FISKE
STAFF WRITER

RICHMOND — A booming economy left the state government with a $150 million surplus for the budget year that ended June 30, Gov. Jim Gilmore told legislators on Monday.

The Republican governor said he would propose that some of the money be spent next year to fulfill his campaign pledge to hire additional elementary school teachers.

Gilmore, however, disappointed many Democrats by declining to propose that any of the surplus be spent to help localities build and renovate schools. The governor said he will end several months in a study commission's report on school construction needs before deciding whether the state support should expand.

The governor spoke before a joint meeting of the House and Senate money committees.

"It is my pleasure to report that the Virginia economy is thriving

Gov. Jim Gilmore pledged during his campaign to hire 4,000 new instructional teachers over four years.

and our revenue outlook exceeds every position," Gilmore said.

The governor revealed that the recession gave 34.5 percent during the last fiscal year — much of the growth attributed to capital gains

Please see **Surplus,** *Page A16*

The *Times Union*, Albany, New York, May 5–9, 1997

The words "When home is a war zone" create a dark and frightening tone, introducing the difficult subject of spousal abuse. The victim's face stares at the reader, partnering with the headline to create the tense mood. Like

HUMPDAY

DINNER ON THE RUN

SILICON VALLEY
L*SV*FE

LIVING WELL

HEALTH & FITNESS ▼

The surest sign of possesing no sense of direction

IT'S a jungle out there. At least that may have been the impression of motorists who believed a billboard that popped up alongside Interstate 880 last week. The billboard, facing southbound traffic between Brokaw Road and the 101 interchange, proclaims, "MarineWorld/Africa USA, 5 miles ahead." That'd be just about downtown San Jose.

ABOUT TIME: Ground will be broken on a couple of non-jungle attractions downtown this week, a pair that we've been awaiting for longer than we like to think. The first —the Tech Museum of Innovation —will have its ceremonies at noon Tuesday. Some high-tech robots, including a 30-foot monster designed by Chico MacMurtie, will do the actual moving of the dirt at the Park Avenue and Market Street site. And even Silicon Valley legend Bill Hewlett has said he'll make the effort to attend, so could you do any less?

The second, the Veterans Memorial, gets its start Friday at 10 a.m. when its first of many flags — a 20-by-30-foot garrison flag — will be hoisted at the site in Guadalupe River Park near the Center for the Performing Arts, again facing Park Avenue. The Veterans Memorial Committee so far has raised about half the $550,000 necessary to complete the memorial, and figures that flying the flag will remind donors to kick in the other half. (To contribute, write P.O. Box 8409, San Jose 95155.)

It's been a joint operation between Cleveland and San Jose for the past 10 years or so, but the Ohio half of the San Jose - Cleveland Ballet didn't get around to publicly acknowledging its California contribution on its printed materials until the "Blue Suede Shoes" ballet opened there last month. "Cleveland San Jose Ballet," they call it there, but it's nice to finally see San Jose mentioned, no matter what the billing. Perhaps some day, even the ink-stained wretches at the Cleveland Plain Dealer will catch on.

FACES AND PLACES: It's a surprising world. When disc jockey Sean O'Callaghan boarded a Princess Cruises liner in Greece for a KBAY-AM promotional cruise, he discovered the chaplain aboard was the Rev. John Snyder, S.J., O'Callaghan's cousin. They hadn't seen each other in 41 years.

Tony DePalma of Monte Sereno took son Marc, 10, and daughter Alison, 12, golfing with him at Pruneridge and felt right proud of himself when he hit from the rough to the green for a birdie on the third hole. But by the ninth hole, it was Alison's show: an eagle. Onlooker Karen Wallich, the course's operations manager, immediately whipped out her pen to sign Alison for a tournament.

The death last week of longtime Santa Clara baseball coach Bob Fatje reminded Louis Duino, the Merc's sports editor emeritus, of a little-known role Fatje played in diamond history. A fan as well as a coach, Fatje was watching a training session of the old San Francisco Seals in pre-majors Seals Stadium. A young shortstop was making a number of errant throws, finally bouncing one off Fatje in the stands.

Bill Hewlett said he'll make the effort to attend.

ILLUSTRATION BY DAVID FRAZIER

Nasal

destroyers

surround

sniffling,

sneezing

humans

to exact

their toll

gesundheit!

BY KATHLEEN DONNELLY

There's good news and there's bad news about our spate of recent rains, says Dr. James Wolfe, chairman of the division of allergy and immunology at Santa Clara Valley Medical Center.

"The good news is that while it rains there's very little pollen in the air," says Wolfe, explaining that trees that usually release their pollen in early spring are somewhat thwarted by damp days.

"The bad news," he continues, "is with all this rain, there is the potential for very high pollen counts this spring season, particularly grass pollens, and olives, and oaks, and other trees."

The 18 to 15 percent of the population who suffer from seasonal allergic rhinitis, more commonly known as hay fever, will remember the record-breaking pollen counts of 1995, when a combination of a warm, dry February followed by a rainy spring made for one of the worst allergy seasons in the Santa Clara Valley. The season, which typically lasts from early February to mid-June, stretched

See GESUNDHEIT, Page 4E

FOOD ▼

Crunchy,

versatile

mix—ins liven

up dishes from

salad to

seafood

go nuts

BY JOYCE GEMPERLEIN FOOD EDITOR

I'm getting nutty in the kitchen. Pecans, peanuts, walnuts, macadamias, almonds, pistachios, cashews and hazelnuts are showing up in everything from salads to seafood.

"Dramatic" is the word chefs are using to describe the effect they are getting from combining nuts with other foods. Crushed, nuts become a crunchy coating for sautéed or broiled meats. Toasted and tossed into a salad, they dress up the most pedestrian greens.

"I think nuts are fantastic in all kinds of dishes," says Hugh Carpenter, a cooking teacher and author of a series of books with his wife, photographer Teri Sandison. In the couple's latest book, "Hot Chicken" (Ten Speed Press, $17.95), nuts figure prominently.

One reason for nuts' popularity is that diners are becoming conscious

See NUTS, Page 4E

INSIDE: WINE OF THE WEEK ■ NIBBLE ■ STRESS BUSTER ■ TO YOUR HEALTH a victim of war, the face is damaged, torn apart, and put back together, echoing the feeling of the victim—the cycle of violence that happens over and over again as described in the story. Torn paper scattered around the face contains the hour-by-hour abuse of the victim. On the original color page, dark tones of black, gray, brown, and purple give the feeling of bruises. Symmetry calms. By centering the victim's face, the designer attempts to bring order to the chaotic swirl of abuse and at the same time, draws the eye down the page to the start of the story. All the pieces fit— from the mood and meaning of the story to the headline type treatment and image, to text placement and style, to color palette, all working in WED-like harmony to enhance the meaning of the story.

San Jose Mercury News, June 26, 1996

The story is about the irritating sniffling and sneezing associated with allergies (see p. 146). This page feels as if it's "sneezing." Its upside-down head and sprinkling of exclamation points enhances the feeling of unexpected surprise. What a wonderful way to connect with the reader—creating a familiar feeling we all know. On the original color page, the single word *gesundheit* is large, tall, and red, making it loud, just like a response to a sneeze. The red exclamation points dance around the head, as if the page was sneezed upon, the result being the scattering of type. The placement of the exclamation points creates a fast and irregular pace in the package. But the marks are placed strategically, pulling the eye from the open mouth, around the image and down to the headline and text, drawing the reader into the story itself.

Notes

1. George Orwell, "Why I Write," in *Collected Essays* (London: Secker and Warburg, 1961), 438.

2. WED is comparable conceptually to the *Maestro Concept*, which was developed and promoted by Buck Ryan while teaching at Northwestern University.

3. The others included, prominently, Jackson Dykman of the *Washington Post*, Lynn Staley, of the *Boston Globe* and later *Newsweek*, Nigel Holmes of *Time* and later an independent consultant, Brenda Shoun of the *Orange County Register*, and Kenneth Irby, Bill Boyd, and Don Fry of The Poynter Institute.

4. William Strunk, Jr. and E. B. White, *The Elements of Style*, 3d ed. (New York: Macmillan, 1979), 23

5. Joan Didion, "Why I Write," in *The Writer and Her Work,* ed. Janet Sternberg (New York: W. W. Norton, 1980), 21.

11

Writer in the Newsroom

Donald M. Murray

A Lifetime Apprenticeship

Sixty-one years ago Miss Chapman looked down at me and said, "Donald, you are the class editor." So much for career planning.

Forty-seven years ago, after having survived infantry combat, college, and a first marriage, I found myself in the city room of the old *Boston Herald*, determined to learn the newspaper craft and get back to writing great poems.

Now, at seventy, I return each morning to my writing desk apprenticed to the writer's craft. Monday morning I write my column for the *Boston Globe*; Tuesday through Sunday I draft yet another book on writing, a novel, a poem. Unemployed, I am blessed by not having to take weekends and holidays off, do not suffer any vacations. "Nulla dies sine linea" [Never a day without a line]: Horace, Pliny, Trollope, Updike.

Chaucer said, "The lyf so short, the craft so long to lerne." I now know he did not speak with complaint but with gratitude.

The Japanese artist Hokusai testified: "I have drawn things since I was six. All that I made before the age of sixty-five is not worth counting. At seventy-three I began to understand the true construction of animals, plants, trees, birds, fishes, and insects. At ninety I will enter into the secret of things. At a hundred and ten, everything—every dot, every dash—will live."

My bones may creak, I may live on a diet of pills, I may forget names, but when I shuffle down to my computer I see Miss Chapman standing in the corner of the room, nodding encouragement.

A lapsed Baptist, I bear witness to the salvation of a writing life. I do not testify for all writers, just this apprentice to a craft I can never learn. The sculptor Henry Moore said:

"The secret of life is to have a task, something you devote your whole life to, something you bring everything to, every minute of the day for your whole life. And the most important thing is—it must be something you cannot possibly do!"

I evangelize. I wish you failure. I hope you have not yet learned to write but are still learning. If you are confident of your craft and are writing without terror and failure, I hope you will learn how to escape your craft and write so badly you will surprise yourself with what you say and how you are saying it.

The writer's day begins when the writing ends. About 11:30 in the morning I turn off my computer and go out in the world to observe and imagine, day dream and night dream, report and remember, think and reflect, rehearse and note, performing all the tasks that bring me to my desk early in the morning, ready to end the writing day with a draft before noon.

I usually know the next morning's writing task—not what I will say and how I will say it, but the territory I will explore. I am in a state of susceptibility. Fragments of language and images come to me in their own way, on their own time. I do not press; I live in wait. The fragments that sparked this talk—"bear witness," "selfish delights"—were scribbled on a 3-by-5 card during a performance of the Borodin Trio: dreadful performance of Mozart, good Mendelssohn, great Shostakovich.

I do not consciously seek; I lie in wait, accepting the lines and images that float through my mind, sometimes making mental notes, sometimes scribbled ones.

I live in a curious and delightful state of intense awareness and casual reflection that is difficult to describe. Perhaps it is like those moments in combat when the shooting and the shelling stop and you can hunker down behind a rock wall and rest. In a poem I wrote a few weeks ago, I found myself saying that I was "Among the dead, the dying, / more alive than I have ever been."

At that moment in combat I celebrated life, noticing the way a blade of grass recovers from a boot, studying how the sky is reflected in a puddle in the mud, even enjoying the perfume of the horse manure the farmer will use to nurture the spring planting—if there is a spring.

My writing has made me a better reporter on my life. I pay attention to my living. Minnie Mae and I go out shopping, and in the supermarket I realize she has become her mother. I seize that moment and explore it in a column published in the *Boston Globe* on March 21, 1995.

A reporter might know what the moment meant and know what to say about it. Writers cultivate not knowing, nurture ignorance, welcome the terror of the blank screen when they do not know what they know. Writers write for surprise, for the discovery of what they did not know they knew, as I did in this column:

It didn't come on gradually, the way I might have expected. It happened in an instant.

I had a cart full of groceries and was heading out the door at the Market Basket when I realized Minnie Mae was not behind me. I turned, and her mother was at the cash register.

She had paid for her groceries, but she was putting her money away, sorting out her coupons, and holding up a line of eye-rolling shoppers.

This had always made Minnie Mae furious. In the mid-1950s when her mother lived with us in New Jersey, Minnie Mae would get jumping-up-and-down mad when her mother did the checkout line routine.

I thought this was funny and said, "Hi, Katie"—her mother's name—when Minnie Mae got in the car. She wasn't amused.

She didn't realize she had become her mother.

When she exits from a store, museum, theater, she comes to a full stop outside the door. Her mother did that.

When I hit a pot hole in the road she gasps. Her mother did that.

When she watches television she just "rests her eyes." Her mother did that.

When I serve supper or dessert, she always says, "Don't give me too much." Her mother drove Minnie Mae crazy when she said that—night after night after night.

Still Minnie Mae refuses to admit her transformation. She does not think it funny. She does not even think it interesting, worth exploring—in a sociological, scholarly manner, of course.

I think it hilarious. I cannot keep from giggling, cannot refrain from quoting Minnie Mae on her mother's idiosyncrasies from thirty years ago, cannot resist repeating what Minnie Mae said then: "If I ever do what my mother just did, tell me. I will never become my mother. Never."

Then, leaving a restaurant one day, I stop to talk to this person, to nod at another, to grab a hand, to joke with a waitress, I look up in the mirror that stretches across a wall.

I am my father.

I couldn't be. He didn't have hair. He wore a watermelon under his shirt. He had this great smile and these glasses that kept you from seeing his eyes, and he wore the smile and specs as a mask. You never were quite sure what was going on behind the salesman's smile.

He snored. He sent out envelopes stuffed with newspaper or magazine clippings. No note. He gave people mottoes or inspiring quotations. He kept notebooks of lists and kept score on his life. He was on the telephone with his friends every night. [I thought we should have buried him with a phone in his hand.]

My editor cut this out. No problem. If it is important, it will return.

I vowed I would never be like my father. But there he was in the mirror.

I remember the lines from the Robert Lowell poem "Middle Age" in which he says his father left "dinosaur / death-steps on the crust, / where I must walk."

My daughter Anne is visiting with Karl. She shows me her new book of lists. We shop and I knew where she would turn and why. She instructs me on my computer and I hand her yellow Post-its before she asks for them. She laughs and says her colleagues think she is crazy the way she marks things.

I don't. She does it the only right way. The way I do it. The way her grandfather would have done it if he had lived long enough to use Post-its.

He would have loved computers. And e-mail. He would have been online morning and night, checking up on friends in Florida and Alabama and Idaho and Iowa and Utah and New Hampshire, as I have just done.

Minnie Mae has become her mother and I have become my father and Anne, God help her, is becoming her father and mine.

If you read my mail, you would know this is hard news: front page news on the human condition. Readers create their own drafts as they read mine, they read the family history of their own blood. Reporters and writers—indeed all artists—set up shop where there is birth and death, success and defeat, love and loneliness, joy and despair.

After I leave my writing desk, I lead a double life. I am a mole, living an ordinary life of errands, chores, conversations with friends, reading, watching TV, eating, and—at the same time—I am a spy to my life, maintaining an alertness to the commonplace, the ordinary, the routine where the really important stories appear.

I am never bored. I overhear what is said and not said, delight in irony and contradiction, relish answers without questions and questions without answers, take note of what is and what should be, what was and what may be. I imagine, speculate, make believe, remember, reflect. I am always traitor to the predictable, always welcoming to the unexpected.

This paying attention is not always comfortable. Reporting on the self can bring terror as well as celebration, pain as well as pleasure.

And in writing those words in a draft of this essay, I am forced by some primitive writer's force to confront my greatest terror and I write the column that was published in April 1995:

> The morning our 20-year-old daughter Lee took sick with her last illness, I was trying to write a letter of sympathy wondering what I could say, asking myself if it would make any difference.
>
> Five days later I knew. It made a difference.
>
> I discovered it was better to reach out than turn away, to say the wrong thing than say nothing.
>
> But in living through Lee's loss and others I also discovered I had something to say to others who suffered the loss of someone they loved.
>
> Pain is better than forgetting.
>
> It is almost 18 years but Lee is still with us. The pain is not so much lessened as it has become familiar, like the pain that continues in the leg that has been amputated. Her death is part of us.
>
> I steel myself pretty well for the expected moments of pain. Her birthday in March, her deathday in August, Thanksgiving, Christmas, even, these days, listening to an Albinoni oboe concerto knowing it is not her practicing in the next room.
>
> But there is no protection from the blindside hit. Lee waves from a passing car. She appears ahead of me on a street in Siena, wearing a backpack. I rush to catch up with her but she turns a corner and is gone.
>
> She stands in the shadows, just outside the living room. I hear her counsel when I have a problem, and pay attention. At the concert I sit beside her in the center of the orchestra as she invited me to sit beside her during an orchestral rehearsal at the University of Massa-

chusetts and we are again surrounded by music.

It is not all tears. We laugh at the same old jokes—and some new ones. Every submarine sandwich I eat, I share it with Lee. It was her favorite.

When I was dying of a heart attack, Lee stood—in the blue jumper she had made—waiting at the end of a brightly lit tunnel, smiling.

But, I often say in a letter of sympathy, people will want you to get over it, snap out of it, buck up, forget.

Of course we have to get on with life, to find salvation in routine that suddenly seems trivial, to fulfill our responsibilities to the living. But not to forget.

It would be the most terrible sadness if the memory of that person who has died were erased.

It is far better to remember, to mourn, to weep, to rage, than to allow the one who is gone to disappear.

In a way I welcome the pain. I hurt; I remember.

So, I say in my sympathy letter, they should learn to accept the pain, even in a way welcome it, by comparing it to the terror of forgetting.

And as an elder of the tribe who has experienced loss, I write for them to remember in their own way, to mourn in their own way, to do what would be appropriate for the person who has gone, and, more important, to do what needs to be done for the living.

I could sleep on the floor of the waiting room as I slept in battle. Minnie Mae could not sleep. No right, no wrong.

The night Lee died we went to a musical in which her sister was appearing in the chorus. Lee would have wanted that, no matter if others approved.

We—her immediate family—chose cremation because it was what we thought she would have wanted and it was, we discovered, what each of us wanted for ourselves. We paid no attention to the relative who said, "I don't know how you could burn her up."

We did what we had to do.

We could not handle a formal funeral, bringing the family from afar, after her quick dying, so we had a private service at the grave side.

I wept—frequently—and Minnie Mae did not. No guilt, no public measuring of pain. I dream of Lee and Minnie Mae does not. That does not mean that one of us mourns more deeply than the other. No guilt. No keeping score.

We love in our own way; we grieve in our own way.

And in this terrible loss we have found strength. When we are tested by other events, we have a measure of our ability to survive.

And we were also reminded that life is fragile.

In my letters reaching out I tell others what Lee's passing taught us: to listen to each other and to ourselves, to live the gift of life with caring and celebration. Today. Right now.

I am a bit uncomfortable sharing that column even after it has been published. On my first typewriter at the *Boston Herald*, the capital *I* had been filed off. We were told never to write personal pieces, but I have found that the more personal I am, the more universal I become.

Much of my writing day is finished when I get up at 5:30 in the morning, read the *Globe*, grab a bagel with old cronies far younger than I am, walk, and sit down at my writing desk.

I write easily, and that is no accident. I remind myself that John Jerome said, "Perfect is the enemy of good" and follow William Stafford's advice that "one should lower his standards." I write fast to outrace the censor and cause the instructive failures that are essential to effective writing.

I write to say I do not know. That is my terror and my joy. I start a column with a line or an image, an island at the edge of the horizon that has not been mapped. And I do not finish the columns unless I write what I do not expect to write 40 to 60 percent of the way through. My drafts tell me what I have to say. This is true of my nonfiction books, my fiction, my poetry. I follow the evolving draft.

One evening in 1944 I dug a foxhole and found my comrades were the bones of World War I soldiers. I have been trying to deal with that ever since and have written poems directly on the subject. The other morning, when I expected to write a page of nonfiction, a poem that pays homage to all the soldiers who came before me and after appeared on my screen.

Draft after draft, what I had to say came clear as a print in the darkroom grows shadows that come clear in developer. As I listen to the poem—and my first readers—I add, cut, change a word, shape the line, always listening to the poem, to what it is telling me. In this concentration of craft, I am lost to the world. As Bernard Malamud said, "If it is winter in the book, spring surprises me when I look up."

Flight of Dreams

A sudden
lightness
in the air

I am
on patrol

between Houfalize
and St. Vith

high on fever
fear
Calvados
my unexpected
living

pink light
before dawn

and in black
winter trees
gray German
shadows

a sudden
rising

winged
and dark
as the trees
where they
slept

dreams
of soldiers from
other wars

struggling
upwards

just before
light

My goal these days is "nulla dies sine quingentis verbis" [never a day without 500 words]. I count the words. More than 802. It is 11:30 and so I pack up, ready for the next writing day to begin.

I look back at that thin—no longer skinny—young man in the *Boston Herald* city room so long ago and realize that I did with dumb instinct what I do by design today.

After walking on my first byline when the cleaning women put the first edition down to protect a scrubbed floor, I developed a healthy disinterest in what I had published.

I felt no loyalty to what I had said and how I had said it. When I learned how to write a story the way the editor wanted it, I experienced a playful desire to unlearn it, to see if I could do it differently.

I kept saying I wonder what would happen if . . .

And today each draft is an experiment. I try short leads and long leads, telling the story all in dialogue or with no dialogue, starting at the end and moving backward, using a voice that I have not tried before, making up words when the dictionary fails.

I sought mentors, asking people at other desks how they were able to write a story I admired. I asked the best reporters if I could go along on my own as they reported a story. They were surprised and said yes; but when the union got wind of it, I was told to knock it off.

I looked at the assignment book and free-lanced stories that were not scheduled to be covered. I tried features on my own and surprised editors with stories they did not expect—and often did not want.

I wrote weddings and fashions for a suburban weekly, volunteered to review books, free-lanced on Saturday for the sports department, took graduate writing courses at Boston University and wrote stories so experimental I could not even figure out what they meant.

I drove Eddie Devin, the best editor on the city desk, home at 1 A.M., put a fifth of whiskey on the kitchen table, handed him a week's carbons of my stories, and was taught how I could improve.

He was older than I was; now my mentors are younger than I am. My principal mentor is Chip Scanlan. No whiskey and no carbons, just fax and America Online; but I'm still learning how I can improve. This essay was radically revised after he read a draft I thought was final.

I read compulsively to see what other writers can do and I still do today; I hunted down craft interviews such as the *Paris Review Writers at Work* series and copied down the lessons I learned about my craft, and I still do that today.

I was stupid stubborn, an inherited quality in a Highland Scot and a necessary quality in a writer. In one prize fight I was knocked down thirteen times and won.

I believed—and still believe—it is my job to educate editors—by example. I propose new ways of writing old stories by showing them a draft or at least a lead. When they didn't listen I wrote it their way—and when possible wrote it my way and submitted it somewhere else.

I was and am a cross-writer, exploring the possibilities of fiction and poetry, books and articles, columns and textbooks. Each genre illuminates the other.

I realize I had energy—and still do. My energy comes from the writing. I write and I find myself saying what I do not expect, in a way I haven't quite said it before. I am energized by surprise.

People think I write from an unhealthy compulsion, but I write from an obsessive passion, gloriously victimized by Miss Chapman's command that I was to be class editor. Annie Dillard said:

> There's a common notion that self-discipline is a freakish peculiarity of writers—that writers differ from other people by possessing enormous and equal portions of talent and willpower. They grit their powerful teeth and go into their little rooms. I think that's a bad misunderstanding of what impels the writer. What impels the writer is a deep love for and respect for language, for literary forms, for books. It's a privilege to muck about in sentences all morning. It's a challenge to bring off a powerful effect. You don't do it from willpower; you do it from an abiding passion for the field. I'm sure it's the same in every other field.
>
> Writing a book is like rearing children—willpower has very little to do with it. If you have a little baby crying in the middle of the night, and if you depend only on willpower to get you out of bed to feed the baby, that baby will starve. You do it out of love. Willpower is a weak idea; love is strong. You don't have to scourge yourself with cat-o'-nine tails to go to the baby. You go to the baby out of love for that particular baby. That's the same way you go to your desk. There's nothing freakish about it. Caring passionately about something isn't against nature, and it isn't against human nature. It's what we're here to do.

I write because I love writing.

And Minnie Mae, who makes leftovers from leftovers, reminds me that nothing is wasted when you are a writer. Remember that line the editor cut from my column, the one about my father being buried with a telephone in his hand? Well, listen to what surprised me this morning:

Long Distance

> Father was always on the phone,
> listening to strangers.
>
> After I left home, we made
> peace on the telephone
>
> and became good at distance,
> a careful reaching out.
>
> When he died, I told Mother
> we should bury him with a phone
>
> at his ear. Mother laughed,
> but disapproved.
>
> The phone rings. It is Dad,
> calling long distance.

That poem told me what I had lived but not really known until it was spoken by the poem: that my father, who listened to strangers better than he listened to his son, became close to me when I became a stranger, living far away and talking to him on the telephone long distance. And now that he is a quarter of a century dead and I live in the decade of life in which he died, we are closer than ever.

The poem was a surprise and it offered me a strange comfort, a different vision of the life I lead.

I wish you such surprises.

And I wish you a craft you can never learn—but can keep learning as long as you live.

For Further Reading

From Don Murray's library of several thousand books on writing, he suggests these personal favorites to writers in the newsroom who want to explore our craft.

Books on Writing in General

Lamott, Anne. *Bird by Bird—Some Instructions on Writing and Life*. New York: Pantheon, 1995.

Plimpton, George. *Writers at Work: The Paris Review Interviews*. Series. New York: Viking, 1992.

On Nonfiction

Jerome, John. *The Writing Trade—A Year in the Life*. New York: Lyons and Burford, 1995.

Rhodes, Richard. *How to Write: Advice and Reflections*. New York: William Morrow, 1995.

Scanlan, Christopher, Karen Brown, Don Fry, Roy Peter Clark, and Keith Woods, eds. *Best Newspaper Writing*. St. Petersburg, Fla.: Poynter Institute. Published annually since 1979.

Zinsser, William. *On Writing Well*. New York: Harper Collins, 1990.

On Fiction

Burroway, Janet. *Writing Fiction: A Guide to Narrative Craft*. New York: HarperCollins, 1995.

Rule, Rebecca, and Susan Wheeler. *Creating the Story: Guides for New Writers*. Portsmouth, N.H.: Heinemann, 1993.

On Poetry

Oliver, Mary. *A Poetry Handbook*. Orlando, Fla.: Harcourt Brace, 1994.

Wallace, Robert. *Writing Poems*. New York: Watson-Guptill, 1995.

Articles and Books on Writing by Donald M. Murray

This is the most complete bibliography of writing on writing by Donald M. Murray. It does not include the newspaper stories, editorials, and columns; magazine articles; juvenile and adult nonfiction books; forewords and introductions to books by other writers; reprints of his articles on writing; short stories and novels; or poems he has published. Murray's works are listed chronologically.

Books

A Writer Teaches Writing. Houghton Mifflin: 1st ed., 1968; 2d ed., 1985.

Write to Communicate: The Language Arts in Process. Educational Division, Reader's Digest, 1973. (A program for grades 3–6 in four kits. One of two editors/authors. Edited every part of the program and wrote 41 short books.)

Learning by Teaching. Heinemann, Boynton/Cook: 1st ed., 1982; 2d ed., 1989.

Writing for Your Readers. Globe Pequot Press, 1983; 2d ed., 1992.

Write to Learn. Holt, Rinehart, Winston: 1st ed., 1984; 2d ed., 1987; 3d ed., 1990; Harcourt Brace: 4th ed., 1993; 5th ed., 1995.

Read to Write. Holt, Rinehart, Winston: 1st ed., 1985; 2d ed., 1990; Harcourt Brace Jovanovich: 3d ed., 1993.

Expecting the Unexpected. Heinemann, Boynton/Cook, 1989.

Shoptalk, Learning to Write With Writers. Heinemann, Boynton/Cook, 1990.

The Craft of Revision. Holt, Rinehart, Winston, 1991; 2d ed., 1994.

Crafting a Life—in Essay, Story, Poem. Heinemann, Boynton/Cook, 1996.

Writing to Deadline: The Journalist at Work. Heinemann, 2000.

My Twice-Lived Life: A Memoir. Ballantine Books, 2001.

Monographs

Colleague in the Classroom: Making Textbooks Work in the Composition Course. Holt, Rinehart, Winston, 1986.

Writer in the Newsroom. The Poynter Institute for Media Studies, 1995.

Chapters

"How to Get Started as a Free-lance Writer." In *Prose by Professionals.* The Society of Magazine Writers. Doubleday, 1961.

"Write to Read." In *Teachers, Tangibles, Techniques: Comprehension of Content in Reading.* The International Reading Association, 1974.

"What is Pre-Writing?" In *The Questions Teachers Ask*, ed. R. Baird Shuman. Hayden, 1977.

"Internal Revision: A Process of Discovery." In *Research on Composing: Points of Departure*, ed. Charles R. Cooper and Lee Odell. National Council of Teachers of English, 1978.

"Writing as Process: How Writing Finds Its Own Meaning." In *Eight Approaches to Teaching Composition*, ed. Timothy R. Donovan and Ben W. McClelland. National Council of Teachers of English, 1980.

"The Feel of Writing—and Teaching Writing." In *Reinventing the Rhetorical Tradition*, ed. Aviva Freedman and Ian Pringle. The Canadian Council of Teachers of English, 1980.

"Out of Silence, a Voice." In *English in the Eighties*, ed. R. Baird Shuman. National Education Association, 1980.

"Conference Guidelines." In *Rites of Writing.* University of Wisconsin at Stevens Point, 1981.

"First Silence, Then Paper." In *Forum: Essays on Theory and Practice in Teaching Writing.* Boynton/Cook, 1983.

"When Not Writing Is Writing." In *Writer's Block—The Cognitive Dimension*, ed. Mike Rose. Southern Illinois University Press, 1983.

"Writing Badly to Write Well." In *Sentence Combining: A Rhetorical Perspective.* Southern Illinois University Press, 1984.

"Newswriting." In *Writing for Many Roles*, ed. Mimi Schwartz. Boynton/Cook, 1985.

"Getting Under the Lightning." In *Writers on Writing*, ed. Thomas Waldrep. Random House, 1985.

"The Essential Delay: When Writer's Block Isn't." In *When a Writer Can't Write—Studies in Writer's Block and Composing-Process Problems*, ed. Mike Rose. Guilford Press, 1985.

"Write Before Writing" and "Teaching the Other Self." In *To Compose: Teaching Writing in the High School*, ed. Thomas Newkirk. The Northeast Regional Exchange, Inc., National Institute of Education, U.S. Department of Education, 1985.

"What Makes Students Write." In *Writing Now*. 1986.

"Process Approach to Newswriting" (with Christopher Scanlan); "Problems and Solutions" and "Consultive Editing." In *How I Wrote the Story*, ed. Christopher Scanlan. The Providence Journal Company, 1st ed., 1983; 2d ed., 1986.

"Importance of Bad Writing—And How to Encourage It." In *Conversations in Composition*, ed. Albert C. DeCiccio and Michael J. Rossie. Merrimack College, undated.

"Reading While Writing." In *Only Connect: Uniting Reading and Writing*, ed. Thomas Newkirk. Boynton/Cook, 1986.

"How the Text Instructs: Writing Teaches Writing." In *The Writing Teacher as Researcher: Essays in the Theory and Practice of Class-Based Research*, ed. Donald A. Daiker and Max Morenberg. Heinemann Boynton/Cook, 1990.

"Writing After a Career of Writing." In *Nieman Reports*. Autumn 1990.

"Memo to a New Feature Writer." In *The Complete Book of Feature Writing*, ed. Leonard Witt. Writer's Digest Books, 1991.

"Use Genre as Lens." In *Elements of Writing*. Holt, Rinehart, Winston, 1991.

"How Poems Think." In *The Teacher as Researcher*, ed. Thomas Newkirk. Workshop 4 By and For Teachers. Heinemann, 1992.

"How to Get the Writing Done." In *The Subject Is Research: Processes and Practices*, ed. Wendy Bishop. Heinemann Boynton/Cook, 1993.

"Letter to a Young Article Writer." In *The Best Writing on Writing*, ed. Jack Heffron. Story Press, 1994.

"Where Do You Find Your Stories?" In *Presence of Mind—Writing and the Domain Beyond the Cognitive*, ed. Alice Gladen Brand and Richard L. Graves. Heinemann Boynton/Cook, 1994.

"Knowing Not Knowing." In *Taking Stock: The Writing Process Movement in the '90s*, ed. Lad Tobin and Thomas Newkirk. Heinemann Boynton/Cook, 1994.

"Tekst 8: Radgivningstimer: Det Andfet Jeg." "Tekst 9: Radgivningstimer: Problemer Og Losninger," "Tekst 10: Skrivegrupper: At Laese Som EnSkribent," "Tekst 12: Kvalitetskriterier: En Checkliste," *Laer Og Skriv*. Christian Kock. Undervisningsninisteriet, Copenhagen, 1994.

"Minnie Mae Cooks a Poem." In *All that Matters—What Is It We Value in School and Beyond*, ed. Linda Rief and Maureen Barbieri. Heinemann, 1995.

"Rewriting Teaching." In *The Art of Classroom Inquiry: A Handbook for Teacher-Researchers*, ed. Ruth Shagoury Hubbard and Brenda Miller Power. Portsmouth, N.H.: Heinemann, 1993.

Articles

"The Explorers of Inner Space." *Dial*, Spring 1968.

"Give Your Students the Writer's Five Experiences." *The Leaflet*, November 1968.

"Finding Your Own Voice: Teaching Composition in an Age of Dissent." *College Composition and Communication*, May 1969.

"Your Elementary Pupil and the Writer's Cycle of Craft." *Connecticut English Journal*, Fall 1969.

"The Explorers of Inner Space." *English Journal*, September 1969.

"The Interior View: One Writer's Philosophy of Composition." *College Composition and Communication*, February 1970.

"Teach Writing as Process Not Product." *The Leaflet*, Fall 1972.

"Why Creative Writing Isn't—Or Is." *Elementary English*, April 1973.

"Dominant Impression." *Exercise Exchange*, Fall 1972.

"The Maker's Eye: How a Writer Reads His Draft." *The Writer*, October 1973.

"What Can You Say Besides 'Awk'?" *California English Journal*, December 1973.

"Introduce the Writing Process—Tomorrow." *Classroom Practices in the Teaching of English*. National Council of Teachers of English, 1973.

"Why Teach Writing—and How?" *English Journal*, December 1973.

"Perhaps the Professor Should Cut Classes." With Lester Fisher. *College English*, November 1973.

"What, No Assignments?" *Alberta English*, Midwinter 1974.

"Our Students Will Write—If We Let Them." *North Carolina English Teacher*, Fall 1977.

"Teach the Motivating Force of Revision." *English Journal*, 1978.

"Write Before Writing." *College Composition and Communication*, December 1978.

"Writing Process/Response Exercise." *Exercise Exchange*, Spring 1979.

"When You Think You've Finished Writing." *English Journal*, February 1979.

"What Makes Readers Read?" *English Journal*, March 1979.

"The Qualities of Good Writing." *English Journal*, March 1979.

"The Listening Eye—Reflections on the Writing Process." *College English*, September 1979.

"The Writing Process." *Beginning an AP Course in English Language and Composition*. Educational Testing Service, Princeton, N. J., 1979.

"Revision: In the Writer's Workshop and In the Classroom" with Donald Graves. *Education Journal*, Boston University, May 1980.

"Reflections." *Language Arts*, May 1980.

"Questions to Produce Subjects." *English Journal*, May 1980.

"The Listening Eye: Reflections on the Writing Conference." *College English*, September 1979.

"Listening to Writing." *Composition and Teaching*, December 1980.

"The Politics of Respect." *Freshman English News*, Winter 1981.

"Editors Must Find New Ways to Develop and Retain Writers." *Bulletin of the American Society of Newspaper Editors*, April 1981.

"Making Clear—The Logic of Revision." *Journal of Basic Writing*, Fall/Winter 1981.

"Which Books on Writing and Editing Should Be in the Newsroom?" *Bulletin of the American Society of Newspaper Editors*, September 1981.

"Teaching the Other Self." *College Composition and Communication*, May 1982.

"Interview with Myself." *New York Writing Project Newsletter*, Spring 1982.

"The Teaching Craft: Telling, Listening, Revealing." *English Education*, Fall 1982.

"Response of Laboratory Rat—or, Being Protocoled." *College Composition and Communication*, May 1983.

"From What to Why—The Changing Style of Newswriting." *Style*, 1983.

"Writing—and Teaching—for Surprise." *College English*, January 1984.

"When Students Learn to Write." *New Hampshire Times*, February 25, 1984.

"Tricks of the Nonfiction Trade." *The Writer*, 1985.

"One Writer's Secrets." *College Composition and Communication*, May 1986.

"Rehearsing Rehearsing." *Rhetoric Review*, 1987.

"Reading for Surprise." *The Whole Language Newsletter*, February 1988.

"What A Beginning Writer Needs to Know." *The Writer*, January 1990.

"Cultivating Surprise." *The Writer*, April 1990.

"All Writing is Autobiography." *College Composition and Communication*, February 1991.

"One Writer's Curriculum." *English Journal*, April 1991.

"Receiving a Poem." *The Writer*, August 1991.

"How Writers See the Unseen Text." *The Colorado Communicator*, November 1991.

"A Writer's Habits." *The Writer*, January 1992.

"Letter to a Young Article Writer." *The Writer*, January 1993.

"The Writing Conference." *Encyclopedia of English Studies and Language Arts*, 1994.

"Pushing the Edge" and "A Preface on Rejection." *Writing on the Edge*, Spring 1994.

"The Craft of Telling." *The Writer*, June 1994.

"Writing At Seventy: Still Lost in the Work." *Muse* 8, no. 1, 1994.

"My One-Desk Schoolhouse." *A Word to the Wise*. Heinemann, 1994.

"Let the Draft Teach—Response to Reprinting 'Writing Fiction: A Self-Interview.'" *The Quarterly, Center for the Study of Writing,* University of California, Berkeley, 1995.

"Memo to a Beginning Essay Writer." *Marginal Comments.* University of New Hampshire, 1994.

"Tricks of the Trade" in two parts. *Notes in the Margins,* Stanford University, 1994.

"Before Writing: Remember What Makes Writing Easy." *Carolina Teacher,* 1995.

Interviews

"Mucking About in Language I Save My Soul." Interview with Driek Zirinsky. *Writing on the Edge,* Spring 1993.

"Focusing on Quality." Interview with Art Young. *Writing Teacher,* November 1994.

12

The Editor's Ambiguous Power

Karen Brown Dunlap and Foster Davis

The early morning caller sounded cheerful and casual. As he introduced himself, we tried to place him. He said he was an assistant city editor with a couple of problems, and wondered if we'd heard of others solving them. First, he had a senior reporter who once excelled but now turned in drab stories. He also had a promising young reporter who left holes in her work. Facts were missing or wrong. She came with good clips after two years in another newsroom, but she wasn't measuring up.

"I feel like changing jobs or going back to drinking," he said. We laughed. "Why not talk to the veteran," we suggested, "find out what he wants to do, what would motivate him?" He'd done that. The veteran wanted to do long take-out pieces, stories that didn't fit in the newspaper's plan. Why not coach the young reporter on her errors? Take them step by step. He had, but she didn't get it. She made the same mistakes over and over, forcing him to rewrite.

His problems reached beyond the two reporters. What did his editor say? Nothing. His editor was always in meetings and just said "deal with" the problem cases. Was it time to think of moving the reporters or firing them? "No way," he said. Company tradition and fear of legal actions meant the two weren't going anywhere. "I wasn't kidding," the caller said, his voice much slower and deeper. "I feel like leaving the industry or going back to drinking."

Power isn't always what we think it is.

Too often we imagine that the powerful newsroom leader mimics Lou Grant, who ruled his domain. When he stormed into the newsroom all eyes turned to him. He growled and everyone jumped. He gave orders and the staff obeyed, and seldom did higher-ups trouble him.

Chances are things don't work that way for you, just as they weren't that way for the caller.

You are constantly in a squeeze play. You must retain your dignity despite second-guessing from bosses and reporters. You risk having your news judgments contradicted and your editing lapses highlighted. You wanted to be an editor to inspire great journalism. Instead you sometimes see yourself in a job that offers little intellectual stimulation and is emotionally draining.

Where is the power in all this? Remember, as an editor you have the opportunity to make a difference in your newsroom. This chapter suggests that you take a new look at power. Examine four areas of strength. You can:

- Focus on your purpose;
- Find the forms of power that suit you;
- Decide on your limits;
- Discover your assets in the newsroom.

Consider each to get away from your forlorn thoughts, and into effective leadership.

Focus on Your Purpose

Consider the man in the cave. He won great battles by conquering enemies who far outnumbered him. He stood for his beliefs and won, but then a new threat appeared and he ran away, dejected, to hide in a cave. As he sulked, the voice from on high came to him asking: "What are you doing here?"

The question wasn't to scold; it was a reminder about mission. Why had the man fought? Why was he now in a cave? What changed his mission? Things weren't out of control; the man just allowed himself to believe they were. A reminder about his mission got him out of the funk and back in the battle.

Regularly remind yourself of your purpose as a journalist. Recall your strengths and build on them. Keep check on your weaknesses. Struggle to overcome them. Keep before you the ways in which you can make a difference and act on them.

Find the Forms of Power That Suit You

Paul Pohlman of The Poynter Institute and members of the Human Resources Center at the University of Chicago have described five types of power.

Legitimate power. This is the formal position that we so often think of as the only source of power. It seems so authoritative, efficient, and impressive. Power comes through appointment that brings a title, responsibility, and a domain. The implication is that one needs only to act and others will respond accordingly. The military makes legitimate power clear to a recruit. Within three weeks the drill instructor turns a clueless trainee into an expert on the chain of command. She is able to make distinctions based on stripes on the arm and bars on the shoulder. In any situation she knows who is in charge of what, how to respond to orders, and what to expect if she doesn't respond appropriately.

As editor, you have rank, but don't expect the stripes alone to inspire enthusiastic compliance. Many people don't respond well to orders. Journalists rank high on this anti-authoritarian list. They want to be inspired, convinced, encouraged, but not commanded. The stripes do give a good foundation. You'll have some sense of your territory of control and a megaphone allowing you to be heard. These are important in gridlock and on deadline. Otherwise, you'll spend a good deal of time relying on other sources of power.

Expert power. Look around your newsroom and think about the people who command respect because of what they know. Look more widely around the company and think of the folks who are indispensable, even though they don't have ranking titles. They are essential because of what they can do. Others approach them because they need their help.

In the quiet recesses of the *St. Petersburg Times* news library, Debbie Wolfe caught the hint of a wave. She moved from being a deskless "clip puller" to news researcher by designing a unique study of journalism and the growing number of computer research services. Next she became a resource for reporters, by showing them how to find new sources online. From there she began teaching online reporting skills and started to plan training programs for the newsroom. The more she did, the more she found to do. Her job title changed to technology training editor, and at that point she had gained official power. Notice, though, that the title followed her newly acquired expertise. She gained power and position because of what she learned.

Expert power can cut two ways for an editor. You ought to have a store of craft knowledge that allows you to help writers improve, but editors trip on being too expert. They become know-it-alls who spout answers when they ought to be listening, and they make changes when a few key questions would help the reporter grow. The ideal is to improve your knowledge constantly. Then you will draw others to you because of what you know and the manner in which you help them grow.

Trade-off power. People gain power through their ability to provide the things that others need. While it smells of sleaze, of wheeling and dealing, it can be the pivotal factor in your success or frustration. Trade-off power calls on you to get to know supervisors and other staffers well enough to provide what they need to meet their goals. It also involves your well-thought-out response to those who are diligent and to those who regularly give less than their best.

Consider your trade-off power. You wield perks and penalties. Use them fairly and wisely and you are a fine leader. Show partiality or over-react, and the newsroom loses respect for you. Use them haphazardly and you've wasted them. Don't use them at all and you'll see the staff ignoring your directions. You'll be among the mass of editors who moan about reporters regularly missing deadlines.

The perks you offer begin with a sincere thank you for a job well done. They move on to a casual show of gratitude spoken loudly enough for others to hear, to choice assignments, better story play, and your all-out effort for monetary rewards. Think of the other perks available for you to trade.

The penalties are equally important: a private word of disappointment such as, "I know you can do better," a clearly written evaluation that spells out areas to improve, or a reluctance to entrust prized story assignments until weaknesses are addressed.

Trade-offs work with supervisors, too. Healthy relations develop when people work together toward the same goal. Implicit in that is a trade-off: "Since we're working toward the same end, if you help me toward my goal, I'll help you toward yours." Invest the time in knowing what your supervisors and colleagues are trying to achieve and look for opportunities that serve all.

Differences can complicate the trade-off process. It takes effort to look beyond differences in style, background, gender, race, ethnic group, and sexual orientation, but you can and should overcome divisions.

Paula Madison took the challenge. She's vice president of news at WNBC-TV, New York City. An incident during her teen years affected her sense of news. Growing up in Harlem, Madison witnessed a major police shoot-out, but none of the news outlets reported it. Years later as a reporter, she chafed at the white, middle-class orientation of her station's news coverage. One day she asked her news director to take a short tour of the city with her. They started on a subway, and her supervisor noticed there was no air conditioning. That was his first lesson on how his morning commute in a fine car differed from the experiences of many in the city. By the end of the tour, the two were talking about ways to broaden the station's view of city life. Madison took a risk in approaching her boss, but the trade-off was better understanding and better news coverage.

Referent power. When the reporter was a child, she was frustrated by the complexity of the English language. There were too many rules, and too many exceptions to them. Her mother taught English, but her explanations seemed mysterious, too. Still, her example helped. When the child found a question she couldn't answer, she'd think, "How would Momma say this?" She usually got it right.

In most businesses you find a few people whose behavior makes them models for others. They gain power through example. People gravitate to them for advice, or emulate them from afar. Referent power is similar to expert power, but there is a difference. We often admire the expert knowledge, without wanting to imitate the experts. Referent power flows from personal qualities that lead to respect.

Years after his death, Jim Millstone's pictures could still be found in the *St. Louis Post-Dispatch* newsroom. He had been an outstanding reporter and then assistant managing editor. He was a tough editor. High praise from him amounted to this: "I see no major problem with your story." Millstone sought excellence in each story. He sought to help interns and young staffers. He cared about his staff. When one reporter, worried about her mother's health, was struggling with a big story, Millstone told her to go home and relax. The story was important, but the person was more important.

Millstone had formal power, and he was an expert on stories, but his real power grew out of the respect others had for him.

Do others seek to model you? If they did, what qualities would they emulate? What type of conduct would you see?

Value power. This power comes from a person who exhibits strong values that are shared by others. Mahatma Gandhi, Martin Luther King, Jr., and Mother Teresa gained influence because of their commitment to certain values. That power is found in news organizations, too.

Editors who worked with Nelson Poynter tell of his approach in teaching the value of readers. Periodically he'd request a change in some aspect of the *St. Petersburg Times*, maybe in design or in the type of coverage. A staffer would explain the difficulties that the change would cause. After listening patiently, Poynter would pull a dime from his pocket and say, "Here's my dime. I'm the reader. Get it done." His appeal was not to his power as publisher, but to his commitment to readers, to do whatever was required to serve them. Editors responded by finding a way to make the changes, by remembering the importance of the reader, and by finding jars to save the dimes.

Power comes from being faithful to values in times of testing. Millstone valued accuracy and would hold a story until he was sure the report was true. Could you do that? In the face of competition from online, print, and broadcast news can you uphold the value of accuracy? News leaders wrestle with infotainment, trash news, and dumbing down the news. Do you have clear values about what is fit to print or produce? Can you explain and defend your stance? Ultimately, leadership is about forming, explaining, and maintaining values. Where do you stand?

Decide on Your Limits

You will be tempted to be all things to all people: friend to old friends, good soldier to the boss, problem solver for HR staff, wise voice to your community, savior to your writers, and godlike figure to rookie reporters. Yield to the temptation, and you will serve none of them well. An editor wears many hats. David Boardman, an editor at the *Seattle Times*, listed "Twenty Hats of a Great Editor" demonstrating that you will need to tap your life skills as much as your craft skills.

You will be stretched, but before you're stretched too thin, give thought to your limits. What are your unyielding principles and what will you negotiate? You will be called on to defend your reporters. How far should you go? Coworkers will come to you with personal problems. When does providing a sympathetic ear become a full-time job as a psychiatrist? How do you avoid becoming a crutch? Many new leaders find the biggest challenge is their relationship with friends they now supervise. Invariably your friendship will change. You have confidences that you can't share and you approach each other from different positions. Accept the change, but respect the friends. As you develop new colleagues at a different level, strive for a healthy connection with old friends.

Finally, let's talk about the sandwich in which you find yourself. Your reporters press from one side, management presses from the other. The only way to avoid being squished is to maintain your character. Decide which battles you'll fight. You can't fight them all and you'll lose effectiveness if you tackle everything with the same fervor. Decide what things you will fight for and how you will fight. Will your style focus on outrage or negotiation? When should you change your style? You won't know the answer for many situations until they arise, but think through processes that will guide your reactions. One of the first rules of martial arts is to take a balanced stance. When you're balanced you can move in any direction quickly and with power. Don't let the world squeeze you. Stay firm, keep your balance, choose your battles wisely, and fight valiantly.

The Twenty Hats of a Great Editor, *by David Boardman*

How to be a full-service editor instead of a fixer.

Reporter: You must be a journalist in your heart and soul. Nowhere is this more essential than in the editing of investigative stories. If you haven't been a reporter, even for a year or two, go be one. And even as an editor, there's plenty of opportunity to help your reporters out with a little reporting. While the reporters are talking to sources, surf the Web for good background information for them. Even if you don't have a direct hand in the reporting of a story, you can play reporter with your reporters. Be curious. Ask them questions. Most importantly, show plenty of interest in what they're doing.

Coach: Don't be Woody Hayes or Bobby Knight; don't throw chairs or punch your reporters. Be Phil Jackson, when he coached the Chicago Bulls, or Gary Barnett, when he guided the resurgence of Northwestern football. A good coach puts players in the right position for their skills, clearly lays out expectations, provides the necessary tools and guidance, shoulders blame for failures, and is free with praise for successes.

Teacher: When you offer advice, do so in a way that helps your reporter take away something to use in the future. Watch for patterns—too much reliance on passive verbs, too few quotes, imprecise language—and use those to teach.

Student: Respect what your reporters know, and what you can learn from them. Let them know you're open to learning, and don't try to pretend you know things you don't. Develop a symbiotic student/teacher relationship that works both ways.

Psychiatrist: Learn what makes your reporters tick. Some need a deadline to be productive; others get too nervous under pressure. Some need constant consultation and reassurance; others like to be left alone. Understanding them and their motivations will help you help them.

Maestro: Think of the story as a song and yourself as the orchestra conductor. It is possible to edit extensively, to leave your own mark on rhythm and pacing of a story if that's necessary, and still to respect and retain the reporter's melody. You know which words and phrases reflect extra thought and effort on the reporter's part; if they work, keep your grubby hands off them. Train your ear by reading good writing aloud.

Reader: Read, read, read whatever you can get your hands on. Read other newspapers, magazines, and Internet lists for story ideas. Read non-fiction for story ideas and research methods. Read fiction for literary strategies and character development. Read mystery novels for narrative techniques.

Librarian: When you find great stories elsewhere, share them with your reporters. Do the same with books.

Diplomat: When you have to say something the reporter would rather not hear about a story, say it gracefully. Focus first on what works, then on what doesn't. And use precise, helpful language. "Can you think of a specific example to make your point clearer to the readers?" for example. Not, "This lead sucks."

Photo Editor: As much as you might implore your reporters to think about pictures to go with their stories, chances are they won't give it proper attention. And no matter how strong your photo staff, you're more likely to get the right pictures with your stories if you're heavily involved. You shouldn't step on the real photo editors' toes, of course, but you should freely suggest photos that capture the essence of the story or provide information best communicated through photography.

Graphics Editor: Again, you should be constantly thinking about what information can be presented graphically. Often, in investigative stories in particular, information is better presented in charts, graphs or maps than text.

Defense Attorney: A good editor defends reporters against angry sources, jealous colleagues, skittish newspaper executives, etc. Your reporters must believe you'll stand with them when the heat is on.

Prosecuting Attorney: Sometimes, you must play district attorney on the behalf of readers and put your reporters on the witness stand. After all, your primary responsibility—for your sake, your reporters' sake, and your newspaper or station's sake—is to the readers. Sometimes, that means giving reporters the third degree (in a respectful manner, of course, and liberally using the pronoun *we*): How do we know this? Can we say this more clearly? Do we have statistics to support this conclusion? What's our best quote? What's our central point here, the one thing we don't want readers to miss? Is this fair? And so on.

Humorist: Keep it light. Yes, investigative stories can be matters of life and death. But even in those cases—in fact, especially in those cases—a well-timed wisecrack can ease the pressure and help maintain a good working environment.

Evangelist: If you're an editor of investigative reporters, you should be the Jerry Falwell of your newsroom, constantly spreading the gospel of investigative reporting up, down, and across your organization. Most importantly, you should be helping your bosses understand why it's worth their while to invest the time and money good investigative reporting requires. Find good stories done by other papers or stations, show them around, and start discussions on how you can do similar—or better—work in your newsroom. And once your reporters are off for a month or two or six working on a big investigation, you must be their public-relations flak inside the newsroom, especially with other editors and reporters complaining about the amount of time your folks are getting.

Babysitter: Literally and figuratively. If your reporter's a dad or a mom who's up against a deadline and can't find child care, offer to watch the kids. Similarly, do whatever you can to ease the stress of the conflicts of daily life for the people who work for you. In a figurative sense, you should babysit your reporters. Keep abreast of their daily activities, through daily conversations and a master electronic file. On long-term projects, have them give you a weekly synopsis or memo on the week's activities and developments.

Clergy/Confessor: Covet whatever or whomever you like. And if you pray to idols, that's your business. But there's one commandment you must follow: Thou shalt not lie. Never, ever deceive anyone in the newsroom; it will surely come back to haunt you. And always be especially straightforward with your reporters. Also, be someone to whom your reporters can confess their sins without fear of undue retribution or punishment. If they're unsure of a fact, concerned about a mistake, afraid of something, you want them to feel comfortable telling you.

Hit Man: A great editor is not afraid to "pull the trigger," to be willing to publish a story that's likely to foment negative reaction and to take the heat when it comes down. There's another side of pulling the trigger, also, one reporters don't talk much about but that's just as important: the willingness to cut your losses, to call it quits or to change direction on a story that just isn't panning out. If your reporters are doing meaningful, genuine investigative reporting, it has to be okay for them to discover that there is no story, or that the story is different than you or they thought it was at the beginning of the process.

Midwife: When a reporter's finally ready to give birth to a story, he or she needs a midwife to help with the delivery. That can mean anything from setting out a deadline schedule to buying him or her a burger and a beer in those tense hours just before publication. Most importantly, be there with and for the reporter.

Recruiter: If you have the opportunity to recruit and hire, this is one of your most important roles. Don't sell it short. Build and maintain a network of quality journalists around the country and make that network work for you when you have an opening. The best thing any editor can do is to hire good people.

Discover Your Assets in the Newsroom

Now think again about the people and situations around you. Where can you find help in exercising your power?

First, look to your supporters. Cultivate them carefully and fairly. Too much attention to them and they become your pets, furthering division in the newsroom. Become dependent on their approval and you'll find them manipulating you. Keep your balance. The bigger tendency is to take them for granted while focusing on the problem folk. Take stock of those co-operative souls, lend them an ear, and regularly express appreciation.

The quiet leaders in your newsroom form another powerful group. Who are they? Susan Ager, columnist for the *Detroit Free Press,* described them as the "soul of a newsroom. They go about their work, not calling much attention to themselves, but if they were gone it would make a big difference." These are the people who calm disturbances, who encourage the frustrated and enlist support by giving a word or two of advice. Often they are the newsroom veterans, but they don't have to have long tenure. In a sense they have referent power. Something about their personal qualities draws people to them. They are respected; they have influence. Turn to them. Bounce your ideas off them. They will help you think through your plans and, if they approve, provide an advance support network.

Don't forget the negative version of the quiet leaders. They stir discontent. They spread gossip, question decisions, see unfairness at every turn. They may not talk to you, but they are talking to everyone else. Challenge them. Encourage them to be a part of the solution rather than a part of the problem. If that fails, at least you can understand their discontent and address it.

Go to other critics. It takes a tough skin to hear them out, but you can learn from them, and often find ways to address their legitimate concerns.

The Humbling of an Editor

She swelled with pride when she became editor of a weekly newspaper within a year of finishing college. She had the title and the power. Then she learned what the power really offered. It meant, she said,

> Writing all the stories when reporters let me down (She used her middle and maiden name for some bylines, her first and married name for others to make the staff look larger);
>
> Coaxing the page designer to stay for one more issue when he became melancholy and threatened to quit;
>
> Joking with the delivery guys on publication day so they wouldn't entertain themselves with funny cigarettes and fail to deliver the paper;
>
> Setting type at 2 A.M. when equipment stalled and the real typesetter's husband demanded that she come home.

That experience wasn't fun, but it taught her something about the ambiguous power of editors. An editor must play many roles to get the job done. But she can make a difference.

How would all this help a discouraged early morning caller? Maybe he will remember that his job is bigger than two problem reporters. Maybe he will renew himself by recalling how he had helped others and by looking for support from those around him. Maybe he could coax the older reporter into taking on the younger reporter as a project. Perhaps it is time for him to take a stand with a higher-up to find new ways of managing the two situations. Maybe it time to come out of the cave, and fight on.

Editors' note: This essay first appeared in *The Effective Editor*, published by The Poynter Institute and Bonus Books, 2000.

13

Credible Photojournalism in a Credulous Age

Kenneth Irby

"If they don't believe it, what's the purpose?"

Such was the sage advice of Professor Harris Smith, a witty and some-times gruff picture editor during the '70s at Boston University who was devoted to insuring the trustworthiness of news photography.

Now on the threshold of the twenty-first century, it seems fashionable to dispute the integrity and value of photojournalism and the wisdom of Professor Smith. Many contributors to critical thinking circles—from the camps of reflective practitioners and of practical scholars—choose to write photojournalism off.

In an echo of *Time* magazine's infamous cover declaring "God is dead," Dirck Halstead, *Time*'s White House photographer and founder of the Digital Journalist website, is credited with the provocative epitaph: "Pho-tojournalism as we know it is dead."

We live in a time of instantaneous visual imagery. Digital cameras, the image-management software PhotoShop, and advanced telecommunica-tions devices such as satellite dishes and digital cell phones make the world a very different place in which to produce photojournalism. Just as quickly as a photojournalist can capture an image on digital media, it can be transmitted for the world to see. And all this sophisticated digital tech-nology makes it extremely easy to manipulate images—and hide the ma-nipulation.

But photojournalism is not dead. It is alive and changing. And our challenge is to strengthen and undergird photojournalism and to ensure its credibility by holding true to our ethical responsibilities.

The old issues are being encountered with a new twist. In April 2000, photojournalists encountered a classic instance of the tensions and anxi-eties surrounding photographic credibility in a credulous age. It involved the juxtaposition of two photographs of young Elián González at the climax of one of the world's most-followed news stories. The photojournalist nearest the center of that case was Alan Diaz of the Associated Press's Miami bureau. Diaz has devoted himself to professionalism and ethical principles—and saw both challenged and defended by his peers in the Elián case.

"While film may be dead, photography as a form of communication is not," Diaz says. "The ethical issues are as real today as they were when I started in this business."

I will return to the Elián case and discuss it in detail below.

Stewards of Credibility in a Visual World

Our responsibility as purveyors of visual information is great. Our world is intensely visual, and so news is intensely visual. Countless citizens (as readers and viewers) come to understand the world through still and moving pictures. If it is not on CNN or MSNBC or in *USA Today*, the *Chicago Defender*, or the *Weekly Challenger*, then it did not happen.

A few years back, *Newsweek* magazine published an editorial, "Visualizing the News," that stated, "Everyone knows that there are three key ingredients to a good magazine piece: reporting that informs, writing that enlightens, and photos that capture the drama that words can't convey."

I agree—as long as reporting, writing, and photography all reflect sound ethical decision making. The duty of all journalists is to report, honestly and accurately, on and about events in our world community. All the ethical dimensions of journalism—weighing the public's right to know against the individual's right to be left alone, minimizing harm, avoiding conflicts of interest, creating a reliable portrait of the world—apply to photojournalism. But the visceral impact of powerful photojournalism can make these ethical issues seem even more troubling. And the ease of manipulation can make good photojournalism seem suspect.

Almost always, the ethical decision presents the greatest struggle for the photojournalist, pitting his or her own conscience and life experience against the public's need to know or desire to be vicarious witnesses.

"I am a human being first and must conduct myself as a conscious observer," says Gabriel Tait, a *Detroit Free Press* photographer. "My choices have an impact on other peoples lives. . . . I still struggle with the issue of whether or not we are causing more harm than good."

That issue gained high visibility after Tait photographed the body of four-month-old Miracle Jackson, wrapped in a plastic bag, being taken from the scene of her murder. Without full context and the newspaper's purpose clearly articulated, its publication provoked outrage in metropolitan Detroit.

"I struggled with it the moment that I pressed the shutter," Tait says. "We talked about the impact at the light table, and my editors talked at length about publishing the picture. . . . We did the right thing; I believe that in my heart. People needed to see the callous way that this little girl's life was taken."

Like Gabriel Tait, photojournalists around the world are striving to address the challenges and responsibilities of meeting high ethical standards that ensure credibility. And they often debate cases that illustrate their struggle. As the twentieth century yielded to the twenty-first century, one of the richest cases under discussion was the photographic coverage of the seizure of Elián González and his reunion with his father.

Elián González: Contrasting Images, Clashing Interests

On April 22, 2000, Elián González, a six-year-old native of Cuba, was seized by federal agents carrying out a court order that he be returned to his father, Juan Miguel González, a citizen of Cuba. Elián had been rescued three miles off the coast of Florida on Thanksgiving Day in 1999 after the seventeen-foot aluminum boat carrying him, his mother, his stepfather, and as many as a dozen others capsized. They had been fleeing Cuba to seek asylum in the United States. Elián, clinging to an inner tube, and a handful of others survived two days and nights in shark-infested waters. His mother did not.

After her death, his father wanted his son returned to him. The Cuban government backed his claim. The anti-Castro Cuban population in South Florida backed Elián's relatives in the United States who wanted to keep him there. After seven months of litigation, negotiation, and saturated media coverage, the courts backed the father's claim of custody. Because the Justice Department was concerned that Elián's relatives would not turn him over in compliance with the court order, Attorney General Janet Reno ordered agents to seize him from the home of his Miami relatives.

That day on television, and the next day on the front pages of many newspapers, two contrasting photographs showed sharply different images of young Elián. In one photograph, shot by Alan Diaz for the Associated Press, a terrified Elián looks on as an armed Immigration and Naturalization Service agent confronts him and his rescuer, Donato Dalrymple.

The other photo, provided to AP by an attorney for Elián's father, shows a smiling Elián and his father after their subsequent reunion.

Some journalists have challenged the authenticity of these two central images, which were given much prominent play, usually in juxtaposition to each other. Some have questioned whether Diaz's relationship with Elián's Miami relatives had put him in the position of being too close to the story. Some also questioned whether his dramatic photo represented the most telling image of what happened. And some journalists, along with Elián's Miami relatives, charged that the reunion image was phony, created by inserting a previously shot image of a happy Elián next to his father.

Manipulation of photographs is not new, but in the midst of the digital age, altering photos has never been easier. As a result, the practice has become more common and can go unnoticed by the untrained eye. As journalists, we must consider the ethical implications of images we publish. When questions are raised about any news photograph, but especially photographs seen around the world in every media format, we are obliged to study the photographs, how they were made and how they were used.

As controversy over these photographs unfolded, I examined the images and interviewed the key decision makers involved in distributing and publishing them. I talked with critics and skeptics. After weighing the evidence, I concluded that the images described above are legitimate and were appropriately shared with the world. Here's why.

The Seizure Photo

Alan Diaz did a commendable job covering this story. He developed a professional journalistic relationship with the family over five months and agreed to serve as the still photographer in a pool arrangement. As a pool photographer, the photographer and his or her news organization agree to share images with other media groups. On the day Elián was seized, Diaz and others did not have a formal agreement with either the González family or the INS. But it was generally accepted that Diaz had the inside track on the Miami family. Attorney General Janet Reno and the government were aware that there would likely be a photographer inside the home at the time of the raid.

During the frantic predawn raid, Diaz was able to get into the home and photograph the seizure of Elián. Diaz's images have become the basis of debates about photographic ethical decision making and editing. Two of the seven photos he shot were uploaded on AP's satellite digital delivery

Alan Diaz/Courtesy of AP

system. Those two images have come to be known in the media, almost interchangeably, as "The Picture."

One image shows Elián with his mouth open, with a fearful expression and the INS agent confronting him and rescuer Donato Dalrymple in the closet area of the bedroom. The other image, also near the closet, depicts a closed-mouth Elián, facing the machine-gun wielding INS agent, who is reaching toward him as Dalrymple appears to try to block the agent.

While variations in the two images are small, the play of the images points to larger issues. A quick check of newspaper front pages showed about a 50–50 split among those that ran the image of Elián with his mouth open and those that did not.

The *New York Times* did not use the image inside the house but used the picture of Elián being transported from the home by an INS agent, Betty Mills. (One interesting twist: The *Times* corrected the "red-eye" of the subjects' eyes, while the *Los Angeles Times*, using a similar image taken by staff photographer Carolyn Cole, did not.) The *New York Times* published an analysis of the photograph and noted that it quickly became a focal point in the debate over whether the Justice Department had used excessive force.

"There were lots of conversations in our newsroom about using the Al Diaz images," said Mike Smith, deputy photo editor at the *New York Times*. "Merrill Oliver, photo editor, was on duty for us that night, and we had several conversations. It is important to note that we had backed off from using many pictures of the child. We felt like, 'Enough already,' because the political posturing had moved out the real authentic images.

"On Saturday, as we considered the image, we felt strongly that everyone had seen it all day in other forms of media coverage and there was a sensational element to the coverage. I am not saying that Al did anything wrong, but for us, an element did not ring true; the closet images just did not feel right. Al was a little too close and involved with the family."

Diaz disagrees. "I faced ethical challenges every day, and I tried to make the right decisions," he said in an interview. "I conducted myself as a professional."

On the West Coast, Cindi Christie, deputy photo manager at the *Contra Costa Times*, recalled her disappointment that a centerpiece the paper had planned for page one would have to be scrapped in favor of the breaking news.

"I felt bad for our photographer, who had spent several days in Mexico photographing local teens who spent their spring break doing community projects south of the border," she said. "When I came to the office, I saw that there were two very similar photos. The designer, who had come in to work on the Mexico layout, had a working page in progress using the photo of Elián being carried by INS agent Betty Mills. I brought over Diaz's photos, and we discussed other options. Those options were presented at the news meeting. We decided to share our decision-making process with our readers in our 'After Deadline' column."

In the end, Contra Costa decided to run the agent-closet photo on the front, next to the photo of the reunion.

"We didn't think the photos had to run the same size, but we wanted head sizes to be similar or maybe a little larger in the reunion photo. It was such a study in contrasts," Christie said. "We did comment that the little boy certainly was resilient to go from the trauma of the morning raid to a beaming little boy in the afternoon."

"The pool worked as we expected it to," said Nancy Borowitz, senior vice president and spokeswoman for Reuters Communication, which also distributed Diaz's photographs. "We evaluate the newsworthiness of a situation case by case. We made no attempt to hide the photos, and we allowed our viewers and members to evaluate the images for themselves."

The Reunion Photograph

At Andrews Air Force Base outside Washington, Juan Miguel González joined the image propaganda war with photos of a smiling Elián and himself and Elián playing with his half-brother. Neat snapshots, presented as recently developed photographs from Ritz Camera, the photo chain store, showed no traumatic after-effects on the child. Those photographs raised a whole new set of questions, however.

As the images quickly appeared only on AP's service, some editors at other photo services resorted to copying the images off television screens and cropping them (a long accepted form of manipulation) in the course of moving the images along to subscribing news organizations.

In a telephone interview, Vin Alabiso, vice president and executive photo editor for AP, said the reunion images were received by the AP office in Washington and reviewed by a senior photo editor.

AP did not know who took the photos, Alabiso said, other than a person close to the family using Miguel González's "portable 35mm camera." Photos of Elián and his brother were taken by Miguel González, AP said.

"We initially received the Ritz Camera 'big prints,' which we up-linked on Photostream," Alabiso said. "We received the negatives from a repre-

Courtesy of AP

sentative from attorney Greg Craig's office. AP did later share the images with AFP, Reuters, and KRT."

Quickly, questions were raised about the authenticity and the source of the reunion photographs. Some questioned Elián's hairstyle and what appears as a missing tooth in photos taken that morning of INS officer Betty Mills carrying Elián out of the front yard by AP photographer Wilfredo Lee.

"Elián's resiliency struck me," Christie said. "I also thought his hair looked different. Again, I had heard that he had been cleaned up for the reunion. We ran the photo of Elián and Juan Miguel. I didn't count teeth. If anything, I wish our caption had more information about who had provided the photo via the AP. I didn't call AP to question the authenticity of the photo. It didn't hit me that hard where I would doubt the credibility of the news organization providing the photo."

Around the world, especially in Latin America, rumors spread questioning the authenticity of the reunion photos. Longtime photojournalist Ricardo Ferro, owner of Florida Fotobanc and a former photo editor at the *St. Petersburg Times*, was among those challenging the pictures.

"Public opinion is Castro's forte, and his KGB-trained masterminds had this photo in the bag long before the raid, to bring to a simmer the boiling reaction of Al Diaz's photo of the storm troopers and Elián," charged Ferro, who was born in Cuba.

Ferro said there are three key elements to determining the veracity of the reunion photo: Elián's shirt, his haircut, and his teeth. "It is a big photo, where his brother and stepmother are in the foreground," Ferro said. "The photo was cropped to show Elián and his father smiling. The Batman shirt that he is wearing in the photo—about a month before the raid, Castro made a comment on Cuban TV, played in Miami, that the Miami family was dressing the child with imaginary idols and mentioned the Batman shirt."

Ferro said one of Elián's Miami relatives is a hairdresser. "She had tightly cropped the sides of Elián's hair only three days before the raid. If you look closely at the raid photos, you can see that clearly," he said. "A week before the raid, Elián had lost a lower front tooth." Based on the missing tooth and the haircut, Ferro strongly contests the authenticity of the reunion photo, which he calls a "Cuban government-released photo."

Harry Walker, director of photography for Knight-Ridder Tribune News Service, said he suspects the Miami family's allegations of fake handouts could have been a ploy to discredit the father and the Cuban government. Maria Mann, director of photography for North America for Agence France-Presse, notes there was probably plenty of propaganda on both sides.

"We were pretty sure that what the family wanted was to counter with their own propaganda move," Mann said. "We treat those images like we treat images from TASS, (the Russian government news service). As they relate to the news, we have an obligation to share them. I did not think that there was any digital manipulation."

What This All Means

Image integrity today is a major issue for magazines, newspaper, websites, and fashion publications. As the commercial world attempts to create a more perfect image by creating fictitious images, people will continue to challenge what they see.

In evaluating the issues, I reviewed the reunion images as well as a range of photos shot by five professionals documenting various aspects of Elián's life. This review included photos shot by renowned Contact Press photographer David Burnett. In the end, I concluded that the reunion image is not a fabrication.

The haircut: A child's hair grows quickly. Since Wilfredo Lee's image was captured with a digital camera at night and blown up, the image suffered some quality loss because of the way the digital camera processes images. There is what professionals call "digital noise" in the image, which made some versions of the image appear lighter on the side, giving the impression that there was less hair. Also, distributing that image electronically as second- and third-generation images contributed to blocking in the darker section, reducing shadow detail, which likely raised the suspicion of manipulation.

To save time in the face of early deadlines for Sunday newspapers, some individuals and organizations resorted to frames captured from television newscasts. That "contributes greatly to image quality degradation," says Walker of KRT.

My level of certainty was reduced after I examined a photograph of the Elián seizure shot by Michael Laughlin of the South Florida *Sun-Sentinel* in Fort Lauderdale. This image shows Elián's haircut in much greater detail than other photographs taken at the scene, highlighting the so-called fade style featuring closely cropped hair right above Elián's ears. The reunion photograph appears to reflect significantly more hair above Elián's ears.

Nonetheless, the less-expensive printing from an inexpensive point-and-shoot camera is very likely to offer high-contrast images that block up and lack clarity in the shadow areas with little or no detail. The ensuing impression is that Elián has more hair in the reunion photo than in the photos taken during the raid.

The missing tooth: Of the many images that have been seen over various forms of media, not one has shown the missing bottom tooth with the kind of clarity needed to question the integrity of the family reunion image. It is possible, but unlikely, that the dark area was caused by a shadow, a dust spot, or a digital artifact in the computer file.

For five months we have seen Elián's every move, but no one image conclusively supports a fabrication plot.

Preserving Photojournalism's Essential Distinction

While standing in line at the grocery store, I was comforted by the exchange of a couple as they discussed a tabloid magazine beckoning to them in the checkout lane. "Look at Oprah, she is thin as a rail," the gentleman said, pointing emphatically at the tabloid. "Now dear," the lady replied in a measured, wifely voice, "you cannot believe that trash. Oprah is fine. I saw her yesterday in the *Tribune* and on her show."

For many, there is still a distinction to be made between journalistic facts as presented in a newspaper of record and the fictionalized representations of a sensational tabloid. But people's suspicions will continue to grow, spurred by their awareness of technological wizardry and skepticism toward the media. We will keep their faith only if we keep faith with our responsibility for ethical decision making.

We must defend the honor of the craft of photography and the integrity of journalism by challenging our sources when necessary, by developing processes that mandate reflective and responsible decision making, and by sharing our knowledge with the UCRs—Users, Citizens, and Readers—of the world.

"Amid all of this technological razzle-dazzle, one thing remains the same," says Jens-Kristian Søgaard, renowned picture editor at Denmark's largest daily newspaper, *Morgenavisen/Jyllands-Posten*. "We maintain our high ethical standard, mustn't we? After all, what good does it do us if we produce great work that nobody believes? I think that it is our duty to maintain high ethical standards."

As the Elián case makes clear, the best ethical decisions are rooted in advance training and critical thinking, so that good decisions are borne by both reflex and reflection. "At that moment, I was not thinking about ethics," Diaz says. "I was doing my job as a photographer. I had played this experience out in my mind hundreds of times. That was when I thought about ethics and what I would do. I was not going to hurt or harm anyone in the process, but I was going to get the picture."

14

Reading the News in the Inkless World of Cyberspace

Mike Wendland

It was the smell I missed the most. That delicious, woodsy, slightly acidic odor that flooded my memory with images of printing presses and the ratcheting clatter of Teletype machines and the sight of a newsroom littered with cups of stale coffee and blue clouds of swirling cigarette smoke.

I know. I know. Newspapers now have separate printing plants. Teletype machines have long been gone. And smoking is taboo.

But those feelings and memories, caught up in the smell of newsprint, were what I missed the most during my experiment. On January 1, 2000, it was easy. With a smug delight, I canceled my newspaper subscriptions. I usually read a local weekly, a local daily and, from the newsstands a few times a week, the *New York Times* and the *Wall Street Journal*. I stopped buying all of them.

"May I ask why you are canceling?" asked a very polite clerk in the circulation department of the *Detroit Free Press*.

"Because your dead tree paper is now obsolete in the Internet age," I replied, somewhat rudely, as it now strikes me. But I meant it. I was sure that there was nothing I could get delivered to my doorstep that was better than what appeared on my computer screen.

But I had to prove it to myself before I could persuade others. I needed to really know by experience how well I could stay informed by reading news only online or on my handheld Palm organizer or Web-enabled wireless phone.

I also limited my exposure to regular television news during the experiment. I'd occasionally catch the network news and snippets of my local news while I ate dinner. I frankly didn't miss television at all. But then, even though I have worked in television for much of the past two decades,

I have seldom watched it. Television is too passive. I just don't have time to stop everything and sit still for a TV newscast.

From January 1, until the end of June, I surfed the Web several times a day, reading the electronic editions of my regular papers and several others.

Let me tell you: For a guy who has devoted the last few years of his professional life preaching new media and the Internet, I was amazed at how frustrated I was without my printed newspaper.

I missed it. I really missed it.

The crinkly feel of it. The sheer enjoyment and relaxation it brought me when I would sit in my big, comfy blue leather chair and read it by a crackling fire. I can't tell you how many times I wished I had had it with me in the bathroom, too.

All those things are subjective. I guess I'm a lot more of a touchy-feely guy than I thought I was.

On an objective level, in terms of the main goal of my decidedly unscientific but personal experiment, I can say with certainty that after half a year of consuming only online news, I didn't miss very much.

I read all I wanted and then some about Elián. I probably have a better sense of the ups and downs of the markets because of the immediacy of online market coverage. I know about the corrupt cops in Los Angeles. I was well aware that Rudy Giuliani had prostate cancer and that Matt Drudge released the e-mail addresses of 300 reporters. All the news happenings during the first half of the year flashed across my computer screen.

But still, there was this gnawing concern that I had somehow missed something. For five months I had this vague, restless worry that I was ignorant. Online news left me unsatisfied. Incomplete. Almost paranoid that I wasn't following enough hyperlinks.

Every day I would try to read—if that's what scrolling up and down a computer screen can be called—the online editions of the *New York Times* and the *Washington Post*, as well as CNN.com, ABCNews.com and the Web edition of my local papers, the *Detroit Free Press* and the *Detroit News*.

I subscribed to a free news-alert service from MSNBC that beeps and flashes a little red dot on the computer screen whenever major news breaks. The Saturday morning that Elián was taken by immigration service agents, the beeping woke me up and I trudged in the dark to my home office to read, at 5:50 A.M., what all the commotion was about.

I used a service called AvantGo to download news from a variety of other sources directly onto my Palm handheld computer. The only time I found it worthwhile was when I was on an airplane, jammed in the middle seat between two huge businessmen. There was no room to turn the pages of a real newspaper, let alone a magazine.

So I whipped out my Palm and, with my arms all scrunched together, tap-tap-tapped with the stylus to make my way through the news I had downloaded before leaving home. The guy on my right wasn't very happy. "Do you have to keep making that noise?" he grumbled. There was the slightest little beep every time the stylus hit the scroll bar, and it apparently kept him from sleeping. On my shoulder. Tough. I kept tapping.

I also tried reading online news on a wireless Qualcomm phone billed as Web-enabled. It was ridiculous. The screen is so small that at best, you can read half a headline. "Firefighters race" (turn the thumb-wheel) "high winds" (turn the thumb-wheel) "in Los Alamos" (turn the thumb-wheel) "blaze."

Whew. To read the morning paper on one of these is to risk a repetitive stress injury to the thumb. Besides, as with the Palm VII wireless communicator that I also experimented with, it often took three to four minutes to make a wireless connection to the news server, then a couple of minutes longer to download the Web pages. By then, it was barely news anymore. I don't have the patience for wireless news.

And I also tried to watch streaming video on the Internet, from MSNBC, CNN.com, and other sources. It was laughable. Even with a broadband, super-fast cable connection, the video appeared herky-jerky. Often the audio was out of sync with the video. And it all appeared on about an inch-by-inch box on the computer screen. Until the Internet can deliver full-screen, full-motion synchronized audio and video, TV on the Internet will never be more than a novelty.

Here's what I couldn't get online:

• *Local news*: Even though I read the online editions of the local papers, they didn't feel local. I had to really hunt to find articles of local interest. On a computer screen, with just links of a uniform size for navigating, there is a lack of perspective about what's important. And it's often hard to distinguish between local and world news on a computer screen. My wife, who is very new to the Internet, never did get the hang of finding local news. "It's all a big jumble," she said, clicking off in disgust one night. I sometimes had to resort to printing out articles from the online edition of my local paper to appease her.

• *Serendipity*: I really missed the surprise of a newspaper. Leisurely turning the pages of a newspaper and finding delightful, fascinating little articles that are just, well, there. Articles I just ran across, instead of having to click on. Sometimes I found that online. But not often. I logged on for quick hits of information and then clicked off. Reading on the Web may be called *browsing*, but it always seemed hurried to me.

• *Advertising*: This was a real issue with my wife. She missed several big sales at the local department store. Flower Day at the local farmer's market happened without her this year. Newspaper coupons that would have saved her money at the supermarket went unclipped. I am convinced that this alone is why newspapers need not worry about becoming extinct. Advertising is more than just ads. Coupons are a sort of currency. Advertising is just as much news as a bylined article. I don't think I ever found a banner ad on an Internet site that interested me enough to click on it.

• *Convenience*: There is no getting around the fact that reading news online is cumbersome. You have to sit down at a computer, log on to the Net and click and scroll, all the while sitting in a chair that is not nearly as comfortable as the easy chair out in the family room. Online is too formal, I have decided. With a newspaper, it's right there. Put it down. Go to the fridge for a Diet Pepsi. Come back. Pick it up. Put it down. Stuff it in your briefcase. Rip out an article and paste it on the family bulletin board.

• *Impact*: This is tough to describe. For some reason, I remember stuff better when I read it on paper. That is probably the result of my conditioning and may not be a problem with younger people raised on the Net. But with a newspaper, it's easier to go back and reread an article that you saw last week, if it hasn't been used to wrap up the garbage or been tossed in the recycling bin. I bookmarked some interesting Web articles, but they were never as easy to find as my stack of newspapers used to be. And whenever I used to look at the stack of newspapers piled on the lower shelf of the end table in my family room, I felt secure, deep down, that if I needed information, it was there.

Again, this experiment was personal and anecdotal. But it was also life changing.

When the experiment ended in July, I was like a drunk on a binge. I resubscribed for home delivery to my local paper and stuffed quarters and dimes into newsstands for the nationals. I brought back bales of newspapers. I read voraciously, even the sports pages. Even those advertising inserts that are disguised as news. Even the food sections, the comics, the real estate pages.

The first week or so, as I walked down my driveway at sunup, serenaded by the birds, and pulled the morning daily out of the bright yellow tube next to my mailbox, I was filled with delight. On that first day, I put it up to my nose and inhaled. Deeply. My wife laughed when I came back to the kitchen with a black newsprint smudge on my nose.

But here's what happened, how this experiment changed my life. I fell back in love with newspapers. Real newspapers. Hold in your hand and crinkle the pages newspapers. So much so that I went back to work at one. I am now the technology columnist for the *Detroit Free Press*, writing about how the Internet and computers are changing lives.

I still am enthralled by online news. But I no longer see it as the future of journalism or even a threat to dead tree papers. It is a tool. An information tool meant for quick hits and handy printouts. A supplement to newspapers, a way to update between editions, to archive stories for easy reader retrieval.

Just today, as I write this, I had a column appear in the *Free Press*. Because I'm down at Poynter in St. Petersburg, I went to the Net and read freep.com, the online edition of the paper. I found my piece, read it, and was pleased to see the editors hadn't cut anything or made any changes. But then I e-mailed my editor. "Where did it appear? Was there any art with it?" I asked.

In other words, what did it look like in the paper?

Until I could see it, take in with a single glance its placement on a page in relation to the other stories of the day, until I could hold it, it was just words on a screen. The paper made it real.

Again, that's subjective. A part of my conditioning. I understand. Maybe someday as the so-called Generation D (*D* for digital) that is raised on the Net becomes the majority, my reading preferences will be in the minority.

But hey, by then, I'll be dirt, symbolically part of the process that fertilizes trees and makes newsprint. And I'm sure that printed newspapers will still be around. Maybe with a part of me, too.

15

The Sayings of Chairman Mel

Melvin Mencher

Make journalism out of your experience.
Use your moral outrage.
Get a good quote up high.
Follow the buck.
Don't miss a deadline.
Be a self-starter. Devise your story ideas.
Be counterphobic. Do what you fear or dislike doing.
Work seven days a week, eighteen hours a day.
If they like you, you're doing something wrong.
Misspell a word and the reader presumes you're stupid. You are.
Don't trust an expert.
Keep your opinions to yourself.
Check the numbers.
Don't report from the office chair.
Follow the facts wherever they take you.
Read your copy closely before turning it in.
Know everything.
Put human interest in your copy.
Good writers abound. Be a good reporter.
Don't fear using the word *said*.
Write tightly.
Get the details.
Dig, dig, dig.
Don't tell us when you can show us.
You can always get a job if you know how to write a lead.
Do not fear telling the truth.
When in doubt, check it out.
Don't take the easy way out.
Follow your hunches and your hormones.
It is immoral not to be excellent in your craft.

Afterword for the Paperback Edition

Roy Peter Clark and Cole C. Campbell

This new edition arrives at another crucial moment in the history of American journalism. A perfect storm has gathered since September 11, 2001, a convergence of geo-political, economic, technological, and demographic forces that confront journalists with unprecedented challenges and opportunities.

Terrorist attacks on American soil provoked a war in Afghanistan and then another in Iraq, conflicts that continue to divide the nation. Journalists have operated along the fault lines of American political culture—their fairness, competence, even their patriotism called into question.

Out of ambition and duty, reporters and photographers have put themselves in harm's way. They sustained injuries during the coverage of 9/11, they faced grave dangers in Afghanistan, and hundreds of them were embedded with military forces invading Iraq. At least two prominent journalists, David Bloom and David Kelly, died in Iraq. Another, Daniel Pearl, was assassinated by terrorists in Pakistan.

The role of the journalist in a democracy is always problematic, but never more so than in wartime. Correspondents covering World War II became loyal propagandists for the American cause. A generation later, young reporters in Vietnam reported stories that contradicted official versions of the war. In our time, the news media have come under attack from the left for not being more skeptical of the government's justifications for war, and from the right for persistent liberal bias and for not flying the flag.

While many journalists showed physical and moral courage in reporting from Afghanistan, Pakistan, and Iraq, a few betrayed the trust of their companies, their profession, and their readers. Jayson Blair of the *New York Times* and Jack Kelley of *USA Today* fabricated important stories over significant periods of time. Recurring scandals and the sagging credibility of the news business resulted in leadership changes at both of these news organizations and a tightening of standards almost everywhere. The *New York Times* introduced reforms including the hiring of a Public Editor to air reader grievances. On every front, there has been a call for more "transparency" in the news business.

New media technologies continue to revolutionize the ways that citizens access information. This has been especially true for younger readers, who seem alienated from traditional forms of news, instead attaching themselves to their favorite websites, weblogs, chat groups, video games, and forms of entertainment that mix news, music, and comedy. Audiences for news have shrunk in all media, except for the ethnic media, the alternative press, and the Internet. Network news programs limited their coverage of the 2004 presidential conventions to a single hour in favor of popular "reality" shows.

Weeks before the 2004 presidential election, CBS News got a black eye for a seriously flawed investigative story. Dan Rather reported that President George W. Bush did not follow orders while serving in the National Guard. The report was based on documents that had come from a questionable source and could not be authenticated. The botched story caused outrage in the news business and among citizens, fueling accusations of liberal bias in the mainstream press.

While there are external threats to the values and craft of American journalism, the greater dangers may be coming from within. As media companies get bigger and bigger, news operations get squeezed in the quest for higher profit margins. The public service mission of journalism is held hostage to the demands of Wall Street.

Journalism is only one of many professions embedded (to use the word of the day) in a business. Medicine is another. Accounting is another. History and current events continue to show that when business values are allowed to dominate professional standards, it not only hurts the profession, but it hurts the business. Accusations of greed plague the drug companies. Accounting scandals helped destroy Enron. It remains to be seen whether the insatiable appetite for short-term profitability will permanently damage the long-term future of the news media.

None of these important issues requires the revision of a single line in these essays. The hope for the future of journalism and democracy is located, as it always is, at the crossroads of values and craft. Only a profound sense of mission and purpose—tested against the challenges of the day—can inspire journalists to strive for new levels of excellence during difficult times.

Journalists cannot do it alone. We need the support and correction of a disenchanted public that already doubts our competence and our motives. The essays in this book can satisfy two audiences: the journalists who seek to serve the public, and the citizens who turn to them with hope and discontent.

Contributors

G. Stuart Adam, provost, Carleton University, Ottawa; Ph.D. in political studies, Queens University, Kingston; former dean of the Faculty of Arts and former director of the School of Journalism, Carleton University; former newspaper reporter and desk editor for the *Toronto Star* and editorial writer for the *Ottawa Journal*; former free-lance producer for CBC-TV Public Affairs.

Pegie Stark Adam, consultant and teacher of newspaper and magazine design in the United States and abroad; Ph.D. in mass communications, Indiana University; former director of Visual Journalism for The Poynter Institute; former associate professor of journalism at the University of Florida; former graphics or art editor for the *Detroit News*, the *Detroit Free Press*, and the *St. Petersburg Times*; coauthor, with Mario Garcia, *Eyes on the News* (Poynter, 1990).

Paula Bock, staff writer for the *Seattle Times*, leader of newsroom writing group; recipient of national and regional prizes for reporting on social issues, the arts, human interest features, and travel; graduate of Harvard University; studied in Taiwan on a Rotary Fellowship; visiting teacher at The Poynter Institute; volunteer work at refugee camps in Southeast Asia.

Cole C. Campbell, Poynter Fellow, The Poynter Institute; former editor in chief, *St. Louis Post-Dispatch*, *Virginian-Pilot*, *Tar Heel: The Magazine of North Carolina*, and *Daily Tar Heel*; John S. Knight Fellow, Stanford University; author, *Competitive Debate* (Information Resource Associations, 1974).

Roy Peter Clark, senior scholar, former dean, and founder of the Writing Center at The Poynter Institute; founding director of the National Writers Workshops; Ph.D. in English, SUNY–Stony Brook; former writing coach, reporter, feature writer, and critic, *St. Petersburg Times*; author, *Free to Write: A Journalist Teaches Young Writers* (Heinemann Educational Books, 1986) and coauthor, with Donald Fry, *Coaching Writers*, (St. Martin's Press, 1992); former editor, *Best Newspaper Writing* series; editor of the Poynter Papers and author of several serials published in North American newspapers.

Foster Davis, a consultant in newspapering to The Poynter Institute and various newspapers, especially in South Africa; former managing editor, *St. Louis Post-Dispatch*; numerous editing posts, including assistant managing editor, *Charlotte Observer*; reporter and producer, CBS News; coauthor, with Karen Brown Dunlap, of *The Effective Editor* (Basic Books, 2000). Foster Davis died of cancer in 2001. This book is dedicated to him.

Karen Brown Dunlap, dean, The Poynter Institute; Ph.D., mass communications, Tennessee State University; former reporter for the *Nashville Banner*, *Macon News*, and the *St. Petersburg Times*; former editor of *Warner Robins (Ga.) Enterprise*; faculty, University of South Florida; former editor, *Best Newspaper Writing* series; coauthor, with Foster Davis, of *The Effective Editor* (Basic Books, 2000).

Jill Geisler, group leader of Leadership and Management Programs, The Poynter Institute; former reporter, anchor, and editorial writer at WITI-TV, Milwaukee, and one of the nation's first female TV news directors; regional Emmy winner; national and regional Edward R. Murrow awards from the Radio and Television News Directors Association, Society of Professional Journalists' Excellence in Journalism and Public Service awards; Associated Press Carol Brewer award for service to journalism; Headliner Award from Women in Communication.

Kenneth Irby, group leader of Visual Journalism, The Poynter Institute; chair, Visual Task Force, Unity '99 conference; board member, Visual Edge digital photography conference; the National Press Photographers Association's Joseph Costa Award for outstanding initiative, leadership, and service in photojournalism; former photographer and deputy director of photography, *Newsday*, serving as photo editor for three Pulitzer Prize–winning projects; former photographer and assistant photo editor, *Oakland Press*; Multicultural Management Fellow, University of Missouri.

Melvin Mencher, former professor of journalism, Columbia University Graduate School of Journalism; author of *News Reporting and Writing* (WCB/McGraw-Hill, 1996, 7th edition) and other journalism texts; former professor of journalism, University of Kansas; former reporter, *Albuquerque Tribune*, United Press, *Albuquerque Journal*, *Fresno Bee*; Nieman Fellow, Harvard University.

Donald M. Murray, professor emeritus of English, University of New Hampshire; columnist, *Boston Globe*; former writing coach, *Boston*

Globe, Providence Journal, and others; Pulitzer Prize winner for editorials, *Boston Herald;* author of nine books on writing and teaching, including *Writing to Deadline* (Heinemann, 2000) and *Write to Learn* (Harcourt Brace, 1995).

James M. Naughton, president and managing director, The Poynter Institute; 18 years as national, metro, managing and executive editor of the *Philadelphia Inquirer;* supervised work that won ten Pulitzer Prizes; covered the White House for the *New York Times;* former reporter for the *Cleveland Plain Dealer;* graduate, University of Notre Dame.

Jay Rosen, chairman, Department of Journalism, New York University; Ph.D. in communication, New York University; associate, the Kettering Foundation; former director, the Project on Public Life and the Press; former fellow, Joan Shorenstein Barone Center, Harvard University, and Gannett Center for Media Studies, Columbia University; press critic and writer for print and online publications; author of several works on public journalism, including *What Are Journalists For?* (Yale, 1999).

Bob Steele, senior faculty and group leader of the Ethics Program, The Poynter Institute for Media Studies; Ph.D., mass communication, University of Iowa; former reporter, executive producer, and news director for television stations in Maine and Iowa; coauthor, with Jay Black and Ralph Barney, *Doing Ethics in Journalism* (Society of Professional Journalists, 1993).

Mike Wendland, Poynter Fellow and technology columnist for the *Detroit Free Press;* technology correspondent for MBC Newschannel TV; Internet reporter for "Net News Daily," broadcast by CBS radio; former on-air reporter for WDIV-TV in Detroit; winner of 20 Emmy Awards as head of investigative team; author of *The Wired Journalist: A Newsroom Guide to the Internet* (RTNDA Foundation, 1996).

Keith Woods, faculty in Ethics, The Poynter Institute; M.S.W., Tulane University; project director for "Media Diversity Beyond 2000," a joint effort between Poynter and The Ford Foundation that seeks to discover and highlight what makes diversity efforts succeed; former editorial writer, columnist, city editor, news reporter and sportswriter, *Times-Picayune,* New Orleans.

Index

Titles of related interest from the University Press of Florida

Al Burt's Florida:
Snowbirds, Sand Castles, and Self-Rising Crackers
Al Burt

Art and Journals on the Political Front, 1910–1940
Virginia Hagelstein Marquardt

The Changing South of Gene Patterson:
Journalism and Civil Rights, 1960–1968
Roy Peter Clark and Raymond Arsenault

The New Africa:
Dispatches from a Changing Continent
Robert M. Press

Frolicking Bears, Wet Vultures, and Other Oddities:
A New York City Journalist in Nineteenth-Century Florida
Jerald T. Milanich

Kick Ass:
Selected Columns of Carl Hiaasen
Carl Hiaasen

Media, Culture, and the Modern African American Freedom Struggle
Brian Ward

Magazines That Make History:
Their Origins, Development, and Influence
Norberto Angeletti and Alberto Oliva

Maximum Insight:
Selected Columns of Bill Maxwell
Bill Maxwell

Orange Journalism:
Voices from Florida's Newspapers
Julian M. Pleasants

Radio and the Struggle for Civil Rights in the South
Brian Ward